ONE DAY

The
Devotional

AT A TIME

for

Overcomers

NEIL T. MIKE & JULIA

ANDERSON | QUARLES

Regal

A Division of Gospel Light
Ventura, California, U.S.A.

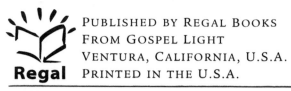

PUBLISHED BY REGAL BOOKS
FROM GOSPEL LIGHT
VENTURA, CALIFORNIA, U.S.A.
PRINTED IN THE U.S.A.

Regal Books is a ministry of Gospel Light, a Christian publisher dedicated to serving the local church. We believe God's vision for Gospel Light is to provide church leaders with biblical, user-friendly materials that will help them evangelize, disciple and minister to children, youth and families.

It is our prayer that this Regal book will help you discover biblical truth for your own life and help you meet the needs of others. May God richly bless you.

For a free catalog of resources from Regal Books/Gospel Light, please call your Christian supplier or contact us at 1-800-4-GOSPEL or www.regalbooks.com.

Cover Design by Kevin Keller
Interior Design by Rob Williams
Edited by Deena Davis

Library of Congress Cataloging-in-Publication Data
Anderson, Neil T., 1942-
    One day at a time / Neil T. Anderson and Mike & Julia Quarles.
        p. cm.
    Includes bibliographical references.
    ISBN 0-8307-2400-1 (pbk.)
1. Christian life. I. Quarles, Mike H. Quarles, Julia. III. Title.

BV4501.2.A4735 2000   00-022501
248.4—dc21

Rights for publishing this book in other languages are contracted by Gospel Light Worldwide, the international nonprofit ministry of Gospel Light. Gospel Light Worldwide also provides publishing and technical assistance to international publishers dedicated to producing Sunday School and Vacation Bible School curricula and books in the languages of the world. For additional information, visit www.gospellightworldwide.org; write to Gospel Light Worldwide, P.O. Box 3875, Ventura, CA 93006; or send an e-mail to info@gospellightworldwide.org.

Contents

Introduction 5

Section One 13
The Gospel Means Good News

Section Two 49
Understanding the True Nature of Your Heavenly Father

Section Three 83
Freedom from the Past

Section Four 117
Overcoming the Biggest Barrier to Freedom

Section Five 147
Beloved, Now You Are a Child of God

Section Six 181
The Chains of Bondage Have Been Broken

Section Seven 215
Discovering the Grace of God

Section Eight 251
Living Free in Christ by Faith

Section Nine 289
The Freedom of Forgiveness

Section Ten 325
Winning the Battle for the Mind

Who I Am in Christ 363

The Overcomer's Covenant in Christ 364

I am thankful for my physical heritage. Church was a regular experience for me, but somehow during those formative years of my life, I was never confronted with the need to make a decision about my relationship with God. I never really understood the gospel. I was 25 years old before I finally realized who God is and why Jesus came; it would be another 15 years before I finally realized what it meant to be a child of God.

PHYSICALLY ALIVE, SPIRITUALLY DEAD

Genesis 2:7 says, "The Lord God formed the man from the dust of the ground and breathed into his nostrils the breath of life, and the man became a living being." Adam was alive in two ways: He was alive physically—his soul was in union with his physical body. But he was also alive spiritually—his soul was in union with God.

In Genesis 2:16,17, "The Lord God commanded the man, 'You are free to eat from any tree in the garden; but you must not eat from the tree of the knowledge of good and evil, for when you eat of it you will surely die.'" Adam disobeyed God and he ate of that tree. Did he die physically? No, but he did die spiritually and was instantly separated from God. Physical death would also be a consequence of sin, but that wouldn't come until years later.

From that time on, everyone who is born into this world is born physically alive but spiritually dead, separated from God. Paul says in Ephesians 2:1, "As for you, you were dead in your transgressions and sins." During those early and formative years of our lives, we had neither the presence of God nor the knowledge of God's ways. We had no choice but to learn how to live our lives independently of God.

Too many people have experienced rejection, abandonment or abuse in their early childhood and have learned to believe the lies, "I am of no value," "I don't measure up," "I am unlovable." Even those of us whose childhoods seemed wholesome often struggle with a poor sense of worth because we are raised in such a competitive society.

Without exception, all the people I have counseled have had an unscriptural belief about themselves and their loving heavenly Father. In order to grow in Christ we must recognize false beliefs from the past, renounce them as lies and reprogram our minds with the truth of God's Word.

IN CHRIST WE ARE SPIRITUALLY ALIVE!

Jesus came to undo that separation from God. He said in John 10:10, "I came that they might have life, and might have it abundantly" (*NASB*). In the early years of my Christian experience, I thought eternal life was something I got when I died, but 1 John 5:11,12 says, "And this is the testimony: God has given us eternal life, and this life is in his Son. He who has the Son has life; he who does not have the Son of God does not have life." Every Christian is alive in Christ *right now*. To be alive means that your soul is in union with God. Throughout the New Testament you will see repeatedly the truth that you are "in Christ," or that Christ is in you. It is this spiritual life that gives us our essential identity.

OUR NEW IDENTITY

Colossians 3:10,11 says that we "have put on the new self, which is being renewed in knowledge in the image of its Creator. Here there is no Greek or Jew, circumcised or uncircumcised, barbarian, Scythian, slave or free, but Christ is all, and is in all."

The tendency is to get our identity from the things we do, or we identify ourselves by means of racial, religious, cultural or social distinctions. According to Paul, none of these natural identities apply anymore because our physical heritage, social standing or racial distinctions no longer serve as the basis for our identity. Our new and true identity lies in the fact that we are all children of God and we are now alive and free in Christ.

The practical significance of this essential truth cannot be overstated. A Christian is not simply a person who gains forgiveness, who gets to go to heaven, who receives the Holy Spirit, who puts on a new nature. A Christian, in terms of his deepest identity, is a saint, a child born of God, a divine masterpiece, a child of light and a citizen of heaven. Peter writes that we are "a chosen people, a royal priesthood, a holy nation, a people belonging to God, that you may declare the praises of him who called you out of darkness into his wonderful light. Once you were not a people, but now you are the people of God; once you had not received mercy, but now you have received mercy" (1 Peter 2:9,10).

LEARNING OUR NEW IDENTITY

Nobody can fix his or her past, but I believe that by the grace of God we can all be free from our pasts. We are no longer just a product of our past. We are primarily a product of the work of Christ on the Cross. But remember, when we were dead in our trespasses and sins we had learned to live our lives independently of God. Our identity and perception of ourselves were formed and programmed into our minds through the natural order of this world. That's why Paul says in Romans 12:2, "Do not conform any longer to the pattern of this world, but be transformed by the renewing of your mind. Then you will be able to test and approve what God's will is—his good, pleasing and perfect will."

Renewing our minds does not come naturally; there is no automatic "clear" button that erases past programming. We have to consciously know the Word of God so that we can understand who we are from God's perspective. And who are we? First John 3:1-3 says,

How great is the love the Father has lavished on us, that we should be called children of God! And that is what we are! The reason the world does not know us is that it did not know him. Dear friends, now we are children of God, and what we will be has not yet been made known. But we know that when he appears, we shall be like him, for we shall see him as he is. Everyone who has this hope in him purifies himself, just as he is pure.

WHO WE ARE DETERMINES WHAT WE DO

The most important belief we can possess is a true knowledge of who God is. The second most important belief is to know who we are as children of God. People cannot consistently behave in a way that is inconsistent with how they perceive themselves. If we do not see ourselves as God sees us, then to that degree we suffer from a false identity and a poor understanding of who we really are.

It is not what we do that determines who we are. It is who we are that determines what we do as illustrated by a letter I received from a missionary.

I am writing in response to reading *Victory over the Darkness*. I am sure you have received many letters, at least I hope you have, because that means people like me have had their eyes opened to God's truth.

I am a missionary, and even though I have been a Christian for 21 years, I never understood God's forgiveness and my spiritual inheritance. I have been bulimic since 1977. I was in Bible college at the time I began this horrible practice. I never thought this living hell would end. I have wanted to die, and I would have killed myself had I not thought that was a sin. I felt God had turned His back on me and I was doomed to hell because I couldn't overcome this sin. I hated myself. I felt like a failure.

But the Lord led me to purchase your book and bring it with me. I began reading it last week. I feel like a new Christian, like I have just been born again. My eyes are now open to God's love. I realize I am a saint who sins, not a sinner. I can finally say I am free of Satan's bondage and aware now of the lies he has been filling me with. Before I would confess to God, beg His forgiveness when I binged and purged, yet the next time I fell deeper into Satan's grasp because I couldn't forgive myself and I couldn't accept God's forgiveness. I also thought the answer lay in drawing closer to God, yet I went to Him in fear and confusion, acting as a sinner who couldn't be loved. No more!

Through the Scriptures and the way you presented them, I am no longer a defeated Christian. I don't consider myself a bulimic; I consider myself a saint, salt of the earth, Christ's friend, a slave of righteousness. Food has no power over me. Satan has lost his grip on me.

As troubled people began sharing their stories with me, I noticed that none of them knew who they were in Christ nor understood what it meant to be a child of God. If the Holy Spirit was bearing witness with their spirit (see Rom. 8:16), why weren't they sensing it? Christians are not sinners in the hands of an angry God! They are saints in the hands of a loving God who has called them to "draw near with a sincere heart in full assurance of faith, having our hearts sprinkled clean from an evil conscience" (Heb. 10:22, *NASB*).

OUR NEEDS ARE MET IN CHRIST

Paul says, "And my God shall supply all your needs according to His riches in glory *in* Christ Jesus" (Phil. 4:19, *NASB*, emphasis added). He is not necessarily addressing our physical needs, but rather our "being" needs, and they are the ones most wonderfully met *in* Christ Jesus.

The secular world has identified these needs but is pitifully inadequate to meet them. Trying to pick ourselves up by our own bootstraps and stroking one another's ego is not going to get it done. What a privilege we have to tell the world how Christ has come to meet our most critical and foundational needs: life, identity, acceptance, security and significance.

It is my prayer that at the conclusion of this devotional you will have entered into the experience that is assured us in Galatians 4:6,7, *NASB*: "And because you are sons, God has sent forth the Spirit of His Son into our hearts, crying, 'Abba! Father!' Therefore you are no longer a slave, but a son; and if a son, then an heir through God." In other words, I'm praying that you will experience a bonding relationship with your heavenly Father.

As you read, study and meditate upon God's Word, be aware that Satan does not want you to know the truth that will set you free. You may actually struggle in your thought life with opposing arguments to the truth of what God has to say about who you are. Let me encourage you to stand against that. If a lie is formed in your mind that is contrary to what the Bible is trying to tell you, then renounce that lie and accept the truth of what God says.

A SIMPLE PLAN TO REALIZE YOUR FREEDOM IN CHRIST

Christians who struggle with addictive behaviors begin to think they are powerless to overcome their sin. That is not true. Every born-again believer is alive in Christ and dead to sin (see Rom. 6:11), and they can do all things through Christ who strengthens them (see Phil. 4:13). These daily devotionals are intended to help renew your mind to the truth of who you are in Christ and to help you realize the freedom He has already purchased for you.

In a few places where it might be confusing as to which of us is speaking, we have added the name of the speaker after "I." However, the vast majority of these devotionals are written from Mike's perspective and experience. He and his wife, Julia, coauthored with me the books *Freedom from Addiction* and *Freedom from Addiction Workbook*. Those books and this devotional would be far more effective if you also read my first two books, *Victory over the Darkness* and *The Bondage Breaker*. We also make reference a number of times to the "Steps to Freedom in Christ." That is a counseling tool that can be purchased from our office or in any Christian bookstore. Many can work through those steps on their own, but others need someone to help them. Don't be afraid to call for help.

Each devotion ends with some probing questions that we hope you will give some thought to as you interact with the material. At the end is a space for you to journal your thoughts. Consider this space as a time and place to interact with God. Be as honest as you can about your true thoughts and feelings. If you have doubts, share them. If you are having a bad day, tell God about it. He already knows the thoughts and intentions of your heart, so why not be honest with your heavenly Father who loves you and will never leave or forsake you. It is my prayer that the truth of God's Word will set you free to be all that God wants you to be.

Neil T. Anderson

THE GOSPEL MEANS GOOD NEWS

DAY 1

Thought for Today: The gospel is not a call to do something, but an announcement of what has been done.

For I am not ashamed of the gospel, for it is the power of God for salvation to everyone who believes, to the Jew first and also to the Greek.
ROMANS 1:16, NASB

Do you want to be free? Have you tried everything within your power to overcome your past and still you can't rid yourself of negative thoughts, feelings and behaviors? Perhaps you could identify with a lady I once counseled. She was one of the most fearful, confused individuals I have ever known. She lived in constant turmoil. Every circumstance in her life seemed to keep her off balance. After each counseling session she would say, "Just tell me what to do! Write out a list of what you want me to do."

Too many Christians believe that living the Christian life is a continuous routine of involvement in well-meaning programs. They believe they could live the victorious Christian life if only they could discipline themselves to read their Bibles, pray more, attend church regularly and fellowship with other believers. Those are good Christian disciplines, but to believe that such personal involvement and effort is the means to fix life's problems is to get the proverbial cart before the horse. Human effort is not what it takes to live the Christian life or to be free from our past and to overcome addictive behaviors.

Victorious Christian living comes by accepting what Christ has already done for us, understanding who our heavenly Father is and who we are "in Christ" and then choosing to live by faith in the power of the Holy Spirit, according to what God says is true. The most well-structured programs cannot set us free, and no amount of human effort can accomplish what Christ has already accomplished for us.

Many of us have been brought up to believe that anything we get out of life we have to work for. The good news is, Christ has already accomplished everything that needs to happen in order for us to be free. For the lady I was counseling, this idea was simply too good to be true. She had tackled every personal problem with sheer determination. Through her own energy, effort and time she had managed to overcome some natural obstacles, but now she had a problem she couldn't resolve—a husband who was addicted to alcohol, sex and gambling.

There are many natural barriers that can be overcome by hard work and human ingenuity, but we can't save ourselves and we can't set ourselves free. The Christian life cannot be lived by our own strength and resources. God in His goodness and His desire for us to learn the truth will bring us to the end of our resources in order that we may discover His.

There is only one Christian life, and that is the life of Christ. What Adam and Eve lost in the Fall was spiritual life. That is what Jesus came to give us—eternal and spiritual life. Jesus is our spiritual life. We are not saved by how we behave; we are saved by what we believe. We live the Christian life by faith, trusting in the finished work of Christ and staying dependent on His presence and resources.

The gospel is not a call to do something. The gospel literally means "good news," announcing that what was needed for us to live the victorious Christian life has already been done. Jesus defeated the devil at the cross, forgave our sins and gave us a new life in Him. Consequently, every born-again believer is alive and free in Christ. We just need to believe the good news and live accordingly by faith in God. We are saved by faith (see Eph. 2:8,9) and we also live by faith (see 2 Cor. 5:7).

It's not that you won't do good works after you become a Christian; bearing fruit is the natural consequence of being alive and free in Christ. The two biggest errors Christians make are trying to become someone they already are—a child of God (see 1 John 3:1-3), and trying to get something they already have—freedom from sin and death (see Rom. 8:1,2).

There is nothing you can do to save yourself or to set yourself free other than to believe that Christ has already accomplished that for you. When you reach that point of understanding, you have appropriated the good news. If you are a victorious Christian, you did what Jesus said to do in Mark 1:15. You repented of your former way of life and believed the good news that Christ died on the cross for your sins and was resurrected in order that you may have new life in Him.

The disciples asked Jesus, "'What must we do to do the works God requires?' Jesus answered, 'The work of God is this: to believe in the one he has sent'" (John 6:28,29).

Probe

Has Christ already set you free (see Gal. 5:1)? Are you depending on what *you* do to live the Christian life in freedom or on what *Christ* has done?

Journal

_____

_____

_____

_____

_____

DAY 2

Thought for Today: The gospel transfers you from one kingdom to another.

For he has rescued us from the dominion of darkness and brought us into the kingdom of the Son he loves, in whom we have redemption, the forgiveness of sins.
COLOSSIANS 1:13,14

When I visited Russia in 1997, I entered into a totally unfamiliar culture. The people and the way they lived were different from anything I had ever experienced. The language, the customs, the religious services, the food, the lodging and the transportation system were all different. Although the people in the church were friendly and responsive, and many of them wanted to communicate with us, we couldn't understand a word they said without a translator.

Even the laws were different. In America we can travel freely around the country. Not in Russia. In the Goldie Hawn movie, *The Girl from Petrovka*, a Russian girl in Moscow didn't have the correct papers that permitted her to be there. She was sentenced to five years in prison for her "crime." When I was a visitor in Russia, I was subject to the laws of that country—I was in a different kingdom from the one I had left.

When you became a Christian, you were transferred from one kingdom to another. "For he has rescued us from the dominion of darkness and brought us into the kingdom of the Son he loves" (Col. 1:13). "For our citizenship is in heaven, from which also we eagerly wait for a Savior, the Lord Jesus Christ" (Phil. 3:20, *NASB*). While it is true that we have to obey the laws of this country, we have been transferred into a spiritual kingdom whose king is the Lord Jesus Christ.

The kingdom of Christ is a spiritual and eternal kingdom invisible to the physical eye. We live in His kingdom by faith, not by sight. Jesus said that we can't point out this kingdom to anyone. "Nor will they say, 'Look, here it is!' or, 'There it is!'" Yet He also said that the kingdom is very real. "For behold, the kingdom of God is in your midst" (Luke 17:21, *NASB*).

The power available to us is the same power that raised Christ from the dead. The apostle Paul prayed that we might perceive "the surpassing greatness of His power toward us who believe. These are in accordance with the working of the strength of His might which He brought about in Christ, when He raised Him from the dead, and seated Him at His right hand in the heavenly places" (Eph. 1:19,20, *NASB*).

On my trip to Russia I could have attempted to live as though I were still in Atlanta, Georgia, but I wouldn't have fared too well. If I had tried to check into a hotel without a passport, I would have been deported. As citizens of the kingdom of God, we don't have to be governed by the old, defeated powers of this world. In the kingdom of God, the same power that raised Christ from the dead and defeated Satan is available to us every day. It is this power that enables us to live in freedom and victory over the world, the flesh and the devil.

This power is available to us as we live by faith in God's kingdom and trust Him in every aspect of our lives. We are not just helpless victims subject to powerful forces in this fallen world. We are subjects in God's kingdom and citizens of heaven, and His resurrection power is available to us. The writer of Hebrews said that we should be moved to awe and reverence because we have received "a kingdom that cannot be shaken" (Heb. 12:28).

As children of God, we have been made joint heirs with Jesus Christ. We are to reign in this kingdom with Him and through Him. "Those who receive the abundance of grace and of the gift of righteousness will reign in life through the One, Jesus Christ" (Rom. 5:17, *NASB*).

Paul says in Romans 6:1-4 (*THE MESSAGE*): "So what do we do? Keep on sinning so God can keep on forgiving? I should hope not! If we've left the country where sin is sovereign, how can we still live in our old house there? Or didn't you realize we packed up and left there for good? . . . We entered into the new country of grace—a new life in a new land!"

This world offers many things that appeal to the flesh, but you cannot satisfy the flesh. The more you try, the more it craves. The temporal attractions of this world are flimsy, fleeting and superficial. Those who succumb to those temptations do a lot of posturing, positioning, boasting and bragging. This world has been judged and, eventually, we will lose every worldly possession and position.

The kingdom of God is characterized by love, joy, peace, patience, kindness, goodness, faithfulness, gentleness and self-control (see Gal. 5:22,23). We can have these fruits of the Spirit only by the grace of God. "May it never be that I should boast, except in the cross of our Lord Jesus Christ, through which the world has been crucified to me, and I to the world" (Gal. 6:14, *NASB*).

Probe

Are you aware of your rights and responsibilities of living in God's kingdom? Now that you are alive in Christ, how can you live as though you are dead to sin (see Rom. 6:11)?

Journal

_____

_____

_____

_____

_____

DAY 3

Thought for Today: The gospel brings you out of darkness into light.

But you are a chosen generation, a royal priesthood, a holy nation, His own special people, that you may proclaim the praises of Him who called you out of darkness into His marvelous light.

1 PETER 2:9, NKJV

When I was in Russia, I was shocked to see that almost everything was rundown, broken, old and dirty. Most of the cars and trucks would be classified as junk heaps in America. Nothing seemed to be clean, and weeds grew unrestrained everywhere. A large number of people lived in multi-story apartment buildings that looked like slum tenements and would probably be condemned in the States. What we take for granted as basic essentials for living, such as ice cubes, napkins and toilet paper, were almost impossible to obtain.

These people were oppressed. I was saddened by the people's sense of hopelessness and helplessness. Why did such a spirit prevail? Because Russian citizens had lived under Communist persecution and oppression all their lives. They didn't know anything different.

When a Russian pastor traveled outside Russia for the first time and stepped off the plane in Europe to see well-kept yards, clean streets and homes and the beautifully landscaped boulevards, he broke down and wept. He didn't know what he had been missing all his life until he saw the free world.

People who are in bondage live in darkness, and they don't know what freedom is like because they have never experienced it. Many don't know how to get out of bondage and others aren't even aware that it is possible in Christ. "Jesus therefore said to them, 'For a little while longer the light is among you. Walk while you have the light, that darkness may not overtake you; he who walks in the darkness does not know where he goes'" (John 12:35, *NASB*). When Jesus came into the world, He brought eternal life and "the life was the light of men" (John 1:4, *NASB*). In fact, Jesus was the light of the world, and He came to rescue us from the domain of darkness. "I have come as light into the world, that everyone who believes in Me may not remain in darkness" (John 12:46, *NASB*).

Every Christian has been brought out of darkness into light. However, we have the choice of walking in darkness or light. When we believe the truth and follow Christ, we walk in the light. But if we believe the lies of the enemy and follow the ways of the world, we walk in darkness. "Again therefore Jesus spoke to them, saying, 'I am the light of the world; he who follows Me shall not walk in the darkness, but shall have the light of life'" (John 8:12, *NASB*).

How do we get out of bondage? Jesus said, "You shall know the truth, and the truth shall make you free" (John 8:32, *NASB*). Truth sets us free. We live in bondage when we believe the lies of this world and walk in darkness. Like the people in the former Soviet Union, some have lived in the darkness for so long that it seems normal to them.

If you believe the truth and are walking in the light, then you are free. To walk in the light is the same as confession, which means to agree with God. "If we walk in the light, as he is in the light, we have fellowship with one another, and the blood of Jesus, his Son, purifies us from all sin. . . . If we confess our sins, he is faithful and just and will forgive us our sins and purify us from all unrighteousness" (1 John 1:7,9).

Jesus said that some people like darkness more than light because their deeds are evil and they fear the exposure of the light (see John 3:19,20). Jesus came to bring us out of darkness into His light; He came to set captives free, restore sight to the blind and release the oppressed (see Luke 4:18). The captives will be freed and the oppressed released when they recover their sight and see the truth. It is the truth of God's Word that sets you free, and you will stay free if you walk by faith according to what God says is true.

In Charles Wesley's great hymn, "And Can It Be That I Should Gain?" the fourth verse describes the freedom found in Christ this way:

> Long my imprisoned spirit lay fast bound
>   in sin and nature's night;
> Thine eye diffused a quickening ray,
>   I woke, the dungeon flamed with light;
> My chains fell off, my heart was free;
>   I rose went forth and followed Thee.[1]

Not only has God brought us into His marvelous light, He has made us fit to walk in it. We are now a chosen generation, a royal priesthood, a holy nation, God's own special people (see 1 Pet. 2:9). In fact, we are not just *in* the light; God has *made* us light. "For you were once darkness, but now you are light in the Lord. Live as children of light" (Eph. 5:8). We are not called to act like someone we really are not, but we are to live according to who we really are—children of light.

The light of the world has come for Russians who know Christ. I was in a church service the Sunday after the new law restricting religious freedom had just been passed. During the worship and praise time, the believers were literally jumping for joy. They still lived in an oppressive society, but these Christians were so excited about having come out of darkness into His marvelous light that they couldn't contain their joy.

Probe

Facing the truth and walking in the light is the first step in recovery and is essential for living free in Christ. Are you walking in the light by living in continuous moral agreement with God? In what ways haven't you been honest with others about who you really are? Ask God to show you, and when He does, confess it. Be honest with God and those you live with.

Journal

_____

_____

_____

_____

_____

_____

Note
1. Charles Wesley, *Worship and Service Hymnal* (Chicago: Hope Publishing Co., 1968).

DAY 4

**Thought for Today: The gospel is true truth and real reality—
anything contrary is false.**

*Let God be true, and every man a liar. As it is written: "So that you may
be proved right when you speak and prevail when you judge."*
ROMANS 3:4

Jamie Buckingham told a story about his mother-in-law's witnessing to him. He resisted her with many intellectual arguments until she said, "Let God be true, and every man a liar." That did it for Jamie! Shortly after that he became a Christian.

The world wants us to believe that homosexuals are born that way and that alcoholism is a disease. But God's Word tells us differently (see 1 Cor. 6:9-11). The world spends billions of dollars to fund man-made projects, but Jesus tells us that a penny invested in His kingdom from a poor widow means more (see Mark 12:42,43). The corporate world implies that we must put self first if we're going to get ahead, but Jesus tells us that everything gained by self-centered living will be lost. We can't take it with us (see Matt. 10:39).

To be successful do we need a trim body, a new car, the latest computer, a fat bank account? The apostle Paul discovered that such gains are nothing but rubbish compared to knowing Christ Jesus our Lord (see Phil. 3:7,8). In order to be wise, do we need the wisdom of this world? Paul says that those who pursue knowledge are "always learning and never able to come to the knowledge of the truth" (2 Tim. 3:7, *NASB*). The message of the Cross is foolishness to those who are perishing (see 1 Cor. 1:18); the foolishness of God is wiser than man's wisdom, and the weakness of God is stronger than man's strength (see 1 Cor. 1:25). The world has worshiped the creation rather than the Creator, and exchanged the truth of God for a lie (see Rom. 1:18,25).

Christians who are not walking in freedom are living in bondage to the lies they believe about God and themselves. I have a friend who was a dedicated Christian. He had a wonderful wife and three children. He served in a Christian ministry and was well respected. But he had struggled with sexual feelings toward other men from the time he was a child and, on a few occasions, acted on those feelings. As a result, he lost his ministry and family and battled depression for years.

He tried everything he knew to get free, but he couldn't get over the fact that he had these feelings. Eventually, he believed the lie that he was a homosexual. He was a Christian but he resigned himself to this continual struggle he couldn't seem to win.

When he read *Victory over the Darkness*, *The Bondage Breaker* and *Freedom from Addiction* and went through the Steps to Freedom in Christ, he realized he had desperately wanted acceptance and love from his father, which he never received. The first male who accepted him also seduced him into a homosexual relationship. Satan took advantage of his sexual encounters and his desperate need for acceptance.

Because of his feelings, he became convinced he must be a homosexual. The light came on when he understood the lie he had believed for many years. Finally, he accepted the truth of who he really was in Christ and that God had created us to be male and female. He was able to appropriate his freedom in Christ and start living according to what God says is true. He was able to share his testimony before his church family, telling them he had been duped, and indeed he was.

Many are living in bondage because they believe the lie that they are alcoholics, drug addicts, homosexuals, gamblers, sex addicts, anorexics, bulimics, perfectionists, workaholics and so on. Every born-again Christian is a child of God and may struggle with addictive behaviors. But what a person does or feels doesn't determine who he or she is. The psalmist wrote, "How long, O men, will you turn my glory into shame? How long will you love delusions and seek false gods?" (Ps. 4:2). "Seek false gods" in this passage could be translated "seek lies."

Jesus said, "I am the way and the truth and the life. No one comes to the Father except through me" (John 14:6). If what we believe doesn't agree with His will, His Word and His way, then it's not true. If what you are thinking—or what the world says—is contrary to God's Word, then reject the lie and choose to believe the truth. Remember: "Let God be true, and every man a liar."

Probe

What have you been taught in the world or by others that you now know to be untrue, according to God's Word? How could this knowledge affect the way you live?

Journal

_____

_____

_____

_____

_____

DAY 5

Thought for Today: The gospel brings salvation, and salvation brings release from bondage.

The Spirit of the Lord is on me, because he has anointed me to preach good news to the poor. He has sent me to proclaim freedom for the prisoners and recovery of sight for the blind, to release the oppressed.
LUKE 4:18

Suppose a woman in a certain country made her living as a prostitute. One day the king of that country issues an edict that all prostitutes have been forgiven. That would be good news if you were a prostitute. The woman no longer has to live in fear of being caught and put in jail. But that truth alone wouldn't necessarily change her behavior or her perception of herself. More than likely she would still continue to live in sin because in her mind she is still a prostitute.

What if the king were to make her his bride and bring her into the palace as the queen? Would that change her behavior and her perception of herself? Of course it would! Why would anyone live like a prostitute if she were the queen? Christians are not just forgiven sinners. They are redeemed saints. They are the Bride of Christ (see Eph. 5:31,32).

Christians aren't just forgiven sinners who get to go to heaven when they die, but in the meantime it's a mean time. Thank God for good Friday and the forgiveness of our sins, but that's only half the gospel. The other half is Easter and the Resurrection and the new life we have in Christ. Not only are we new creations in Christ, but Luke 4:18 says that Jesus also came "to proclaim freedom" and "to release the oppressed."

Salvation, by definition, means deliverance—not just deliverance *from* sin and our past, but deliverance *to* a new life in Christ. We are not just forgiven, we are born-again children of God. We can't fix our past; God doesn't even do that. But by the grace of God we can be free from it. Being alive and free in Christ is not just for super-saints. It's the birthright of every child of God.

Salvation is not learning how to cope. Salvation means freedom and new life. Possibly the biggest lie believed by those who are struggling with an addictive behavior is that freedom from addiction is not possible. If we believe we are doomed to remain in bondage, we probably will remain in bondage. Even Jesus said, "According to your faith will it be done to you" (Matt. 9:29).

Neither programs nor human effort can set us free. Freedom from addiction is possible only by the grace of God. The psalmist said, "Many are saying of me, 'God will not deliver him'" (Ps. 3:2). There will always be those who choose not to believe, but too many of us have already experienced the truth that Christ "gave himself for us to redeem us from all wickedness and to purify for himself a people that are his very own, eager to do what is good" (Titus 2:14). Martin Luther describes our salvation this way:

> It unites the soul with Christ as a bride is united with her bridegroom. Christ and the soul become one flesh. And if they are one flesh and there is between them a true marriage—indeed the most perfect of all marriages. It follows that everything they have they hold in common. Accordingly, the believing soul can boast of and glory in whatever Christ has as though it were its own. Thus the believing soul by means of the pledge of faith is free in Christ, its Bridegroom, free from all sins, secure against death and hell and is endowed with the eternal righteousness, life and salvation of Christ its Bridegroom. Here this rich and divine Bridegroom redeems her from all her evil and adorns her with all His goodness.[1]

"It is for freedom that Christ has set us free. Stand firm, then, and do not let yourselves be burdened again by a yoke of slavery" (Gal. 5:1). Christ has done everything necessary for us to be free. He wants us to be free so much that He gave Himself as a ransom to die on a cross. Then He gave Himself to us. We are one with Christ because our souls are in union with Him. There is nothing else God needs to do for us to be free.

Probe

How does salvation bring freedom from our past? Explain the difference between a forgiven alcoholic and a redeemed saint who struggles with old habits that were learned before salvation.

Journal

_____

_____

_____

_____

_____

Note

1. Harold J. Grimm, ed., *Martin Luther* (Philadelphia: Fortress Press, 1957), n.p.

DAY 6

Thought for Today: The gospel gives you new life in Christ.

The thief comes only to steal and kill and destroy; I have come that they may have life, and have it to the full.
JOHN 10:10

When I was presenting a Freedom from Addiction workshop, I noticed a young lady who appeared to be having a problem with what I was saying. During a question-and-answer time, she asked, "Do you mean to tell me that if I believe I am one with Christ, dead to sin and alive to God, it will change my life?"

I responded, "If you really were one with Christ and you believed it, of course it would."

What is our greatest need? Is it to have our sins forgiven? This alone will not necessarily change us or enable us to live free and productive lives.

What Adam and Eve lost in the Fall was their spiritual lives—their relationship with God. Consequently, everyone who has ever been born is physically alive but spiritually dead. "As for you, you were dead in your transgressions and sins, in which you used to live when you followed the ways of this world and of the ruler of the kingdom of the air, the spirit who is now at work in those who are disobedient" (Eph. 2:1,2). Our greatest need, therefore, is *spiritual life*. That is what Jesus came to give us (see John 10:10).

Too many people have preached only half the gospel. We have presented Jesus as the Messiah who came to die for our sins so that when we die we will get to go to heaven. What's wrong with that? First, it gives the impression that eternal life is something we get when we die, which isn't true. "He who has the Son has life; he who does not have the Son of God does not have life" (1 John 5:12). Eternal life is not something we get when we die. Every child of God is alive in Christ the moment he or she is born again.

Here is another example of how we've preached only half the gospel. If you wanted to save a dead person, what would you do, give him life? If that is all you did, he would only die again. To save a dead person you would have to do two things. First, you would have to cure the disease that caused him to die. Since "the wages of sin is death" (Rom. 6:23), Jesus went to the cross to die for our sins. Is that all? Absolutely not. He was resurrected so that we might have life. Now finish Romans 6:23: "but the gift of God is eternal life in Christ Jesus our Lord." The glorious riches of salvation is "Christ in you, the hope of glory" (Col. 1:27). Being alive in Christ and dead to sin is the only assurance of victory (see Rom. 6:11).

Dear Christian, do you realize that you have the life of Christ within you? Your soul is in union with God. "For you died, and your life is now hidden with Christ in God. When Christ, who is your life, appears, then you also will appear with him in glory" (Col. 3:3,4). If this is not true, then you are not a Christian. A Christian is someone who has received Christ into his or her life by faith. Paul makes this point clearly: "Examine yourselves to see whether you are in the faith; test yourselves. Do you not realize that Christ Jesus is in you—unless, of course, you fail the test?" (2 Cor. 13:5).

Would it make any difference how you lived if you were fully aware of this truth? Keep in mind that the truth is true, whether you feel like it or even if you choose to believe it or not. Believing something doesn't make it true, and not believing something doesn't make it false. Truth is true whether we believe it or not. If you know and believe the truth, it will set you free (see John 8:32).

Jesus didn't come just to show us a new way to live; He came to give us His life. "I am the way and the truth and the life. No one comes to the Father except through me" (John 14:6). You have His life if you have put your trust in Christ and received Him as your Lord and Savior. Jesus came so that everyone who believes in Him may have eternal life. "For God so loved the world that he gave his one and only Son, that whoever believes in him shall not perish but have eternal life" (John 3:16). If you have the Son, you have life. "Whoever believes in the Son has eternal life, but whoever rejects the Son will not see life, for God's wrath remains on him" (John 3:36).

You may think your greatest need is to overcome your addiction or deal with a life-controlling problem. But those are just symptoms of the real disease, which is to be separated from Christ. Our greatest need is to be united with our heavenly Father; that is, to be spiritually alive. That life can only be recovered in Christ. "In him was life, and that life was the light of men" (John 1:4). How do we get it? "Everyone who listens to the Father and learns from him comes to me. No one has seen the Father except the one who is from God; only he has seen the Father. I tell you the truth, he who believes has everlasting life" (John 6:45-47).

Perhaps you're thinking, *Well, I have believed in Christ and have received Him, and I am a Christian, but I'm not free from addiction.* I think I can understand; I've been there and done that. My problem was that I didn't understand what it meant for Christ to live in me. I didn't know what it meant to trust in Him to live His life through me. I didn't believe that His life in me was enough for my problems and needs. Now I know that He not only came to give me life, but He actually is my life. For I have died and my life is hidden with Christ in God (see Col. 3:3).

Probe

How can the living Christ who is within you be the answer for your addiction? Explain the difference between trying to get rid of negative behavior and trusting in Christ to be your life.

Journal

_____

_____

_____

_____

_____

DAY 7

Thought for Today: Freedom in Christ is your birthright as a child of God.

It is for freedom that Christ has set us free. Stand firm, then, and do not let yourselves be burdened again by a yoke of slavery.

GALATIANS 5:1

Suppose you are the only child of parents who died in an accident. Your inheritance is $1 million, which has been deposited in your name. You don't have to work for it or wait until you die to receive it. How would you learn to live with your new inheritance? First, you would have to believe that you actually did inherit $1 million. Then you would have to learn how to draw from your bank account. Finally, you would have to learn how to live responsibly with the ability to tap into this new resource.

To be alive and free in Christ is the birthright of every child of God. It is worth far more than any lottery you could win. Nobody can cheat you out of your birthright, but the devil will try to convince you it isn't yours. He can't do anything about your position in Christ, but if he can convince you that it isn't true, you will live as though it isn't. "Therefore, brethren, be all the more diligent to make certain about His calling and choosing you; for as long as you practice these things, you will never stumble" (2 Pet. 1:10, *NASB*). In Dr. Charles Stanley's words, we have "settled for the settled-for life."

The first step to freedom is to believe that freedom has already been provided for you as a result of what Christ has done on the cross. It is not something you have to work for, it is something you have to believe in. It is your birthright. If something is already provided for you, the question is not how to earn it but how will you take possession of it. We can only by faith claim the promises of God and appropriate what He says is true. No matter what God has provided, it is not yours until you have received it by faith. "But as many as received Him, to them He gave the right to become children of God, even to those who believe in His name" (John 1:12, *NASB*).

I counseled a man who told me he was praying that God would deliver him from his alcoholism. I told him that God would not answer his prayer. He looked at me in astonishment, not sure he had heard me right. I told him, "There are two reasons God will not answer that prayer. First, He has already provided for our deliverance. "He has delivered us from the power of darkness and conveyed [us] into the kingdom of the Son of His love" (Col. 1:13, *NKJV*).

Second, it is a prayer of unbelief. If God has already provided something for us, we don't need to beg Him to give it to us. I have seen altars flooded at churches, Sunday after Sunday—people seeking to be delivered from various bondages and life-controlling problems. This doesn't seem to work, since the same people keep coming back week after week.

What seems to be the problem? Is God not interested in setting His people free? That can't be the reason, because Jesus Himself assured us that He came to set the captives free (see Luke 4:18,19). Christ certainly didn't fail in His mission. When He died on the cross, He said, "It is finished!" (John 19:30, *NASB*). In the high-priestly prayer, Jesus said He had completed the work He came to do (see John 17:4).

Furthermore, Paul wrote, "It was for freedom that Christ set us free; therefore keep standing firm and do not be subject again to a yoke of slavery" (Gal. 5:1, *NASB*). We can learn two important facts from this verse. First, Christ has done everything necessary for every Christian to be free. Second, it is possible to revert to our former way of living under the law and stay in bondage. But we do not need to pray and beg God to set us free. That has already been done.

Many Christians who are struggling with addictions are working hard to abstain. It's possible to achieve abstinence and still not be free. That is the condition of a "dry drunk." Freedom is not something we can obtain by working for it. We work "out" our salvation (see Phil. 2:12). Freedom has already been provided for us as a birthright and is gained by receiving it through faith. It doesn't depend on what we do but on what Christ has done. Now that's good news! What are you depending on— your sincere efforts or Christ's finished work on the cross?

You may continue to live in bondage if you fail to believe the truth or do not continue to live by faith according to what God says is true. In the latter case, you are not drawing from your eternal resources! It is every Christian's responsibility to do whatever is necessary to maintain a right relationship with God. Your eternal destiny is not at stake, but you will not experience your victory in Christ if you fail to claim and maintain your position in Christ.

If you have decided to become a Christian by faith but still find your-self living in bondage, what should you do? You need to make sure your relationship with God is right. You can do this by resolving all known personal and spiritual conflicts by going through the Steps to Freedom in Christ. I strongly suggest you read *Victory over the Darkness* and *The Bondage Breaker* by Neil T. Anderson. Many people can go through the steps on their own, but if you can't process the steps by yourself, find someone experienced and qualified to lead you through them.

You need to understand your identity, position and authority in Christ if you want to maintain your freedom. Remember, it was for free-dom that Christ set you free (see Gal. 5:1). Freedom is part of your inher-itance as a child of God. Don't settle for less.

Probe

How can you claim your birthright as a child of God on a daily basis? How can self-help programs and self-efforts actually keep you from experiencing your birthright?

Journal

_____

_____

_____

_____

_____

DAY 8

Thought for Today: The personal presence of Christ
in our lives is the answer.

How blessed is the man who does not walk in the counsel of the wicked, nor stand in the path of sinners, nor sit in the seat of scoffers! But his delight is in the law of the Lord, and in His law he meditates day and night.
PSALM 1:1,2, NASB

I knew a man—a Christian who wanted to live for Jesus—who spent all his family's considerable savings and retirement trying to overcome his problem with homosexuality. He had been in secular therapy for over a year at the advice of friends. I had the privilege of connecting Him with God by taking him through the Steps to Freedom in Christ. He found his freedom through repentance and faith in God, which is something no secular program can do.

It isn't unusual for Christians to seek secular help for their problems. In fact, many Christians who struggle with various addictive behaviors have spent thousands of dollars on secular counseling and treatment programs.

Why do they choose to seek secular help for their problems? Is it because they don't believe or don't know how Christ can set them free? Many churches have not adequately addressed the problems of alcoholism, drug addiction, anorexia, bulimia, sexual addiction, homosexuality and so on. Consequently, churches are referring many of their people to secular support groups, treatment centers, psychiatrists and psychologists. Many of them can help you cope with your problem and encourage you to live more responsibly, but they can't save you or set you free.

Does a sovereign God—who sent His only Son to give us life and destroy the works of the devil—not have an answer? Is not Christ the answer, and doesn't truth set you free? Did He fail in His mission to set the captives free? Surely our problems are not too difficult for God!

To offer an adequate answer, I am not suggesting involvement in a Christian self-help program. That won't work either. Nor am I suggesting a new way to live, based on the words of the Bible, which we follow in our own strength. We certainly need the truth of God's Word to have an adequate base for our faith, but we also need the life of Christ. Jesus is the way and the truth *and the life* (see John 14:6, emphasis added). He has shown us the way and given us the truth by which we live by faith, *and* He has given us His life in order to live it.

The man who spent all his money on secular treatment for his homosexual problem is now so excited about his freedom and his relationship with Christ that he spends most of his time telling others about it. We have no business sharing our faith unless we have a victorious testimony that is a living witness of the resurrected life of Christ within us.

Paul says we shouldn't go to the world's legal system in order to solve our legal problems. Taking our disputes before the ungodly is a bad witness (see 1 Cor. 6:1-6). Should we then rely upon some self-help program and consult the ungodly to solve our spiritual and emotional problems? Read again the words of the psalmist:

> How blessed is the man who does not walk in the counsel of the wicked, nor stand in the path of sinners, nor sit in the seat of scoffers! But his delight is in the law of the Lord, and in His law he

meditates day and night. And he will be like a tree firmly planted by streams of water, which yields its fruit in its season, and its leaf does not wither; and in whatever he does, he prospers (Ps. 1:1-3, *NASB*).

If you want to be blessed, prosperous and free in Christ, you will have to be firmly rooted in Him. Only then can you be built up in Him (see Col. 2:6,7). "See to it that no one takes you captive through philosophy and empty deception, according to the tradition of men, according to the elementary principles of the world, rather than according to Christ. For in Him all the fulness of Deity dwells in bodily form, and in Him you have been made complete, and He is the head over all rule and authority" (Col. 2:8-10, *NASB*).

Probe
In what ways have you looked to the secular world or sought the counsel of unbelievers for answers to your problems? How can you turn to God on a daily basis for truth to live by?

Journal
_____

_____

_____

_____

_____

DAY 9

Thought for Today: The gospel is the power of God unto salvation.

*Yet to all who received him, to those who believed in his name, he gave
the right to become children of God—children born not of natural descent,
nor of human decision or a husband's will, but born of God.*

JOHN 1:12,13

So far in this devotional we have learned that Christ came to set the captives free. Freedom is our birthright—the inheritance of every child of
God. We have seen that salvation means deliverance, or freedom, from
bondage. But none of this will apply to you unless you are a child of God.
Have you believed in Christ and received Him as your Lord and Savior?

Jesus said, "I have come that they may have life, and have it to the
full" (John 10:10). Have you discovered the joy and peace of being spiritually alive in Christ? Perhaps you have believed in the existence of God
and His Son, and have tried to live a good life, but have never consciously invited Him to be your Savior and Lord. No matter who you are or
what you have done, at this very moment you can receive Him into your
life. He offers you the same wonderful life that millions of people
through the centuries have received with life-changing results. He has
already paid the penalty for your sin. He is asking you to put your trust
in Him. Here are four eternal truths that will help you discover how to
know God personally and experience the full life He promises.

1. *God loves you and wants to have a personal relationship with you.* "For
God so loved the world that he gave his one and only Son, that whoever
believes in him shall not perish but have eternal life" (John 3:16). "Now
this is eternal life: that they may know you, the only true God, and Jesus
Christ, whom you have sent" (John 17:3). God wants you to know Him,
but sin is the reason that most people do not have a personal relationship
with Him.

2. *Our sin cuts us off from God so that we cannot have a personal relationship with Him and experience His love.* We were all created to have a per-

sonal relationship with God, yet we have all sinned: "For all have sinned and fall short of the glory of God" (Rom. 3:23). Because we all chose to go our own independent way, our relationship with God was broken. The fact that we are selfish and self-centered is obvious because we either rebel against God or we don't really care about Him. This is evidence of what the Bible calls "sin"; Scripture says that "the wages of sin is death" (spiritual separation from God, Rom. 6:23). We are cut off from God because He is holy (pure and sinless) and we are sinful. A great gap cuts us off from God because He cannot tolerate sin. People often try to find a full and meaningful life through their own efforts. They try to live a good life or be religious. But the Bible clearly teaches that there is only one way to bridge this gap between God's holiness and our sin.

3. *Jesus Christ is God's only cure for our sin.* Through Him you can know God personally and experience His love. Jesus died in our place, for our sins. "But God demonstrates his own love for us in this: While we were still sinners, Christ died for us" (Rom. 5:8). Then Jesus rose from the dead. "Christ died for our sins . . . He was buried . . . He was raised on the third day according to the Scriptures . . . He appeared to [Peter], then to the twelve. After that He appeared to more than five hundred" (1 Cor. 15:3-6, *NASB*).

Jesus is the only way to God. He said, "I am the way and the truth and the life. No one comes to the Father except through me" (John 14:6). God has done the work to bridge the gap that cuts us off from our heavenly Father. He sent His Son, Jesus Christ, to die on the Cross in our place to pay the penalty for our sin. But it is not enough just to know these truths. We must take the next step and "cross the bridge."

4. *We must individually receive Jesus Christ as Savior and Lord.* Then we can know God personally and experience His love. "To all who received him, to those who believed in his name, he gave the right to become children of God—children born not of natural descent, nor of human decision or a husband's will, but born of God" (John 1:12,13). Receiving Christ involves turning to God from self (called repentance) and trusting Christ to come into our lives to forgive our sins so that we can begin our

personal relationship with Him. "Repent and believe the good news!" (Mark 1:15). Just to know in your mind that Jesus Christ is the Son of God and that He died on the Cross for our sins is not enough. We receive Jesus Christ by faith, which is a choice we make based on the truth of God's Word.

Would you like to accept Jesus' invitation to life? By faith you can receive Jesus Christ right now through prayer. God knows your heart and is not so concerned with your words as He is with the attitude of your heart. Millions of people all around the world have already found new life in Christ. The following is a suggested prayer that can help you express your trust in Jesus:

> Dear Lord Jesus, I realize that I am a sinner and spiritually dead. Thank You for dying on the cross for my sins. Thank You for the resurrection life that You came to give me. I now choose by faith to receive You as my Savior and Lord. I choose to believe that You have forgiven my sins and given me eternal life. Please make me the kind of person You created me to be. From this day forward I desire to know You and the power of Your resurrection. In Jesus' name, I pray. Amen.

Probe

Did you just now receive Christ into your life by faith? How can you know that Christ is in your life (see 1 John 5:11-14)?

Journal

_____

_____

_____

_____

_____

DAY 10

Thought for Today: The gospel is not addition, it is transformation.

Therefore, if anyone is in Christ, he is a new creation;
the old has gone, the new has come!
2 CORINTHIANS 5:17

She grew up a very plain and undistinguished person. She felt like a nobody and believed she was a nobody. In high school she got into drugs and sex. She became the girl friend of the president of a Hell's Angels biker's group. While riding across the open range they had a horrible motorcycle accident. Her leg was badly broken and she had a puncture wound that wouldn't heal.

She lay in a hospital for weeks, depressed and suicidal. She had no visitors except for her mother every few days. She kept the shades drawn and wouldn't bathe. Her hair was matted and her eyes were sunken in despair. Her sister, who had just become a Christian, called on the phone. Although the sister didn't know how to present the gospel, she made the young woman in the hospital bed promise that she would pray after their conversation. The injured woman agreed just to get her sister off the phone. But after she hung up, the thought kept coming to her: *You promised to pray.* She did, and God met her in that hospital room. She received Him as her Lord and Savior.

The young woman's mother was astonished the next time she came to see her daughter. She started to turn and walk out, thinking she was in the wrong room. The shades were open and the room was filled with light; her daughter was clean and filled with new life. She was a new person. The Bible says that in Christ we are new creations, the old is gone and everything is new (see 2 Cor. 5:17).

When you receive Christ by faith, you don't just get something new added to the same old person you've always been. Being religiously converted means to change one's values and rules for living. But Christianity is more than a religion; it is a relationship. When we are born again we become someone totally different. We are no longer "in Adam," we are now "in Christ." We were spiritually dead; now we are spiritually alive. Formerly, we had no relationship with God; now we are His children.

The Greek word for "transformed" is *metamorphe* from which we get our word "metamorphosis," which means a change into a different form. When a caterpillar comes out of the cocoon, it doesn't come out as the lowly worm that crawled in. What emerges is a beautiful creature that can fly. The same physical chemicals that made up the caterpillar now make up the butterfly, but the creature is no longer the same. It has experienced metamorphosis—a transformation.

When we put on Christ, nothing external changes other than our countenances; but inside, we have been transformed and are being transformed into His image day by day. His life-giving Spirit has transformed us into children of God. "The Spirit himself testifies with our spirit that we are God's children. Now if we are children, then we are heirs—heirs of God and co-heirs with Christ" (Rom. 8:16,17). When we begin to understand who we are and what we have, we will begin to live like the children of God we truly are.

Many Christians who know they have been born again believe their sins are forgiven and have the assurance of eternal life, yet they still live in bondage to addictive behaviors. Why is this? In many cases they still believe they are the same sorry sinners they used to be. Many people have been told, "Once an alcoholic, always an alcoholic," and they believed it. People have the same problem with salvation. They think, *I was a sinner before Christ and now I am just a forgiven sinner.* Not true! You are now a saint who sins, but the only hope you have of overcoming sin is to believe that you are alive in Christ and dead to sin (see Rom. 6:11).

John Murray describes our salvation and the results of it in terms of regeneration, which is an act of God through the Holy Spirit to new life in Christ. This new life is not merely a neutral state arising out of forgiveness of sin, but a positive implantation of Christ's righteousness in man by which we are "quickened" or made alive (see John 5:21). We are made a new creation (see 2 Cor. 5:17) and given a new life (see Rom. 6:4). Regeneration involves an illumination of the mind, a change in the will and a renewed nature.[1]

You may be thinking, *I don't feel or act like a new creation.* That's the problem. Because we don't feel or act like it, we don't believe it. This is not to infer that changing the way you think and believe is easy. It's not. We will spend an entire section explaining this in "The Battle Is Won or Lost in the Mind." The first step, however, is to know what the gospel means and what salvation has accomplished for you. Don't ever forget that it is *the truth*—not how you feel or how you act—that sets you free (see John 8:32). Believing the lie is what keeps you in bondage. If Satan can get you to believe that you're still the same old person you used to be, then you will still live and behave in the same old way.

Probe

What would happen if you got up every morning and proclaimed: "I am alive in Christ and dead to sin, and I choose to live today by faith, according to what God says is true and regardless of how I feel"? Would you be willing to say that every morning for at least one month?

Journal

_____

_____

_____

_____

_____

Note
1. John Murray, *Principles of Conduct* (Grand Rapids, Mich.: Eerdmans, 1957), p. 204.

DAY 11

Thought for Today: Our life is governed by the fundamentals of our faith.

His divine power has given us everything we need for life and godliness through our knowledge of him who called us by his own glory and goodness.

2 PETER 1:3

When I attended the University of Alabama, Paul "Bear" Bryant was the coach. He set a record for winning more games for major universities than any coach in the history of the game. Why was he so successful? Most people believe it was because he majored in the basics—tackling, blocking, catching, running, kicking. His teams weren't fancy, and some people even thought they were dull. But they were better coached in the basic elements of football than any other team. His teams were fundamentally sound.

If you and I are going to walk in the freedom Christ purchased for us, we need to be fundamentally sound. We need to know who God is and who we are in Christ. We need to understand the gospel and how to live by faith according to what God says is true. Simply stated, "We need to know the truth." I searched for most of my Christian life—without success—for something or someone to help me overcome my addiction.

In October 1988, I had been struggling with my alcoholism for more than eight years. I had been a Christian for 18 years. I was a seminary graduate who served in the pastorate for eight years. Nevertheless, I was addicted to alcohol. I had tried everything I knew to quit, but it only seemed to get worse. I didn't have anywhere else to turn or know of anything else to try.

One Sunday, I was so frustrated and defeated that I didn't know what to do but just get drunk. I picked a fight with my wife and told her she and the other people at our church were a bunch of hypocrites. I was the real hypocrite. I claimed to be a new creation in Christ who loved the Lord and put Him first in my life, but my actions showed otherwise. I didn't fully understand the gospel or who I was in Christ. I saw myself as an alcoholic, a failure and a sinner, so that's the way I acted.

This drunken binge ended as all of them had. I was driving home filled with guilt and despair. I noticed some tapes on the front seat and I popped one into the tape player. It was from a set called "Victorious Christian Living," by Dr. Bill and Anabel Gillham. This particular tape was of Anabel speaking on John 14:20. I thought I knew my Bible pretty well, but I never knew what Jesus meant when He said, "On that day you will realize that I am in my Father, and you are in me, and I am in you." As I listened to the tape I realized that I had never thought about the implications of this verse. If Jesus is in me and I am in Him, how does that change me? If this is true, and I believed it was, then maybe this was the answer I was looking for. At first I didn't fully understand what it meant; but when I learned how to appropriate this truth by faith, I knew who I was in Christ and I was free.

What experience must we have in order to be free? The only experience that had to happen was Christ's death and resurrection two thousand years ago. The only way we can enter into this incredible, revolutionary, life-changing truth is by faith. No experience will *make* that true; it *is* true. When we choose to live by faith according to this truth, freedom works out in our experience.

According to 2 Peter 1:3, we have everything we need for life and godliness. The next verse says we have become partakers of His divine nature. Because we are united with Him, we can be all that He created us to be.

Here are a few of the gospel basics for Christian living. This list represents just a few of the benefits we have in Christ. If you believed them, would your life change?

1. You have been justified—completely forgiven and made righteous (see Rom. 5:1).
2. You died with Christ to the power of sin's rule over your life (see Rom. 6:1-7).
3. You are free from condemnation (see Rom. 8:1).
4. You have been placed in Christ by God's doing (see 1 Cor. 1:30).

5. You have received the Spirit of God into your life that you might know the things freely given to you by God (see 1 Cor. 2:12).
6. You have been given the mind of Christ (see 1 Cor. 2:16).
7. You have been bought with a price; you are not your own, you belong to God (see 1 Cor. 6:19,20).

The first chapter of Ephesians lists some of the spiritual blessings we have in Christ. Paul—under the inspiration of God—realized that many believers couldn't fully grasp all that has been bestowed on them. In Ephesians 1:18,19, Paul says, "I pray also that the eyes of your heart may be enlightened in order that you may know the hope to which he has called you, the riches of his glorious inheritance in the saints, and his incomparably great power for us who believe."

Probe
What keeps us from appropriating all that we have in Christ? Pride? Ignorance? Unbelief? How can these be overcome?

Journal
_____
_____
_____
_____
_____

DAY 12

Thought for Today: Self-sufficiency undermines our sufficiency in Christ.

For what the Law could not do, weak as it was through the flesh, God did: sending His own Son in the likeness of sinful flesh and as an offering for sin, He condemned sin in the flesh.

ROMANS 8:3, NASB

In January 1985, I (Mike) had promised my wife that if I ever got drunk again I would move out of the house. It was about a week later that I did get drunk and agreed to abide by my promise. I had no earthly idea what I was going to do, but I had heard about a Christian treatment center and decided that would be the best thing for me.

I had been struggling intensely with my addiction for more than five years. My wife had given up on me. When she told me good-bye, she said she didn't want me to call her or write while I was gone, and she really didn't want to see me again.

About midnight I boarded a bus in Atlanta and rode all night to Bethel Colony in Lenoir, North Carolina. I was the only person on the bus, so I had a lot of time for reflection. I was beginning to see that it wasn't just my behavior that was so wrong. There was something wrong with my whole understanding of the Christian life. I wanted to do good, but I just couldn't. It was just as Paul described in Romans 7:18,19 (*NASB*): "For I know that nothing good dwells in me, that is, in my flesh; for the wishing is present in me, but the doing of the good is not. For the good that I wish, I do not do; but I practice the very evil that I do not wish."

I was living in the flesh (my own resources), and there was nothing good in my flesh or the power to do good. I really didn't understand what living by the flesh meant as opposed to living by the Spirit. I knew what was biblically right and wrong, and I was trying to live a righteous life under the law, in my own strength. My pride kept saying, "You can do it. Try harder!"

I finally arrived at Bethel after traveling for 16 hours. I was physically and emotionally exhausted, and totally depressed. They assigned me to the laundry room for my service while I was there. It contained one washing machine and one dryer. For the next two months I washed and dried clothes for 20 alcoholics, addicts, street persons and chronic offenders. Many of them came to the center carrying a plastic bag full of the filthiest clothes I had ever seen. But I realized these men were no different from me. All of us had tried to live our lives from our own resources, with our own plans, and we had all failed.

God used my time at Bethel to humble me and show me that in my flesh there was nothing good. It was an extremely valuable lesson and one I had to learn if I was ever going to be free.

In 1997, I was invited to come to Bethel Colony and be the Bible teacher at their Homecoming and Bible Conference. As I was sharing my testimony of how I had found my freedom in Christ, I said, "All my life I have tried to get my act together. Is that what you're trying to do, too?"

I was startled to hear a chorus of affirmation from the men.

"Forget it," I told them, "because it won't work!" I shared how I had learned that my act was no good and that asking God to help me improve it wasn't the answer—our flesh can't be improved or cleaned up. My act was nothing but my flesh, and the flesh profits nothing (see John 6:63). The flesh is hostile to God because it acts independently of Him. Those who live according to the flesh cannot please Him (see Rom. 8:7,8).

The only thing God can do with our flesh is put it on the Cross and start over, and that's what He did. The problem is that we were born sinners and have had a relapse. The standard answer to the question, "How many sins do you have to commit to go to hell?" is "One." But the right answer is "None," because we were born physically alive but spiritually dead and were by nature children of wrath (see Eph. 2:1,3). That's like asking how many moos it takes to make a cow. A cow moos because it is a cow. A sinner sins because he is spiritually dead—separated from God.

God isn't interested in changing your behavior or improving your old nature. Instead, He wants you to realize that in the flesh (your resources) there is no good thing. God wants you to give up on the flesh and trust Him to be your life and your resource. The only life that works is Christ's life within you. The issue is whether you will choose to trust in Christ and His life and resources or trust yourself and your own resources. The choice you make determines whether you walk in the flesh and experience bondage or walk in the Spirit and experience freedom.

Trying harder will only lead to more failure, frustration and bondage. God wants all of us to stop relying on ourselves and our old ways of living. "Now those who belong to Christ Jesus have crucified the flesh with its passions and desires" (Gal. 5:24, *NASB*). We can do this by faith because God has already won that battle. "In Him you were also circumcised with a circumcision made without hands, in the removal of the body of the flesh by the circumcision of Christ" (Col. 2:11, *NASB*).

God doesn't want to change your old futile way of living; He wants you to give up on it and exchange it for Christ's life and find your sufficiency in Him.

Probe
Think of all the ways you have tried to get your act together. Have you come to the point where you can honestly say, "I can't, but I believe God can; therefore, I'm going to trust in Him"?

Journal

_____

_____

_____

_____

_____

UNDERSTANDING THE TRUE NATURE OF YOUR HEAVENLY FATHER

DAY 13

Thought for Today: God is love.

We have come to know and have believed the love which God has for us. God is love, and the one who abides in love abides in God, and God abides in him.
1 JOHN 4:16, NASB

A pastor's wife who carried a huge load of responsibility for her church never felt that what she did was good enough. She didn't feel accepted by her husband or the people in the church, and she struggled with many relationship problems. Finally, she was driven to seek some help.

The counselor gave her an exercise in which she answered questions about her feelings toward God. After the exercise, the counselor said, "You see God as someone who is very strict and unapproachable. You respect Him greatly, the way you would respect the head of a girl's school, but He isn't someone you would want to get close to."

She hadn't thought of it that way but agreed that the counselor was right. She had a distorted concept of God and of who she was in relationship to Him, which contributed to her burnout. Nobody wants to be intimately involved with someone who is deemed to be strict or unapproachable.

Do you know who your heavenly Father is and what He's really like? The Bible teaches that God is love, but do you always feel that He loves you? Anxiety disorders, depression and chemical addiction are the three most prevalent mental health problems in America, in that order. Those who struggle with mental illness almost always have a distorted concept of what God is like. To be mentally healthy, one must have a true knowledge of God.

Our understanding of God is something we develop over time. The way we have been raised and educated will greatly contribute to our knowledge of Him. Many people project an image of their earthly fathers onto their heavenly Father. For example, one young woman said she couldn't trust God because "love leaves." She believed this because every significant person she had ever loved had left her, including her father and her husband.

Because every human image has flaws, we often derive an inaccurate picture of who God really is. If we see God in the form of our earthly father we may think of Him as a stern judge, a harsh taskmaster, a strict schoolteacher, a disapproving parent or a remote ruler. Can you see how your concept of God could affect how you relate to Him?

An improper concept of God could lead a person to focus on what he or she should do to please God in order to gain His love and acceptance. Some think God will love them more if they perform better. If they make a mistake, they feel unloved and rejected because of their belief that God is a disapproving parent who can never be pleased. That view would make the love and acceptance of God conditional, which it isn't.

Which parent, friend, teacher, or boss is God most like? Hint: That's a false question, because God isn't like any of them. Although people may appear to be godly because they are becoming like Him, they are created in His image, not He in theirs. No mortal can give us the unconditional love and acceptance that God does. "Though my father and mother forsake me, the Lord will receive me" (Ps. 27:10).

If you performed better, would God love you more? Of course not! The love of God is not dependent upon us or how well we perform. We don't do the things we do with the hope that God may one day accept us. God has accepted us; that is why we do the things we do. We don't labor in the vineyard with the hope that God may someday love us. God loves us, and that is why we labor in the vineyard. We don't get our act together in order to receive God's love; we receive God's love in order to get our act together. "You see, at just the right time, when we were still powerless, Christ died for the ungodly. Very rarely will anyone die for a righteous man, though for a good man someone might possibly dare to die. But God demonstrates his own love for us in this: While we were still sinners, Christ died for us" (Rom. 5:6-8).

The mental essence of addiction is self-consciousness, and the answer to addiction is God-consciousness. Several years ago the *Wittenberg Door* interviewed writer-priest Brennan Manning, who commented:

The only lasting freedom from self-consciousness comes from a profound awareness that God loves me as I am and not as I should be, that He loves me beyond worthiness and unworthiness, beyond fidelity and infidelity, that He loves me in the morning sun and the evening rain without caution, regret, boundary or breaking point; that no matter what I do, He can't stop loving me. When I am really in conscious communion with the reality of the wild, passionate, relentless, stubborn, pursuing love of God in Jesus Christ for me, it's not that I have to or I've got to or I must or I should or I ought. Suddenly I want to change because I know how deeply I'm loved.

God doesn't love you because you're lovable. God loves you because God is love. It is His nature to love you.

Probe
Does your understanding of God compel you to pursue Him? Why or why not? What experiences have you had that would cause you to think that God doesn't love you?

Journal

_____

_____

_____

_____

_____

DAY 14

Thought for Today: God has accepted you just the way you are.

Wherefore, accept one another, just as Christ also
accepted us to the glory of God.
ROMANS 15:7, NASB

Several years ago, I received a phone call from my daughter. She informed me that she was moving in with her boyfriend. I didn't think this boyfriend was an answer to a father's prayer, so I didn't receive this as good news. I felt strongly that I needed to warn her of the dangers of doing this, but more importantly, I wanted her to know that I loved her just the way she was. I couldn't accept her behavior, but I could accept her.

I wrote her a six-page letter. In the first four pages I told her I loved her and accepted her, no matter what she did. She was my daughter and I loved her unconditionally. In the last two pages I warned her of the consequences of living outside of God's will and that if we live according to the flesh, we will reap corruption.

A few days later she called me on Father's Day. She told me she loved me and appreciated the letter and my concern for her. She also said she let her boyfriend read it. A few years later they married. When she became pregnant with her first child, she called me and said, "Dad, if I am going to raise a child, I would like to do it around Christian parents. So could we move to Atlanta and live with you until my husband gets a job?" I agreed, and they moved in with us for five months.

One Saturday morning at the breakfast table, my daughter told me why they were willing to move in with us. "Because we knew you accepted us," she said.

Have I always accepted my daughter unconditionally? Not until I came to believe that God accepted me unconditionally. After 15 years of struggling and failing as a Christian, I finally understood and was able to appropriate God's unconditional love and acceptance of me. Then I was able to accept myself and other people in the same way.

It's one thing to acknowledge God's unconditional love and acceptance, but it's another thing to personally believe and appropriate God's love and acceptance when we are living in defeat. Mother Teresa believed that our biggest need is to be loved and accepted. She spent her life reaching out to the unlovable, demonstrating God's unconditional love. God's love is most evident when it is most needed. Anybody can love the lovely, but it takes the grace of God to love the unlovable. "If you love those who love you, what credit is that to you? Even 'sinners' love those who love them" (Luke 6:32).

Unless you know that you are loved and accepted unconditionally by God, your pursuit of Him and His righteousness will always be skewed by your effort to gain something you already have.

I received an e-mail from a man who questioned God's love and acceptance. He quoted a lot of verses that appeared to "prove" that God's love and acceptance are conditional. Obviously he had been hurt in the past, probably by some of God's children. God's love for us is not conditioned by our faith but by His character. Christ demonstrated His love for us when He died on the Cross for all our sins. "This is how we know what love is: Jesus Christ laid down his life for us. And we ought to lay down our lives for our brothers" (1 John 3:16). Our acceptance doesn't depend on what we do but on what God has done. If God's acceptance depended upon our righteousness, none of us would be accepted.

The subtle motivation behind many of our pursuits is to gain the approval and acceptance of others or, in a negative sense, to avoid rejection. Even in the best of human relationships we will feel the sting of criticism and rejection, because we are not living with perfect people. Only in our relationship with God can we find unconditional love and acceptance, because it is the nature of God to love us. As we mature in Christ, the love of God should become our nature as well. "Dear friends, let us love one another, for love comes from God. Everyone who loves has been born of God and knows God. Whoever does not love does not know God, because God is love" (1 John 4:7,8).

We live in a performance-based society. We compete against and compare ourselves with one another. It's hard to believe the kingdom of God is any different, but it is. God's love for you is not based on your performance but on His nature and Christ's performance when He took our place on the cross. Everything sinful in your life was put on the Cross, and God has removed your sins as far as the east is from the west. In Christ you are forgiven and made acceptable in His sight just the way you are. There is nothing you could do to make yourself more acceptable to Him. That is the grace of God.

Probe

What specific events in your life have caused you to question God's unconditional love and acceptance? Other than the Cross, what more proof would you need to be convinced that God loves you and has accepted you into His family?

Journal

_____

_____

_____

_____

_____

DAY 15

Thought for Today: Nothing you can do can make God love you less, and nothing you can do can make Him love you more.

For I am convinced that neither death nor life, neither angels nor demons, neither the present nor the future, nor any powers, neither height nor depth, nor anything else in all creation, will be able to separate us from the love of God that is in Christ Jesus our Lord.
ROMANS 8:38,39

I vividly remember when I understood that God loved me and accepted me unconditionally. I was struggling with alcoholism, and my sense of worth was at an all-time low. One afternoon in my office, I noticed a Christian magazine, the *Wittenberg Door,* and picked it up. It featured an interview with Brennan Manning, a Catholic priest who was a former alcoholic. He presented a concept of God that I had never heard before. I was astonished to read his portrayal of God's unconditional love and acceptance of us. Throughout the 16 years of my Christian life, I had seen myself as a dirty, rotten sinner who could not measure up. I believed that God was sick and tired of me and my failures. No one had ever taught me differently.

This priest had the audacity to say that our ability to perform doesn't affect God's love for us. No matter what we are capable or incapable of doing, God still loves us unconditionally. Manning said something to the effect that the only lasting freedom from self-consciousness comes from a profound awareness that God loves each of us as we are, not as we should be.[1]

The words flowed like pure water poured out on a man dying of thirst in a dry and wasted land. I drank in this truth, and God's love penetrated into the depths of my being. God was *for* me, not against me. I didn't need to change in order to gain God's love and acceptance. God loved me; therefore, I could change. Manning said that every attempt to change ourselves is motivated either by self-hatred or guilt in some form. This is one of the main reasons that Christians don't experience freedom from their addictions.

Guilt is a powerful motivation, but it doesn't bring the desired result. According to Manning, the biggest mistake we can make is to say, "Lord, if I change, You'll love me, won't You?" But the Lord's reply is always, "Wait a minute, son, you've got it all wrong. You don't have to change so that I'll love you; I love you so that you'll change." This was what I needed to hear. Even though I taught about God's unconditional love and acceptance as a pastor, this was the first time I really understood it and believed it.

As my concept of God began to heal, my relationship with my heavenly Father took on a new dimension. Instead of viewing myself as a sinner trying to perform for God, I saw myself as His child whom He loved and accepted. That's not to say God always approves of our behavior. He doesn't. But even then we have the assurance that His discipline is a proof of His love: "The Lord disciplines those he loves" (Heb. 12:6).

In my bondage to alcohol, I believed that God's acceptance was based on my performance. The problem was, I couldn't perform perfectly. Therefore, I believed I had failed God and disappointed Him. But God's acceptance of us is not based on our performance. It is based on Christ's performance on the Cross.

The great commandment is to love the Lord our God with all our heart, but we have to first appropriate His love in order to return it. "We love because he first loved us" (1 John 4:19). "And so we know and rely on the love God has for us. God is love. Whoever lives in love lives in God, and God in him" (1 John 4:16). Love doesn't begin with us; it begins with God.

When I finally understood God's love and acceptance, one of the first things I did was to sit down and write my three children a letter. I confessed to them that I had been a harsh, legalistic father who showed only conditional love. I had also given them the wrong idea about God.

Wouldn't it be wonderful if there was someone who knew everything about you—every lewd thought and despicable act you never dared to tell anyone—and yet loved and accepted you? *There is!* Why don't you receive it right now? You don't have to fully understand this gracious characteristic of God in order to receive it.

Probe

If you performed better, would God love you more? If you fully understood God's unconditional love and acceptance, would your perception of yourself change? Your perception of God? How would that understanding change your behavior?

Journal

_____

_____

_____

_____

_____

Note
1. Brennan Manning has written several books on the subject, including *The Ragamuffin Gospel* and *Abba's Child.*

DAY 16

Thought for Today: A gracious gift offered freely must still be received.

*Yet to all who received him, to those who believed in his name, he gave
the right to become children of God. . . . From the fullness of his grace we
have all received one blessing after another.*

JOHN 1:12,16

When I was growing up, I struggled with feelings of insecurity and inferiority. It was almost impossible for me to receive love. I would be interested in a certain girl and then pursue her with great determination. If
she liked me, I would immediately lose interest in her. I just couldn't
believe that anyone would really be interested in me. I was programmed
to believe that people would reject me, and if they didn't, I couldn't
receive it. I couldn't receive love that was freely given, because I believed
it had to be earned.

While struggling with alcoholism, I remember a counselor's telling
me that I was more comfortable with chaos than with peace. I couldn't
receive the good things God and people offered me.

Do you have trouble receiving the grace of God? Society has taught
us to perform and achieve in order to earn approval and develop a sense
of worth. But God turns it around and says, "I am the giver. Will you
receive your identity and sense of worth from Me?" Many of us have trouble answering yes because we want to make a name for ourselves and
prove to the world that we're really something worthy of their admira-
tion. There's a name for such foolishness. It's called pride, and it keeps us
from believing and receiving. We believe that we don't need anyone's
help. The truth is, we absolutely need God, and we necessarily need each
other.

God owns the car of life, and He is the driver. He has invited us to stop
running on our own fuel and climb aboard. Pride answers, "Thanks, but
no thanks; I will get there on my own." And off we go until we run out of
gas. But the invitation is always there: "Come to me, all you who are weary

and burdened, and I will give you rest. Take my yoke upon you and learn from me, for I am gentle and humble in heart, and you will find rest for your souls. For my yoke is easy and my burden is light" (Matt. 11:28-30).

When I married Julia, she accepted and loved me, but I couldn't receive it. I was extremely jealous and suspicious. I accused her of ridiculous things. It was as if I was trying to get her to reject me. When she finally did, I would say, "See? I knew all along you would reject me."

I was more comfortable with rejection than acceptance because I thought I deserved rejection. I was suspicious of anyone who loved me, because I couldn't love myself.

We have trouble receiving because we see ourselves as unworthy of any gift we haven't earned. Salvation is a free gift of God. We did nothing to deserve the sacrificial death of Christ on the Cross when we were ungodly sinners. His sacrifice was an act of grace, which by definition is getting what we don't deserve.

Thinking a free gift is too good to be true, we've been conditioned to ask, "What's the catch?" There is only one catch, and many trip over it. In order to experience God's grace, you must receive it. You can't earn it and you don't deserve it. You can only receive it.

The prodigal son in Luke 15 wasted all his money on loose living. Yet, when he finally came to his senses and returned home, he was received like a long-lost son, and a banquet was thrown in his honor. Such a reception was always there for him, but he had to make the decision to come back home. He had to be willing to receive the unconditional love and acceptance of his father. He could have decided that he was going to turn over a new leaf, work hard and redeem himself, thus proving that he could make it on his own. But he finally realized he couldn't, so he came home to his gracious father who would provide for all his needs.

"Don't be deceived, my dear brothers. Every good and perfect gift is from above, coming down from the Father of the heavenly lights, who does not change like shifting shadows" (Jas. 1:16,17). We are deceived if we believe we can earn the approval of God. And we are deceived if we believe He can't love and accept us because we are unworthy of His grace.

Nobody deserves God's grace. If he did, it would no longer be grace. We are saved only by the grace of God.

Probe

Is it hard for you to believe and receive the grace of God? Do you find it easier to give than to receive? Why?

Journal

_____

_____

_____

_____

_____

DAY 17

Thought for Today: God's love is based on an eternal and unchanging covenant.

This is the covenant I will make with the house of Israel after that time, declares the Lord. I will put my laws in their minds and write them on their hearts. I will be their God, and they will be my people. No longer will a man teach his neighbor, or a man his brother, saying, "Know the Lord," because they will all know me, from the least of them to the greatest. For I will forgive their wickedness and will remember their sins no more.

HEBREWS 8:10-12

Because of your sins, failures and lack of commitment, have you ever felt that God has given up on you? Let me tell you a story that illustrates why I believe He won't do that.

Dr. Robertson McQuilkin, a noted Christian author and theologian, was president of Columbia Bible College and Seminary. When he was 57, he learned that Muriel, his wife of 40 years, had Alzheimer's disease. When she reached the point that she could no longer care for herself, Dr. McQuilkin had a difficult decision to make. He could put her in a nursing home and let them care for her, or he could do it himself. Of course, if he cared for her himself he would have to give up his job as head of the Bible college and seminary. His decision was to resign the presidency and care for his wife.

This is how he explained his decision. "As Muriel needed more and more of me, I wrestled daily with the question of who gets me full-time—my wife or Columbia Bible College and Seminary? When the time came, my decision was firm. It took no great calculation. It was a matter of integrity. Had I not promised 42 years before, 'in sickness and in health . . . till death do us part'?"[1]

Dr. McQuilkin goes on to say that he was surprised at people's response to his decision. Husbands and wives renewed their marriage vows. Pastors told the story to their congregations. More than likely, Dr. McQuilkin's decision moved people because it's unusual to see people go to such lengths to honor a covenant.

God has made a covenant with us, too. It is based on His love, which is even more steadfast than Dr. McQuilkin's love for his wife. God's love for us isn't based on our actions but on His unchanging nature. That means His covenant is also unchanging. Keeping the covenant depends on Him, not us.

What exactly is a covenant? According to Webster's dictionary, to make a covenant is to enter into a formal agreement; to stipulate; to bind one's self by contract. Most of us know that a legal covenant is binding. Marriage covenants are also supposed to be binding according to our wedding vows.

Even though many people don't honor their wedding vows, God always honors His covenant: "God is not a man, that he should lie, nor a son of man, that he should change his mind. Does he speak and then not act? Does he promise and not fulfill?" (Num. 23:19). God's new covenant with us is unconditional and made possible only by the death and resurrection of our Lord Jesus Christ. The writer of Hebrews prayed: "May the

God of peace, who through the blood of the eternal covenant brought back from the dead our Lord Jesus, that great Shepherd of the sheep, equip you with everything good for doing his will, and may he work in us what is pleasing to him, through Jesus Christ, to whom be glory for ever and ever. Amen" (Heb. 13:20,21).

What is God's new covenant with us? It is the promise that He will be our God and we will be His people; we can know and relate to Him as our heavenly Father; He has forgiven our sins and will remember them no more; He will put His laws in our minds and write them on our hearts (see Heb. 8:10-12). You can stake your life and base your future on this covenant. Watchman Nee says this about God's covenant with us:

> Promises are given to encourage faith, but often we cannot rise to God's promises. At times we cannot even lay hold of divine facts: appearances seem to belie them. But when this is so, we still have His covenant. And the covenant means more than the promises, more even than the mighty works. It is something God has committed Himself to do. The covenant is a handle given us by God on which faith can lay hold. Morally we have no claim on God. But He has been pleased to bind Himself to a covenant, and having thus pledged Himself to act for us, He is—and I say it reverently—bound to do so. Herein is the preciousness of the covenant. It is this that gives strength to faith when faith is at its weakest.[2]

Because the New Testament covenant is eternal and unchanging, there is nothing that can change it. The covenant was initiated by God and sealed by the blood of Christ on the Cross in order to secure our relationship with God. Our relationship with Him is based on His promises and covenant, not on our ability to perform. Victory is assured when we claim His promises and believe His Word.

Probe

Can you explain in your own words the covenant relationship you have with your heavenly Father? How does this truth influence how you live?

Journal

_____

_____

_____

_____

_____

Notes

1. Robertson McQuilkin, "Repaying a 40 Year Debt," *Christianity Today* (October 8, 1990), n.p.
2. Watchman Nee, *A Table in the Wilderness* (Wheaton, Ill.: Tyndale House Publishers, 1988), n.p.

DAY 18

Thought for Today: Security is found in relationships, not possessions.

Above all, love each other deeply, because love covers
over a multitude of sins.

1 P E T E R 4 : 8

I had a good friend who seemed to have everything going for him. He was worth millions. He had a beautiful, loving wife; wonderful children; an outgoing, winsome personality. But he struggled with a debilitating sense of worthlessness all his life. How could he have such a poor sense of self when he had so many things going for him? He shared that his mother had told him over and over, "I wish you had never been born." He grew up thinking that he was unloved and unaccepted, and it affected every area of his life. All of the other things he had were insignificant in the face of his great need to be loved and accepted.

Learning that God loved and accepted him just as he was, literally changed his life. He gave up his high-paying job and went into full-time ministry to tell others of this great love he had experienced. Mental health experts have said that if people knew they were loved and forgiven, half the mental institutions and prisons would be empty.

Helen Keller, both deaf and dumb, seemed destined to spend her life in institutions until Anne Sullivan took an interest in her. When everybody else had given up on Helen, Anne went out of her way, every day, to show Helen God's love and acceptance. Helen became an outstanding student and eventually graduated magna cum laude from Radcliffe College. Books were written about her, and a movie, *The Miracle Worker*, was made of her life and Anne Sullivan's work with her. The love of God was the miracle that transformed Helen Keller's life.

The director of No Longer Bound, a Christian treatment center near Atlanta, shares one of his biggest problems with the men in his recovery ministry. If they meet a female who will give them the time of day, they will leave the program to be with her. Why? Because their greatest need is to be loved and accepted.

It's the same reason people gravitate to bars. They can get alcohol anywhere, but they go to a bar to hopefully meet someone who will listen to them, accept them for who they are and maybe even love them.

No matter how much fame or fortune we accumulate, everything pales in comparison to being with those who love and accept us.

Who are the most secure people in the world? It isn't those with the most money, material possessions or prestigious positions. G. K. Chesterton said, "There is nothing that fails like success."[1] Security comes from living in loving and committed relationships. Our ultimate security can only be found in an eternal relationship with our loving heavenly Father.

Scripture says, "In His love and in His mercy He redeemed them" (Isa. 63:9, *NASB*), and "I have loved you with an everlasting love; therefore I have drawn you with lovingkindness" (Jer. 31:3, *NASB*). The Bible tells us over 40 times that God's love is everlasting. Prophecy and preaching will cease; tongues and gifts will be no more; knowledge will pass away. But love never fails (see 1 Cor. 13:8). One of the most popular church hymns is "Great Is Thy Faithfulness," which was based on Lamentations

3:21-23 (*NASB*): "This I recall to my mind, therefore I have hope. The Lord's lovingkindnesses indeed never cease, for His compassions never fail. They are new every morning; great is Thy faithfulness."

The love of God is the basis for our redemption. Without His love, we would all be hopelessly lost.

Probe

Think back to the times when you felt very secure and very insecure. What made you feel secure or insecure? What did you believe at the time and what was the nature of your relationship with God and others?

Journal

_____

_____

_____

_____

_____

Note
1. G. K. Chesterton, *Heretics* (London: Bodley Head, 1960), p. 12.

DAY 19

Thought for Today: The Good Shepherd will see that His flock is properly cared for.

I came that they might have life, and might have it abundantly. I am the good shepherd; the good shepherd lays down His life for the sheep.
JOHN 10:10,11, NASB

My book *Freedom from Addiction* had been on the bookstore shelves for nearly a year and was doing very well for a limited market. The accompanying workbook was finished and would soon be available as well. The Freedom in Christ Recovery Ministry, of which my wife, Julia, and I are the directors, was progressing well and I was really excited about it. Regal Books had videotaped a seminar with Neil Anderson, Julia and myself. I had just returned home from conducting a Freedom from Addiction workshop, and afterward I met with the directors of a large rescue mission in our country's capital. On Sunday I preached three services at a church in Virginia and the response was very affirming. I was full of ideas and plans for the ministry and couldn't wait to get back to begin putting them into practice.

But it was not to be. I came down with a bad case of flu the day I got home. I was so sick and weak I couldn't do anything but lie around and moan. When I recovered, I got a stomach virus and was sick for another two weeks. A whole month gone. What a waste! Or was it?

After I recovered from the flu, I plunged back into the ministry. Then my computer, which figured prominently in my work, crashed several times and I had to reinstall the software twice. Then my printer wouldn't print. I couldn't send or receive e-mail. My goals and plans were being blocked in every direction!

I said, "Lord is there something You want me to learn from all this?" Slowly but surely I began to see the picture. God kept drawing me back to Psalm 131: "O Lord, my heart is not proud, nor my eyes haughty; nor do I involve myself in great matters, or in things too difficult for me. Surely I have composed and quieted my soul; like a weaned child rests against his mother, my soul is like a weaned child within me. O Israel, hope in the Lord from this time forth and forever" (vv. 1-3, *NASB*).

It is so easy to get puffed up with our successes and caught up with our plans. God was more interested in my just being His child, like a newly weaned infant who is content to rest safely in his mother's arms. God is our Shepherd who guides, provides and protects. When we stray away from Him, He gently pulls us back. Our business for God may be the greatest enemy of our devotion to God.

Hannah Whitall Smith tells the story of a time when she needed Scripture for encouragement. The only verse she could think of was

Psalm 23:1—"The Lord is my shepherd; I shall not want" (*KJV*). But the verse didn't satisfy her. She thought this passage was just a child's verse, yet no other passages came to mind. It was as if there were no other verses in the Bible. Slowly she began to realize this verse was all she needed.

We are like sheep who need a Shepherd for guidance and protection. It is the Shepherd's responsibility to see that His flock is provided for. "He who did not spare His own Son, but delivered Him up for us all, how will He not also with Him freely give us all things?" (Rom. 8:32, *NASB*). Our Shepherd gave His life for us. He is a Shepherd you can trust because only He has your best interests at heart. "Like a shepherd He will tend His flock, in His arm He will gather the lambs, and carry them in His bosom; He will gently lead the nursing ewes" (Isa. 40:11, *NASB*).

God doesn't help those who help themselves, but He does provide for those who admit they can't do it themselves. His resources kick in when we trust in His strength. "He does not delight in the strength of the horse; He does not take pleasure in the legs of a man. The Lord favors those who fear Him, those who wait for His lovingkindness" (Ps. 147:10,11, *NASB*). A wolf will seek to isolate a lamb from the flock to make it vulnerable. The Lord may just set us down until we get our bearings straight once again.

Probe

If the devil can't make you immoral, he will simply try to make you busy. Have you ever gotten so busy for the Lord that you forgot Him? What happened next?

Journal

_____

_____

_____

_____

_____

DAY 20

Thought for Today: Security is the result of abiding in God's love.

I pray that you, being rooted and established in love, may have power, together with all the saints, to grasp how wide and long and high and deep is the love of Christ, and to know this love that surpasses knowledge—that you may be filled to the measure of all the fullness of God.
EPHESIANS 3:17-19

Anabel Gillham tells the story of how her son taught her about God's love. Her son, Mason, was born profoundly retarded, and it got to the point that he had to be institutionalized because he could no longer communicate or even feed himself. Of course, Anabel and her husband still loved and missed him, so they would often bring him home on weekends.

One Sunday, a little while before it was time to take Mason back, Anabel was at the kitchen sink washing dishes. Mason was sitting at the table with his bib on. There was food scattered everywhere as Mason stared into space, totally detached from his surroundings. Anabel put her dishcloth aside and knelt down in front of her son and said, "Oh, Mason I love you so much. If only you knew how much I loved you." But he didn't respond. He couldn't. When she went back to the sink with tears flowing down her cheeks, God spoke to her heart: "Anabel, that is the way I love you. Even if you couldn't perform one deed or perfectly respond to Me, I would still love you."[1]

Our performance is not the basis for God's loving us!

I continually questioned God's love for me when I struggled with alcoholism. I could preach a sermon on God's love and tell others He loved them, but deep down I thought God had given up on me. I was basing His love on my performance.

Mike Darnell, director of Insight for Living in Montgomery, Alabama, says that he looked out in the yard one day and saw his teenage son shoveling gravel. He was dirty and sweaty. Mike said, "Jeremy, you know that I love you, don't you?" Jeremy told him yes. Then Mike said,

"Do you know why I love you?" Jeremy replied, "No, I can't say that I do."
He had probably asked himself the same question, since he had recently
totaled Mike's pickup truck. Mike told him, "I love you just because
you're my son."

In our ministry we emphasize the spiritual inheritance we all have as
children of God. But did you know that *you* are God's inheritance? "They
are your people, your inheritance that you brought out by your great
power and your outstretched arm" (Deut. 9:29). You are a valuable possession of the Lord. He made a supreme sacrifice in order to obtain you,
and He is not going to abandon His possession. God's Son "gave Himself
for us, that He might redeem us from every lawless deed and purify for
Himself a people for His own possession, zealous for good deeds" (Titus
2:14, *NASB*). At least 10 times we are referred to in Scripture as God's own
possession.[2] One such verse is 1 Peter 2:9 (*NASB*): "You are a chosen race,
a royal priesthood, a holy nation, a people for God's own possession, that
you may proclaim the excellencies of Him who has called you out of darkness into His marvelous light."

You belong to God, and He is irrevocably committed to you. This
commitment is not based on your performance but on God's covenant,
which was sealed with the blood of Christ. God is your provision and
your defense. "What, then, shall we say in response to this? If God is for
us, who can be against us?" (Rom. 8:31).

How much does Jesus love you? In the same way the Father loves the
Son. Jesus said, "Just as the Father has loved Me, I have also loved you;
abide in My love" (John 15:9, *NASB*). To abide means to remain or continue in something or someone. What a privilege to remain, for the rest
of our lives, in God's love. We will never lack the assurance of His presence in our lives if we simply make the mental choice to abide in His love
in good times and in bad.

Probe

How could you develop the habit of abiding in Christ's love? What
impact would it have on your life if you practiced His presence 24 hours
of every day?

Journal

_____

_____

_____

_____

_____

Notes
1. Bill and Anabel Gillham, *Victorious Christian Living* tape series (Fort Worth, Tex.: Lifetime Guarantee, n.y.), audiocassette.
2. See Exodus 19:5; Deuteronomy 7:6; 9:29; 14:2; 26:18; Psalm 135:4; Malachi 3:17; Ephesians 1:14; Titus 2:14; 1 Peter 2:9.

DAY 21

Thought for Today: The God of all comfort wants to bless you.

Because of his great love for us, God, who is rich in mercy, made us alive with Christ even when we were dead in transgressions—it is by grace you have been saved. And God raised us up with Christ and seated us with him in the heavenly realms in Christ Jesus, in order that in the coming ages he might show the incomparable riches of his grace, expressed in his kindness to us in Christ Jesus.

EPHESIANS 2:4-7

Several years ago, my wife and I made arrangements for a young lady to be released from jail in order to get help at a Christian treatment center. While making the arrangements, another young lady who was also in the same jail decided to do the same thing. She had lived on the streets for a number of years and been arrested many times for different offenses. Against his better judgment, the judge ruled that the girl could go to the center if my wife and I would escort her there. We agreed to drive her the 200 miles to the center.

We stopped on the way and Julia bought her some cosmetics, a hairbrush and other personal effects. When we arrived at the treatment center, it was time for dinner and we were invited to eat with everyone. The other women were extremely friendly and helpful to the girl, and the place was pleasant and comfortable. What impressed me the most was the demeanor of the women in the program. All of them seemed to be genuinely happy, and they went out of their way to welcome and look after the newcomer.

The girl was also impressed, but not in the same way. She didn't know how to receive their love and acceptance. Judging by the expression on her face, she looked as though she had landed on another planet. The laughter, the friendliness and the fellowship were all foreign to her. She literally freaked out during dinner. Within an hour after dinner she bolted and returned to the streets where she could relate to her own kind. She could have accepted mean, abusive and harsh treatment from the people at the center, but she couldn't relate to their love and acceptance, which was freely given.

What a tragedy that many people reject the love of God. They don't believe they deserve to be blessed, cared for, loved and honored. Such love is foreign to everything they have ever experienced, so they reject His love and the love of others and return to their old way of life.

Our compassionate heavenly Father is "the God of all comfort, who comforts us in all our troubles" (2 Cor. 1:3,4). When Jesus entered the city of Jerusalem, He said, "How often I wanted to gather your children together, just as a hen gathers her brood under her wings, and you would not have it!" (Luke 13:34, *NASB*).

We have to remind ourselves again and again of God's grace and provision, because the world teaches just the opposite: "There is no free lunch . . . you have to work for what you get . . . you get what you negotiate . . . nice guys finish last . . . it's a dog-eat-dog world out there," and so on.

The kingdom of God is not like the kingdoms of this world. God wants to bless you in many ways:

1. He blesses and surrounds the righteous man with favor (see Ps. 5:12).

2. He will strengthen and bless His people with peace (see Ps. 29:11).
3. He delights in your well-being (see Ps. 35:27).
4. He wants to bless those who keep His commandments with peace and long life (see Prov. 3:1,2).
5. He will meet your needs according to His glorious riches (see Phil. 4:19).
6. He wants to richly provide all things for you to enjoy (see 1 Tim. 6:17).

We have to continually renew our minds to the truth of God's great grace or the messages of this world will drown out the truth of God's Word. It has been estimated that there are 7,000 promises of God in the Bible. Most of us probably couldn't recall 70 of them, because we've never been challenged to learn them, much less memorize them. As a simple exercise, try underlining in Psalm 103:1-8 (*NASB*) all the benefits for those who bless the Lord:

Bless the Lord, O my soul; and all that is within me, bless His holy name. Bless the Lord, O my soul, and forget none of His benefits; who pardons all your iniquities; who heals all your diseases; who redeems your life from the pit; who crowns you with lovingkindness and compassion; who satisfies your years with good things, so that your youth is renewed like the eagle. The Lord performs righteous deeds, and judgments for all who are oppressed. He made known His ways to Moses, His acts to the sons of Israel. The Lord is compassionate and gracious, slow to anger and abounding in lovingkindness.

Probe

What percentage of your day is spent listening to the negative voices of this world compared to the truth of God's Word? (Consider the messages you hear at school and work and from television and radio.) What can you do in a practical way to overcome this negative input?

Journal

_____

_____

_____

_____

_____

DAY 22

Thought for Today: Our sufficiency is in Christ.

And my God shall supply all your needs according to His riches
in glory in Christ Jesus.
PHILIPPIANS 4:19, NASB

For 50 years I tried everything but Christ to meet my needs for acceptance, security and significance. When I was in high school I went out for
all the sports. I made some of the teams but ended up sitting on the
bench most of the time. The only time I got to go into the game was in
the last two minutes if we were safely ahead or hopelessly behind. In college, I searched for fulfillment by trying to get beautiful girls to date me.
I didn't have much success there either.

When I graduated from college, I had a new plan to become somebody. My goal was to make money, lots of money. I became a stockbroker
and began to do quite well. I remember saying to my colleagues, "I like to
make money because I can go places, buy things and do what I want." But
even as an unbeliever I knew that wasn't true. I wanted to make money
because people seemed to respect those who were financially prosperous.

When I became a Christian, I changed my goal again: I wanted to be
successful in ministry. I graduated from seminary and entered the pastorate with the goal of building a large church. But it wasn't to be. None

of my gimmicks, methods, programs or plans worked. My preaching, pleading, promising and threatening produced very little fruit, and my persistent power to persuade produced puny payoffs. The irresistible force had met the immovable object.

The psalmist speaks a sad commentary for those with false pursuits:

> Do not be overawed when a man grows rich, when the splendor of his house increases; for he will take nothing with him when he dies, his splendor will not descend with him. Though while he lived he counted himself blessed—and men praise you when you prosper—he will join the generation of his fathers, who will never see the light of life. A man who has riches without understanding is like the beasts that perish (Ps. 49:16-20).

Years later, my daughter asked, "Dad, what is the greatest lesson you have learned in 57 years?"

My answer: "The greatest lesson I've learned is that I can look to God to meet all my needs, and He has." It took me 50 years to realize that, and it was the most painful lesson I've ever learned. But it was well worth it.

Freedom is found in trusting God's resources, not our own. We are the only ones who can prevent God from meeting our needs. We suffer needlessly when we attempt to be our own god, and Satan will use that attempt to jerk us around. Satan's plan is not to get you drunk, to do drugs or to have an affair, but to get you to live your life independent of God. That is the purpose behind every temptation. We start drinking, using, and having affairs when we play god. Heaven is when we say, "Thy will be done." Hell is when God says to us, "Your will be done."

I wish I could say I learned this great lesson easily, but the truth is I surrendered kicking, screaming, clawing and scratching. I had to try everything else first in order to be convinced that the things I tried couldn't possibly meet my needs. I struggled for years with alcoholism, almost lost my marriage, came to the verge of financial ruin and alienated a lot of friends and family. It was a bitter lesson, but one I had to learn in order to be free in Christ.

Hannah Whitall Smith wrote:

The greatest lesson a soul has to learn is that God and God alone is enough for all its needs. This is the lesson that all God's dealings with us are meant to teach, and this is the crowning discovery of our entire Christian life. GOD IS ENOUGH! No soul can really be at rest until it has given up dependence on everything else and has been forced to depend on the Lord alone. As long as our expectation is from other things, nothing but disappointment awaits us. Feelings may change, doctrines and dogmas may be upset, the Christian work may come to nought, prayers may seem to lose their fervency, promises may seem to fail, everything we have believed in or depended on may seem to be swept away and only God is left—just God, the bare God, if I may be allowed the expression, simply and only God . . . then we must come to the positive conviction that He is, in Himself alone, enough for all our needs and that we may safely rest in Him absolutely and forever.[1]

Probe

When are you most tempted to be self-sufficient? Why is it so hard for you to surrender your will to God's will?

Journal

_____

_____

_____

_____

_____

Note
 1. Hannah Whitall Smith, *The God of All Comfort* (London: James Nisbet & Co., 1906), pp. 242, 243.

DAY 23

Thought for Today: You are in Christ, and Christ is in you.

On that day you will realize that I am in my Father, and you are in me, and I am in you.
JOHN 14:20

I had been a Christian for 18 years when I turned 51 years old, but I was still in bondage to alcohol. I had tried everything I knew to overcome my addiction and everything anyone had told me to do. I had been through the gamut of AA treatment centers (secular and Christian), psychologists, psychiatrists, counselors, addiction specialists and every Christian formula and discipline I had ever heard about. Nothing worked. I was miserable and I made everyone around me miserable.

I was driving home after a drunken binge in Florida, filled with guilt and overwhelmed by a sense of hopelessness. I began listening to a tape by Anabel Gillham on the Scripture passage about being in Christ and Christ being in me (see John 14:20).

I thought, *If Christ is in me and I am in Christ, and Christ is in the Father, what more do I really need?* Why was I driving myself crazy, searching wildly for an answer to my problem, if Christ is in me and I am in Him? Had the answer been there all along and I hadn't seen it? Did I already possess what I needed and I just didn't know it? I couldn't see the proverbial forest, or the One who created it, because I was trying to grow my own tree by my own resources. I was already firmly rooted in Christ (see Col. 2:7) but didn't know it. I was trying to draw my nourishment from programs, treatment centers, counselors and support groups. These resources could help, but only if they supported the truth of my being in Christ and Christ's being in me!

What were the implications of being alive in Christ and Christ living in me? What did that really mean? It meant that my soul was in union with God. If Christ is in me, did I need more power? If I am in Christ, could I be more secure? If Christ is in me, did I need to search for another answer? If I am in Christ, could I do or get anything more to be complete?

I was desperately trying to become somebody I already was, and I was searching for something I already had! God tells us that He has already given us everything we need for life and godliness, because we have become a partaker of His divine nature (see 2 Pet. 1:3,4). God has blessed us with every spiritual blessing in Christ (see Eph. 1:3). Paul says in 1 Corinthians 1:30 (NASB), "But by His doing you are in Christ Jesus, who became to us wisdom from God, and righteousness and sanctification, and redemption." Christ is now our wisdom, our righteousness, our sanctification and our redemption. What more do we need?

To be spiritually alive means that our souls are in union with God. This truth of being united with God is most often conveyed in the New Testament by the prepositional phrases "in Christ" or "in Him." These phrases occur 40 times in the book of Ephesians alone. Here are just a few of the benefits of being alive in Christ.

1. We have been made a new creation (see 2 Cor. 5:17).
2. We have been made sons of God (see Gal. 3:26).
3. We are forgiven (see Eph. 4:32).
4. We are always led in triumph (see 2 Cor. 2:14).
5. All our needs are met according to His glorious riches (see Phil. 4:19).
6. We enjoy true freedom (see Gal. 2:4).
7. We have peace (see Phil. 4:7).
8. We have been made complete in Christ (see Col. 2:10).

What else do you need if you are already complete in Christ? Can you add anything to "complete"? We all need to mature in Him, but that comes naturally (or supernaturally) when we walk by faith, according to what God says is true, in the power of the Holy Spirit. We don't need to get something more; we just need to know the truth of God's Word that reveals who we already are and what we already have.

Here is a personalized version of the prayer Paul prayed for all believers in Ephesians 1:15-19 (adapted from NASB). Read it for yourself and think about its truths:

For this reason Paul, having heard of the faith in the Lord Jesus which exists in me, and my love for all the saints, does not cease giving thanks for me, while making mention of me in his prayers; that the God of our Lord Jesus Christ, the Father of glory, may give to me a spirit of wisdom and of revelation in the knowledge of Him. I pray that the eyes of my heart may be enlightened, so that I will know what is the hope of His calling, what are the riches of the glory of His inheritance in me, and what is the surpassing greatness of His power toward me. These are in accordance with the working of the strength of His might.

Probe

How should believing the truth that you are in Christ and He is in you, change the way you live? Has it? Why or why not?

Journal

_____

_____

_____

_____

_____

DAY 24

Thought for Today: God understands you because He has been there.

For we do not have a high priest who cannot sympathize with our weaknesses, but one who has been tempted in all things as we are, yet without sin.
HEBREWS 4:15, NASB

When I checked into a Christian treatment center, I found myself living with people I had never associated with before. Some had been addicts and alcoholics for more than 30 years. Many had lived on the streets. Some were chronic offenders who had been sent to the center instead of prison. When I arrived, only two of the 20 residents still had driver's licenses. Only one was still married.

I lived with them for two months. We ate together and shared a communal bathroom and worked side by side. I heard their stories of rejection, despair, disappointment, grief and loss. We became friends, and I discovered they were no different from me. Their circumstances were different, but they had the same longings and needs. In retrospect I am very grateful for my time there, not only for what God did in me but also for the privilege of getting to know these dear people. This experience has helped me greatly in my ministry as I reach out to those in bondage. I don't look down on anyone, because I've been there.

At first it's hard for some people with severe dependencies to realize what they have in common with others. Most people struggling with an addiction believe they are different, their problems are unique and no one understands. Believing that you are unique or different from everyone else will keep you in bondage, yet it is true that most people will never fully understand your struggle. Rest assured that God does understand you and the road you have traveled.

Jesus took upon Himself the form of a man (see Phil. 2:7), and He was tempted in all things as we are (see Heb. 4:15). He suffered hardships, endured beatings and felt the sting of rejection, even though He had never done anything wrong. Jesus understands because He has been there.

When I went to Bethel, I didn't go voluntarily. My wife had kicked me out of the house and I didn't have anywhere else to go. But Jesus came to earth voluntarily because of His love for us. I spent two months at Bethel, but Jesus humbled Himself for 33 years on earth and never once claimed to be superior to us. He understands earthly problems.

I went to Bethel entirely for selfish reasons. I was looking for help for myself only. Jesus came to earth to give Himself for us by dying a cruel death on a cross. "Who, although He existed in the form of God, did not regard equality with God a thing to be grasped, but emptied Himself, taking the form of a bond-servant, and being made in the likeness of men. And being found in appearance as a man, He humbled Himself by becoming obedient to the point of death, even death on a cross" (Phil. 2:6-8, *NASB*).

Jesus emptied Himself of all His rights and became a bond servant— a slave—not just to solve your problems but to give you life. He humbled Himself and became obedient to His earthly parents and to worldly authorities so that you could be healed, set free and made whole. He submitted Himself to a painful death on a cross so that your sins would never be counted against you. Jesus Christ didn't come to earth to scold you and threaten you with hell if you don't do better. He came to die that you might live and experience His life.

Does Christ understand why people get drunk, do drugs, abuse their wives, molest children, commit murder, have illicit sex, deal drugs, look at pornography? Of course He does. He understands it far better than the people who do it. He knows they are living in bondage: "Jesus answered them, 'Truly, truly, I say to you, everyone who commits sin is the slave of sin'" (John 8:34, *NASB*). He knows that others in bondage have been promising you "freedom while they themselves are slaves of corruption; for by what a man is overcome, by this he is enslaved" (2 Pet. 2:19, *NASB*).

How does God respond to our sin, which separates us from Him? "For God so loved the world, that He gave His only begotten Son, that whoever believes in Him should not perish, but have eternal life. For God did not send the Son into the world to judge the world, but that the world should be saved through Him" (John 3:16,17, *NASB*). God not only understands completely why people sin and live in bondage, but He also provided a way out by sending His Son to set them free.

Sin is the result of attempting to meet our own needs apart from God. Bondage to sin is the result of choosing to live our lives independently of God. We have been deceived when we try to meet our needs apart from Him. Only God perfectly understands us and only He is capable of meeting our needs. The devil wants us to believe that God is distant and unconcerned. What a lie! The Lord Jesus is in you, dear believer, and deeply concerned that your needs are met and that you live a righteous life "in Him."

Probe

Think of a crisis time when you questioned whether God was present in your life or whether He really understood you. What did you choose to believe about Him and yourself? What difference do you think it would have made had you known the truth about God and yourself and chosen to believe it?

Journal

_____

_____

_____

_____

_____

FREEDOM FROM
THE PAST

DAY 25

Thought for Today: You can't fix your past, but you can be free from it.

*In him we have redemption through his blood, the forgiveness of sins, in
accordance with the riches of God's grace.*
EPHESIANS 1:7

The morning I woke up handcuffed to a hospital bed, my clothes bloody
and torn and my shoes badly scuffed, I didn't have any recollection of
where I had been the night before. It was the most humiliating experience
of my life.

When I started screaming "Where am I?" two women in white uniforms rushed into the room. They informed me that I was in Cooper
Green Hospital in Birmingham, Alabama, where they take drunks, winos
and indigents. I wanted to go home. They said I couldn't because the
Birmingham police had a "hold" on me.

I couldn't remember what happened between the time I closed up
the bar at the downtown Hilton and went to the parking deck to my car.
I'd had a blackout. Had I killed someone while driving under the influence? It was a terrifying feeling. Fortunately, I'd only been arrested for
public drunkenness.

After reading our book *Freedom from Addiction*, a friend commented,
"You must be free to be able to write all that in a book for everyone to
read." It's true that I'm free of my past and able to walk in the light
because of what Christ did for me on the cross. But it's His work, not
mine. God sets us free from the past by forgiving our sins and making us
brand-new creations in Christ. When I finally understood this truth, my
life completely changed.

People who let their past control them are living in bondage. The
essence of the New Covenant is that God has forgiven our sins and He
will remember them no more (see Heb. 8:12). He hasn't forgotten them,
but He has removed them as far as the east is from the west (see Ps.
103:12). He will not use our past against us. The penalty we deserved for

our sins was absorbed by Christ, who died *once* for all (see Rom. 6:10).

I heard a preacher joyfully share his testimony about how God had redeemed him from a homosexual lifestyle. He was a high-school dropout and spent years in a mental institution. He had tried to commit suicide many times. Was he joyful about his past? No! He was joyful about the grace of God that had redeemed him from his painful past. When we're free from our past, we will welcome opportunities to share what God has done to free us and turn our shame into a testimony of His greatness.

Karla Faye Tucker helped her boyfriend kill two people with a pick-ax while they were high on drugs. She surrendered her life to Christ while in prison. For 15 years she lived an exemplary Christian life on death row. Those who knew her testified to the incredible change in her and the joyful way she lived. She maintained her composure as she walked to her execution because she had trusted in Christ's death on the Cross as payment for her horrible sins. Now she is living with Him.

The vast majority of Christians have sinned far less than Karla Faye Tucker, but many can't seem to let go of their past. They're focusing on what they've done rather than on the Cross and what Christ has done. We all have regrets, but brooding over past sins in morbid introspection only brings guilt and despair. Paul wrote in Colossians 2:13,14 about the truth we all must embrace:

> When you were dead in your sins and in the uncircumcision of your sinful nature, God made you alive with Christ. He forgave us all our sins, having canceled the written code, with its regulations, that was against us and that stood opposed to us; he took it away, nailing it to the cross.

Probe

In what ways have you or haven't you made peace with your past? We all have to live with the natural consequences of our sin, but how does the truth that we are forgiven and made new creations in Christ change what we can become in the future?

Journal

_____

_____

_____

_____

DAY 26

Thought for Today: You are not just a product of your past; you are primarily a product of Christ's work on the cross.

*For you know that it was not with perishable things such as silver
or gold that you were redeemed from the empty way of life handed
down to you from your forefathers, but with the precious blood of Christ,
a lamb without blemish or defect.*
1 PETER 1:18,19

Does your past determine who you are today? Are you still chained to your past? Can you escape the past by ignoring or denying it?

It is true that we can't escape the natural consequences of our past, but our experiences do not keep us from being the people God created us to be. Because of the gospel, we have been forgiven and cleansed of all unrighteousness. Christ offers us a new beginning, without guilt or condemnation. We still have the possibility of being victimized in the future, but whether we remain a victim is our choice. We have the means, in Christ, to be set free from the past.

After I found my freedom in Christ in October 1988, I still had to face the presbytery in which I was a member. I didn't look forward to it. The presbytery didn't look favorably on ordained ministers who got drunk. The chairman of the ministers' committee informed me that I would face discipline.

When he gave me the bad news, I thought, *I'm in for more disgrace and public humiliation. But it's OK. No matter what they do or think, I'm still a child of God who is free in Christ. Nothing can change that.* Such a meeting with the ministers' committee would have devastated me in the past, but I received their verdict with joy and peace in my heart.

Many people would have considered me a colossal failure at that time, and God showed me that I *was* a failure when I lived according to the flesh—when I lived by my own strength and resources. If I had walked away from that discipline, continuing to think I was a failure, I would have continued to fail. But my identity and sense of worth no longer came from who I was before I met Christ, and certainly not from the opinion of others. My identity comes from God, and God says that I was redeemed from my futile way of life, which I inherited from my forefathers (see 1 Peter 1:18, *NASB*). By the grace of God, I am now His child and I am complete in Christ.

I have learned that a mistake is never a failure unless I fail to learn from it. Failure comes when I say, "I was pushed." I have to assume responsibility for my attitudes and actions and then receive the incredible forgiveness and cleansing that come from our gracious heavenly Father.

When Satan plays the role of the accuser, he uses the traumas and failures of our past to tell us we're no good—we're worthless, stupid, inferior, inadequate, insecure, guilty. If we believe the father of lies, we will continue to be in chains. Our heavenly Father promises not to use our past against us when He says, "I will forgive their wickedness and will remember their sins no more" (Jer. 31:34).

Many people go to the grave chained to the past because they have covered it up. The good news is that God has redeemed us and set us free. My failure and brokenness is one of the greatest credentials I have for the ministry I do. The same can be true of you. Isn't that amazing? God turns the tables on Satan and uses our sins and failures to bring glory to Himself. Our testimony is that God is the Redeemer and He has redeemed us from our futile way of life.

Perhaps you're thinking, *You don't know what I've done.* No, but God knows, and when Christ died for our sins, He died once for *all* (see Rom. 6:10).

My earthly father lived a very sinful life and didn't think he could ever be forgiven. He was chronically unfaithful to my mother and physically abusive to all of us. He was an angry, tormented man, but he turned to the Lord in his 60s and received Christ and the forgiveness of his sins. When he was on his deathbed, I saw something in him that I had never seen as a child. He had complete peace. He kept reassuring me he was fine, even though he was hours from death. He knew his sins were forgiven and he knew where he would spend eternity. What a difference Christ makes!

Have you received Christ and forgiveness of your sins? If you have, then your past has been taken care of and you don't have to be controlled by it. When you get to heaven, God isn't going to say, "Some of your sins were so bad that the shed blood of Christ on the Cross wasn't able to cover them. We're going to have to work something else out." No, He's going to say, "My grace is sufficient for you; enter into your eternal rest" (see 2 Cor. 12:9; Heb. 4:3). Christ is the One "who gave himself for us to redeem us from all wickedness and to purify for himself a people that are his very own, eager to do what is good" (Titus 2:14).

Probe

What past shame or guilt is keeping you from being the person God created you to be? Why do you believe the lie that you are defined by your past?

Journal

DAY 27

Thought for Today: We are saints in the hands of a loving God.

*But now in Christ Jesus you who once were far away have been
brought near through the blood of Christ.*
EPHESIANS 2:13

I was teaching at a Christian treatment center on the subject of God's
complete forgiveness of our sins. One of the men said, "But I was a
cocaine addict every day for 10 years. I did so much harm and damage to
those around me. How can I ever be guilt free? Every day I am reminded
of all the hurt I caused to the ones I love. I don't see how I will ever be able
to reconcile that."

This man lived every day believing he was a sorry sinner in the hands
of an angry God. He's not alone. Many Christians live their lives waiting
for the hammer of God's justice to fall. Dear Christian, the hammer
already fell! It fell on Christ! He died once for all our sins (see Rom. 6:10).
We are not sinners in the hands of an angry God. We are saints in the
hands of a loving God.

The cocaine addict did deserve punishment, as all of us do. But
Someone else took the punishment for us. "We all, like sheep, have gone
astray, each of us has turned to his own way; and the Lord has laid on him
the iniquity of us all" (Isa. 53:6). God's righteous indignation toward sin
has been satisfied. The biblical word for this is "atonement" or "propiti-
ation." It means to be satisfied, placated or appeased, and moved by
mercy to accept reconciliation. Jesus has made us acceptable because "He
is the atoning sacrifice for our sins, and not only for ours but also for the
sins of the whole world" (1 John 2:2). "This is love: not that we loved God,
but that he loved us and sent his Son as an atoning sacrifice for our sins"
(1 John 4:10).

All of us have fallen short of the glory of God and desperately need a
Savior and Lord. Even as Christians we haven't lived up to our full potential. Satan takes advantage of our lack of perfection to convince us we are

sorry sinners and God is angry with us. God is not angry. He is well pleased and completely satisfied with the death of His Son as payment for our sins.

I can identify with those who struggle with addictive behaviors. I remember how my sins and failures overwhelmed me. I believed I was the worst Christian who ever lived. I was defeated and lived in bondage to lies. When I believed the truth of what the Cross had accomplished, I walked out of bondage into freedom. God has been satisfied by Christ's work alone, and we cannot add to that finished work.

In the story of the prodigal son, the son finally comes to his senses and goes home to his father. "But while he was still a long way off, his father saw him and was filled with compassion for him; he ran to his son, threw his arms around him and kissed him" (Luke 15:20). Why didn't the father let his son finish his prepared speech? Why didn't he tell the boy that he forgave him? Because the son had already been forgiven. He was forgiven when he left home. All he had to do was come home and receive that forgiveness.

Probe

How would it change your life if you believed the truth that you are totally forgiven and completely acceptable to God? How would that belief affect your recovery? In what way?

Journal

_____

_____

_____

_____

_____

DAY 28

Thought for Today: The wall of denial can keep you in bondage.

When I kept silent, my bones wasted away through my groaning all day long. For day and night your hand was heavy upon me; my strength was sapped as in the heat of summer. Then I acknowledged my sin to you, and did not cover up my iniquity. I said, "I will confess my transgressions to the Lord"—and you forgave the guilt of my sin.

PSALM 32:3-5

A young lady who sought counseling was estranged from her parents and had lost all her friends. She had experienced over 20 broken relationships with guys she had once dated. All her roommates had moved out. She didn't get along with anybody. She had been date-raped by her boyfriend in college on three separate occasions. When a counselor suggested to her that she might have some responsibility for being in that situation the third time, she was highly offended and never came back to counseling.

A popular singer was being divorced by his wife because of physical abuse. He said, "I didn't beat her. I did shove her, and she hit her head on something!" He added, "If you knew what I had to live with, you would understand."

People seem to have a hard time admitting they are wrong or have any part to play in their own downfall. In the last half of the twentieth century, we have had one president resign and another one impeached because neither one could admit he had done something wrong.

David committed adultery with Bathsheba and arranged for her husband's death when he found out she was pregnant (see 2 Sam. 11). He covered it up for months. Finally, God sent him a prophet to confront him with his sin. David reveals the inward pain of cover-up and denial in Psalm 32:1-5.

Denial can be the highest wall between you and your freedom. Denial is an unwillingness to face the truth about yourself and take responsibility for yourself and your problem. Since the truth sets you free, denial keeps you in bondage.

When I was at a Christian treatment center, the director would say, "Not all liars are addicts, but all addicts are liars." That is true, because once an addict stops lying and denying, he will be able to face the truth, get help and get free. Denial keeps you from the truth that sets you free.

Which is harder to say when you've done something wrong: "I'm sorry"; "Will you forgive me"; or "I did it"? All Christians are sorry they have sinned; many are just sorry because they have been caught. Others will ask for forgiveness but not specify what they want the other person to forgive them for. True confession is agreeing with God and saying, "I did it." You haven't confessed and assumed your responsibility until you say that.

When God sent Nathan the prophet to confront David with his sin, David admitted his wrongdoing and took responsibility for it (see 2 Sam. 12). If he had not done this, he wouldn't have been able to write Psalms 32 and 51, which have given direction and hope to countless Christians.

When Joshua the high priest was standing before God in filthy clothes, Satan was accusing him. "The angel said to those who were standing before him, 'Take off his filthy clothes.' Then he said to Joshua, 'See, I have taken away your sin, and I will put rich garments on you'" (Zech. 3:4). We risk the possibility of not having our sins taken away if we say, "My clothes aren't dirty. I'm OK. There's nothing wrong with me."

Even secular treatment programs stress the need to be honest. They won't even try to help someone who can't admit he or she is wrong and needs help. I'm not the greatest communicator, but whenever I speak, people say they appreciate the fact that I'm honest, open and vulnerable. When I first heard Neil speak, what impressed me most was not that he was a great communicator and Bible teacher (although he is), but that he was down to earth, didn't take himself too seriously and was frank about his own failures. I remember telling my wife I could work for a man like that.

Secret sin on earth is open scandal in heaven. Before you can appropriate God's truth that sets you free (see John 8:32), you must face the truth about yourself, take responsibility for your attitudes and actions and admit your wrongdoing. "If we confess our sins, He is faithful and righteous to forgive us our sins and to cleanse us from all unrighteousness" (1 John 1:9, *NASB*). This is the first step out of darkness and bondage into light and freedom.

Probe

What secret sin has kept you in bondage? Is there someone you could share it with? Why or why not? Could you be totally honest with God?

Journal

_____

_____

_____

_____

_____

DAY 29

Thought for Today: In reference to sin, the last judgment for the Christian was at the Cross.

Therefore, there is now no condemnation for those who are in Christ Jesus.
ROMANS 8:1

I was attending a conference in the beautiful mountains of North Carolina. It was a great conference in a magnificent setting. The fellowship was wonderful and the messages were encouraging. It was good to be around fellow Christians for a whole week and hear excellent teaching. But something in me put a damper on my enthusiasm.

I had spent most of the previous seven years battling alcoholism. It had damaged me, my marriage and my Christian walk. I'd been through two treatment centers, been arrested for public drunkenness and been called before the church discipline committee for excessive drinking. I had been a Christian for more than 15 years, graduated from a conservative seminary and pastored a church. *I really don't belong here,* I thought. *I wonder what all these people would think if they knew all about me. They would probably run me off.*

I attended a workshop on the book of Galatians, taught by the Rev. Jack Miller, a Presbyterian minister who was the director of World Harvest, the missions organization. The teaching was grace oriented. I don't remember a lot of what Rev. Miller said, but I will never forget this statement concerning our sins: "The last judgment for the Christian was at the Cross. There is no punishment for the Christian. Christ took it all on Himself at the Cross." I had to hold on to my chair to keep from standing up and shouting "Hallelujah!" If I hadn't been a Presbyterian, I think I would have.

I don't have to let my sins and failures weigh me down for the rest of my life. I can hold my head high and enter into life with the knowledge that I am cleansed, free, forgiven and declared righteous because of Christ's death and resurrection. I am neither inferior nor superior to any other believer. The ground is level at the foot of the Cross.

Why had this truth remained outside my heart? Because Christians can have an intellectual knowledge of the truth but not personally believe and appropriate it so that it changes their lives. The focus of my teaching had been on our responsibility and what *we* should do. This isn't necessarily wrong unless it neglects to point out that we cannot do for ourselves what Christ has already done for us.

The most common trait defeated Christians share is that they don't know who they are in Christ. Consequently, many feel guilty when they are not guilty. Unless their consciences are seared, all defeated Christians feel guilty. Are we guilty if Christ died once for all our sins? The finished work of Christ on the Cross declares that we are *"not* guilty."

When King David confessed his sins of adultery and murder, God forgave his sin (see 2 Sam. 12:13; Ps. 32:5). If sin has been dealt with, then so has the guilt associated with it. The prophet Isaiah was consumed with guilt when confronted with the holiness of God. One of the seraphim around the awesome throne of God brought a live coal from the altar. Isaiah tells what happened next: "With it he touched my mouth and said, 'See, this has touched your lips; your guilt is taken away and your sin atoned for'" (Isa. 6:7).

In the Old Testament, the sinner was required to bring a guilt offering to atone for sin. Under the New Covenant, God Himself provides the guilt offering—His Son Jesus Christ. "How much more, then, will the blood of Christ, who through the eternal Spirit offered himself unblemished to God, cleanse our consciences from acts that lead to death, so that we may serve the living God!" (Heb. 9:14).

Does this mean we don't have to confess our sins? No. Confession simply means that we agree with God when we have sinned. It is essentially the same as walking in the light. In other words, it is living in continuous and conscious agreement with God. It is not our confession that atones for our sin. Only Christ can do that, and He did.

At one time I believed that God had given up on me and I was under judgment for my sins. As a result, I gave up. The guilt I felt was only psychological, because I wrongly believed that I was guilty. If I were flying from Atlanta to Los Angeles and missed my connection in Dallas, would I have to spend the rest of my life in the Dallas airport? I would simply catch the next plane to Los Angeles and get on with my life. If it was my fault that I missed the flight connection, I would hopefully learn by the mistake and commit myself to be more responsible the next time.

If you walk outside your house and slip in the mud, do you sit there the rest of the day condemning yourself? Would you blame God for sending the rain that caused the mud, or someone else for not clearing a path for you? If you're a wise and responsible person, you would get up, clean yourself off and get on with what you started out to do. You are spiritually defeated if you hopelessly sit in the terminal of blame or remain in the mud of self-condemnation.

There is no pending punishment or condemnation for the Christian. All of our sins were placed on Christ (see Isa. 53:6). Lay hold of this truth and get on with the abundant life God has provided for you. "The thief comes only to steal and kill and destroy; I have come that they may have life, and have it to the full" (John 10:10).

Probe

Now that we are forgiven, should we go on sinning so that grace may abound? Because the believer is under grace and no longer under the law, Satan has no basis to accuse us. Therefore, is being under the grace of God a license to sin or a means not to sin?

Journal

_____

_____

_____

_____

_____

DAY 30

Thought for Today: Forgiven people embrace the truth as a liberating friend.

If we walk in the light, as he is in the light, we have fellowship with one another, and the blood of Jesus, his Son, purifies us from all sin.

1 JOHN 1:7

Roger was talented, outgoing and seemed to have his life together. He was a respected Christian with an effective ministry. The Christian community was shocked when it came to light that Roger was having homosexual affairs. He lost his marriage and ministry; his credibility was so damaged that he moved out of town, got a new job and started attending a new church.

Roger wanted to be free, but he still struggled with homosexual feelings. A friend encouraged him to read *Victory over the Darkness, The Bondage Breaker* and *Freedom from Addiction.* Roger worked through the Steps to Freedom in Christ. With the help of his friend he was able to understand how early childhood experiences had led him to believe many lies about himself and his sexuality. By the grace of God, he renounced every sexual use of his body as an instrument of unrighteousness, and he was free to be the man of God he was created to be.

With his pastor's permission, Roger shared with the church his testimony of overcoming past sexual struggles and finding his freedom in Christ. Telling his story was the hardest thing he had ever done. He had no idea how the people would respond. He was overwhelmed when people from all over the church came forward and embraced him and told him of their love and acceptance. Roger said it was the most affirming thing that had ever happened to him. That day he learned a fundamental truth about Christianity: "If we walk in the light, as he is in the light, we have fellowship with one another, and the blood of Jesus, his Son, purifies us from all sin" (1 John 1:7).

People will remain in bondage if they believe the lie that they are more secure when they hide their sins and failures. Satan is the prince of darkness, while "God is light; in him there is no darkness at all" (1 John 1:5). The only way to experience your forgiveness and freedom is to walk in the light. Truth sets us free, but lies keep us in bondage. When you expose the lie, it no longer has any power over you. Satan is the prince of darkness and his demons are like cockroaches that only come out under the cover of darkness. Turn on the light and they run for the shadows. God is light, and the Holy Spirit of truth will lead us into that light. As long as your sin remains hidden in the dark, you are bound by it.

In order to successfully process the Steps to Freedom in Christ, you have to be totally honest and open. Only then can you appropriate God's blessing. We can face the awful truth about ourselves because we are already forgiven; God already knows everything about us, yet still He loves and accepts us. "Nothing in all creation is hidden from God's sight.

Everything is uncovered and laid bare before the eyes of him to whom we must give account" (Heb. 4:13). Paul explains how a just God, who hates sin, can still love and accept us (Rom. 3:23-26):

> For all have sinned and fall short of the glory of God, and are justified freely by his grace through the redemption that came by Christ Jesus. God presented him as a sacrifice of atonement, through faith in his blood. He did this to demonstrate his justice, because in his forbearance he had left the sins committed beforehand unpunished—he did it to demonstrate his justice at the present time, so as to be just and the one who justifies those who have faith in Jesus.

Why, then, do we work so hard to cover up our sins when they are already covered by the blood of Christ? Why do we go to such great lengths to hide our failures when God is using them to show us our need of Him? Why is it so difficult to admit our weaknesses when His power is perfected in our weakness (see 2 Cor. 12:9,10)?

I know a Christian counselor who is having a great ministry in the Atlanta area. For years he bore very little fruit in his ministry. Then he finally decided to share his own past problems with addiction. His ministry took off the moment he revealed the truth about himself.

We don't hide our sins in order to be accepted. We are already accepted in Christ; therefore, we can walk in the light. In Christ, we can be honest and real because we are already forgiven and loved. "'Come now, let us reason together,' says the Lord. 'Though your sins are like scarlet, they shall be as white as snow; though they are red as crimson, they shall be like wool'" (Isa. 1:18).

Probe

Why do people try to hide who they are and cover up their weaknesses? What are they afraid of and what do they need more than anything else in the world? Would you be willing to share your experience with someone who is living a defeated life?

Journal

_____

_____

_____

_____

_____

DAY 31

Thought for Today: God's love is most evident when it is most needed.

He has not dealt with us according to our sins, nor rewarded us according to our iniquities. For as high as the heavens are above the earth, so great is His lovingkindness toward those who fear Him. As far as the east is from the west, so far has He removed our transgressions from us. Just as a father has compassion on his children, so the Lord has compassion on those who fear Him. For He Himself knows our frame; He is mindful that we are but dust.
PSALM 103:10-14, NASB

When Mandy made an appointment to counsel with Neil, she had already attempted suicide at least three times. "How can God love me?" she sobbed. "I'm such a failure, such a mess."

"Mandy," he assured her, "God loves you, not because you are lovable but because it is His nature to love you. God simply loves you. Period."

"But when I do bad, I don't feel like God loves me," Mandy argued.

"Don't trust those feelings," Neil said. "God loves all His children all the time, whether we do good or bad. That's the heart of God. When the 99 sheep were safe in the fold, the heart of the shepherd went after the one that was lost. When the prodigal son squandered his life and inheritance, his father still loved him and welcomed him home. Those parables teach us that God's heart is full of love for us."

"But I've tried to take my own life, Neil. How can God overlook that?"

"Just suppose, Mandy, that your son grew despondent and tried to take his own life. Would you love him any less? Would you kick him out of the family? Would you turn your back on him?"

"Of course not. If anything, I'd feel sorry for him and try to love him more."

"Are you suggesting that your heavenly Father doesn't love you as much as you love your children?"

Mandy got the point. She began to realize that God, as a loving parent, understands our weaknesses and forgives our sin.

Have you ever felt that God has given up on you? Do you fear there is a limit to His love and forgiveness, and you're walking on thin ice? Well, let me tell you, there is no limit to God's love; and His covenant with us is based on *His* word and character, not ours.

Our walk of faith can be interrupted by negative circumstances, personal unbelief or satanic deception. If we believe that God has given up on us, we can easily give up on ourselves as well. Tempted to stop living by faith, we slump dejectedly by the side of the road and wonder, *What's the use? Who cares?*

The primary truth you need to know about God for your faith to remain strong is that His love and acceptance are unconditional. When your faith is weak, God still loves you. When you're strong one moment and weak the next, God still loves you. God's love for us is the great eternal constant in the midst of all the inconsistencies of our daily walk. We are tempted not to turn to Him when we need Him the most. But God's love is most evident when it is most needed. "While we were still sinners, Christ died for us" (Rom. 5:8).

Of course God wants us to do good. The apostle John admonishes us to stop sinning. But he follows up with the reminder that God has already made provision for our failure, so His love continues constant in spite of what we do: "But if anybody does sin, we have one who speaks to the Father in our defense—Jesus Christ, the Righteous One. He is the atoning sacrifice for our sins, and not only for ours but also for the sins of the whole world" (1 John 2:1,2).

One reason we are tempted to doubt God's love is because we have an adversary who accuses us day and night. But your advocate, Jesus Christ, is more powerful than your adversary. He has canceled the debt of your sins—past, present and future—and He always lives to make intercession on our behalf. No matter what you do or how you fail, God's capacity to love and accept you completely is greater.

God wants you to accept your identity as His child and live as a child of God should. But even when you forget who you are, He still loves you. He wants you to walk by faith in the power of the Spirit. Should you stumble off the path, He still loves you.[1]

Probe

What do you typically do when you're down? Do you question your salvation? God's love? Christianity? What can you do in advance to help you through the low times?

Journal

_____

_____

_____

_____

_____

Note
1. Neil T. Anderson, *Victory over the Darkness* (Ventura, Calif.: Regal Books, 1990), pp. 117-122.

DAY 32

Thought for Today: Defeated Christians have forgotten who they are.

For if you possess these qualities in increasing measure, they will keep you from being ineffective and unproductive in your knowledge of our Lord Jesus Christ. But if anyone does not have them, he is nearsighted and blind, and has forgotten that he has been cleansed from his past sins.

2 PETER 1 : 8 , 9

How easy it is to forget what Christ has done and who we are in Him, especially when we fail! As soon as we stumble, the "accuser of the brethren" is right there to tell us what sorry sinners and no-good Christians we are. If we believe those lies, we end up defeated in our Christian walk.

A seminary student's wife audited Neil's class Resolving Personal and Spiritual Conflicts. At the conclusion of the class she handed him a letter, which read in part:

> I just want to thank you again for how the Lord used your class to change my life. The last two years of my life have been a constant struggle for the control of my mind. I was ignorant of my position and authority in Christ and equally ignorant of Satan's ability to deceive me. I was constantly afraid. My mind was bombarded with hostile, angry thoughts. I felt guilty and wondered what was wrong with me. I didn't understand how much bondage I was in until I came to your class. . . . For the first time in my life I can identify Satan's attacks and really resist him. I'm not paralyzed by fear anymore and my mind is much less cluttered. As you can tell, I'm pretty excited about this.

She was a Christian long before she audited Neil's class, but her Christian walk had been stymied by the archenemy of our faith. Her mind was plagued by demonic thoughts. She was a child of God, but she was defeated, the unwitting victim of the deceiver. She didn't understand her identity in Christ and was being "destroyed from lack of knowledge" (Hos. 4:6).

She represents many Christians who are ignorant of their spiritual heritage and the battle going on for their minds. Consequently, they are living defeated lives. When struggling believers correctly perceive the nature of their conflict and understand how they can be transformed by the renewing of their minds, they will be able to share the same testimony given above.[1] Satan can't do anything about our position in Christ, but if he can get us to believe it isn't true, we will live as though it isn't. We are defeated if we forget who we are and what we have as a result of being alive and free in Christ (see 1 Cor. 1:30). Peter says that Christians who become ineffective and unproductive have forgotten they were cleansed from their sins (see 2 Peter 1:8,9). Notice what Peter instructs us to do: "Therefore, my brothers, be all the more eager to make your calling and election sure. For if you do these things, you will never fall, and you will receive a rich welcome into the eternal kingdom of our Lord and Savior Jesus Christ" (2 Pet. 1:10,11).

If we don't realize—daily—that we were cleansed from our sins, Satan will try to convince us that we have failed so greatly and sinned so badly that there is no hope for us and that we are doomed to live in misery and despair. If we forget that we're cleansed from our sins, we will establish our own identity and try to live in our own strength. That is a sure prescription for disaster.

When Satan reminds us of our sins, our only defense is the finished work of Christ, which is a guarantee of victory. Satan was defeated at the Cross (see Col. 2:15) when Christ, who knew no sin, became sin for us that we might become the righteousness of God (see 2 Cor. 5:21).

Don't forget what Christ has done for you and who you are in Christ. He has done everything necessary for you to walk in freedom. You are a child of God, who is dearly loved, redeemed, set apart, forgiven and cleansed from all your sins. Romans 8:31-39 puts it so clearly:

What, then, shall we say in response to this? If God is for us, who can be against us? He who did not spare his own Son, but gave him up for us all—how will he not also, along with him, graciously give us all things? Who will bring any charge against those whom God has chosen? It is God who justifies. Who is he that condemns? Christ Jesus, who died—more than that, who was raised to life—is at the right hand of God and is also interceding for us. Who shall separate us from the love of Christ? Shall trouble or hardship or persecution or famine or nakedness or danger or sword? As it is written: "For your sake we face death all day long; we are considered as sheep to be slaughtered." No, in all these things we are more than conquerors through him who loved us. For I am convinced that neither death nor life, neither angels nor demons, neither the present nor the future, nor any powers, neither height nor depth, nor anything else in all creation, will be able to separate us from the love of God that is in Christ Jesus our Lord.

Probe

If God is for you, who can be against you? If God didn't spare His own Son for you, won't He give you all things? If God justified you, who will bring any charge against you? If Christ died for you, who is the one who condemns you? Who or what can separate you from the love of God that is in Christ Jesus?

Journal

_____

_____

_____

_____

_____

Note
1. Neil T. Anderson, *Victory over the Darkness* (Ventura, Calif.: Regal Books, 1990), pp. 155, 156.

DAY 33

**Thought for Today: We sense our freedom in Christ when
we learn to accept ourselves.**

*Accept one another, then, just as Christ accepted you,
in order to bring praise to God.*
ROMANS 15:7

Paul's words admonish us to accept one another just as Christ has accepted us. But have we accepted *ourselves?* When I struggled with my addiction and habitual sin, I constantly berated and condemned myself. I would do OK for a few days or a week, but then I would relapse into my habitual sin and blow it—big time. People didn't tell me what a fool or failure I was and point out my sinful behavior. I didn't need anyone to tell me that; I was my own worst critic. How could I behave the way I did, knowing that God loved me and sacrificed His only begotten Son so that I could be alive and free in Christ?

When I was still struggling with my addiction, I had to drive down a long hill to get to my house. At the bottom of the hill were large concrete pillars that upheld an overpass. I continually struggled with the thoughts: *Just drive into that pillar and it will all be over. Your life is a mockery. It would be best if you ended it now. Everyone would be better off.* The morning after a binge, I would be especially besieged by these condemning thoughts.

When I began to learn about the grace of God and how He loved me unconditionally, no matter what I did or didn't do, I began to see that I was forgiven, loved and accepted. But for a long time I didn't live that truth. Eventually I saw the need to accept myself the way God had accepted me. It was a liberating and life-changing experience.

I've heard many people say, "I can't accept myself." Perhaps you're thinking the same thing right now. On what basis are you not accepting yourself? Is it your past sins and failures? Our inability to achieve perfection is usually the basis for our self-condemnation, as well as the basis of Satan's accusations.

How can you legitimately accept yourself? The same way God has accepted you—just the way you are. You may not feel loved and accepted, even though you have mentally acknowledged the truth that God does accept you according to Romans 15:7. Understand that God couldn't accept our sins, so Jesus went to the Cross and died for them. He couldn't accept our old nature, so Christ was resurrected so that we can have new life and be partakers of the divine nature. On that basis God has accepted us, and on that basis we can accept ourselves.

In receiving God's forgiveness, you are also forgiving yourself. If there is no condemnation for those who are in Christ Jesus, then why do you condemn yourself and why should you receive the condemnation of others? "Let no one keep defrauding you of your prize by delighting in self-abasement" (Col. 2:18, *NASB*). Living with guilt and shame is not conducive to good mental health, nor is it a means to stop sinning. Using guilt to motivate yourself or others to try harder is not God's answer. "These are matters which have, to be sure, the appearance of wisdom in self-made religion and self-abasement and severe treatment of the body, but are of no value against fleshly indulgence" (Col. 2:23, *NASB*).

Good parents aren't always pleased with the performance of their children, but they still love and accept them for who they are. Parents who base their love and acceptance on performance will create a false motivation for growth in a child who tries to gain their arpproval. Nobody can measure up to such standards and will always feel unloved and unac-cepted.

To accept yourself as God accepts you doesn't mean you have reached perfection, and it doesn't mean that you take sin lightly or make excuses for it. It means that you have received God's unconditional love and acceptance. This is an important part of your growth process. We live in a way that is pleasing to God because we are loved and accepted, not to gain His love and acceptance, which we are incapable of doing.

Can you really forgive and accept yourself? Yes you can, because God has already forgiven and accepted you—not because you deserve to be for-given but because He freely forgives. In the same vein, we can accept oth-ers as God has accepted us. Freely we give because freely we have received.

Probe

How have you been affected by significant others in your life who have not accepted you? How has their lack of acceptance affected your self-perception and the way you relate to others?

Journal

_____

_____

_____

_____

_____

DAY 34

Thought for Today: We don't have to justify ourselves; we have already been justified.

Therefore, since we have been justified through faith, we have peace with God through our Lord Jesus Christ.
ROMANS 5:1

In his book _Healing Grace_, David Seamands tells of a man named Stypulkowski, who was a fighter with the Polish underground resistance during World War II. When the war ended, he was in the wrong place at the wrong time and was captured by the Russian army. He and 15 other Poles were taken to Russia to stand trial before the war crimes court. Prior to the trial, the men were put under rigorous interrogation to break them mentally, emotionally and spiritually, so they would confess to anything.

All 15 of the other men broke under the grueling pressure. Only Stypulkowski did not—in spite of the fact that for 69 out of 70 nights he was brutally questioned in a total of 141 interrogations. Not only did he

endure the interrogations, but at one point his interrogator broke and
had to be replaced. Over and over again, his tormentors relentlessly
examined everything he had ever done or hadn't done, scrutinizing everything for its fear and guilt content. They grilled him on his work, marriage, family, children, sex life, church, community life and even his concept of God. This followed weeks of starvation, sleepless nights and cal-
culated terror. Most insidious of all were the signed confessions of his
best friends, all of whom blamed him for something.

Stypulkowski's torturers told him his case was hopeless and advised
him to plead guilty. Otherwise, they said, his fate would be certain death.
But he refused. He said he had not been a traitor and could not confess
to something that wasn't true. He went on to plead not guilty at the trial.
Largely because of a Western observer's presence at the trial, he was freed.
Most impressive was the completely natural way he witnessed of his
Christian faith, which he kept alive by regular prayer. Every loyalty was
subordinated in his loyalty to Christ.

Stypulkowski was not free from weaknesses. His accusers pointed
them out to him again and again. But he was never shattered by their
accusations. He was able to endure them because he daily presented
himself to God and to his accusers in total honesty. He knew that his
only defense was Christ's perfect life, not his. So when his accusers
charged him with some wrong, he freely admitted it. He humbly said, "I
never felt it was necessary to justify myself. When they showed me I was
a coward, I already knew it. When they shook their finger at me with
accusations of filthy, lewd feelings, I already knew that. When they
showed me a reflection of myself with all my inadequacies, I said to
them, 'But gentlemen, I am much worse than that. For you see, I had
learned it was unnecessary to justify myself. One had already done that
for me—Jesus Christ!'"[1]

It's hard to admit that we're wrong if we think we have to justify ourselves. When I struggled with my addiction, I continually tried to explain
and justify my sinful behavior. I blamed others and always had an excuse
for why I was drinking. I judged others as I thought they were judging
me. I wanted to point out their sins and pull them down to my level of

degradation. I thought, "I'm not so bad; others do what I'm doing and many do even worse things!"

Christ died for our sins, not our excuses. If we make excuses, we're saying, "I'm not so bad. I really don't need a Savior." Apart from Christ, all we are able to do is to sin and fail. So when we sin and blow it, we shouldn't be surprised or try to cover it up. We should do as Stypulkowski did and freely admit it. Confession of sin is necessary to experience the benefits of Christ's death for our sins. "If we confess our sins, he is faithful and just and will forgive us our sins and purify us from all unrighteousness" (1 John 1:9).

The opposite of confession is not silence, it is rationalization. Prisons are filled with "innocent" people who say they are just victims of a corrupt judicial system. Every patron in a bar can quit anytime he or she chooses! These people would love to tell you why they need to drown out their sorrows. The thought process goes, *Life hasn't been fair to me, and you would drink, too, if you had my problems.* The only way to convince yourself or others that you can quit at any time is to just do it. If we try hard enough, we can rationalize almost anything. But why should we do that when we've already been justified?

The word "justified" means to be declared innocent or free from blame. It is impossible to justify ourselves, because we are not innocent. We have all sinned and fallen short of the glory of God (see Rom. 3:23). There isn't anything we can do to justify ourselves, but we don't have to. According to Romans 5:1, "Since we have been justified through faith, we have peace with God through our Lord Jesus Christ." In other words, we have already been justified and we already have peace with God. The only defense for our sin and failure is Christ. So when the devil or others point out our sins, we can only agree with them and then point to Christ who is our defense.

Why do some Christians seem to live joyful and confident lives and others seem to be eaten up with guilt and remorse? Joyful, confident Christians look to Christ for their defense. Defeated Christians try to justify themselves or conclude that they really are no-good sinners who fail God every day. Scripture tells us we have been cleansed from a guilty conscience and can come to God with a sincere heart in full assurance of faith.

> Therefore, brothers, since we have confidence to enter the Most Holy Place by the blood of Jesus, by a new and living way opened for us through the curtain, that is, his body, and since we have a great priest over the house of God, let us draw near to God with a sincere heart in full assurance of faith, having our hearts sprinkled to cleanse us from a guilty conscience and having our bodies washed with pure water (Heb. 10:19-22).

We can't save ourselves; we can't cleanse ourselves; we can't justify ourselves; we can't free ourselves. The good news is we don't have to. Jesus Christ has already done it for us. We just need to trust Him to be our defense and believe that we have already been justified by faith.

Probe

What has been your experience with others when you tried to justify your sins and failures? If someone pointed out your shortcomings in the future, how could (or should) you respond?

Journal

_____

_____

_____

_____

_____

Note
1. David Seamands, *Healing Grace* (Wheaton, Ill.: Victor Books, 1988), pp. 121-123.

DAY 35

Thought for Today: Christ died for all our sins—past, present and future.

When you were dead in your sins and in the uncircumcision of your sinful nature, God made you alive with Christ. He forgave us all our sins.

COLOSSIANS 2:13

I experienced freedom from addiction when I finally understood what God had done for me on the Cross and who I was in Christ. A year later I went through the counseling internship at Grace Ministries International in Atlanta, Georgia. It was an exciting time; I had never before experienced such acceptance and encouragement, plus I was learning how to help people find their identity and freedom in Christ.

Toward the end of my internship, the president of Grace Ministries asked me to come on staff. I was speechless. Finally, I said, "I just can't believe you would be interested in someone like me. You know about my checkered past. You know how badly I've failed. I've been through two treatment centers, arrested for public drunkenness and called before the church discipline committee. Why would you be interested in someone like me?" I will never forget his answer. He looked me straight in the eye and said, "That's the kind of man we're looking for."

They weren't necessarily looking for people who had failed badly, but they were looking for those who had been broken of their self-sufficiency and were trusting Christ to be their life. I learned a little more about the grace of God that day. I did go on staff and enjoyed four-and-a-half great years with them.

When I met Neil at a conference, we talked about the possibility of my coming on staff with Freedom in Christ Ministries. I wondered if they would accept me if they knew about my failures and the fact that I was divorced. I gave Neil a tape of my testimony so he would know all about me. Later he told me that my testimony is what convinced him he would like to have me on staff.

Many people live as though God has forgiven them for their past sins but He's keeping a record of present sins and will surely find them guilty for any future sins. When Christ died once for all our sins, how many of our sins at that time were future? All of them were! "Shall we go on sinning so that grace may increase? By no means! We died to sin; how can we live in it any longer?" (Rom. 6:1,2). When we come to Christ, all of our sins are forgiven—past, present and future. That wonderful truth is not a license to go on sinning; it is a gracious means not to sin.

King David, who was an adulterer and a murderer, was called a man after God's own heart (see Acts 13:22). Abraham was a bigamist who allowed a king to take his wife into his harem in order to save his own life, yet he was called a friend of God and an example of faith (see Jas. 2:23). Moses was a murderer, but he was called the most humble man who ever lived (see Num. 12:3). Noah got drunk and lay naked before his son in his tent, yet found favor in the eyes of God (see Gen. 6:8; 9:21,22).

We deny ourselves the blessings of God when we focus on what we have done instead of what Christ has done for us. Without the grace of God and His forgiveness, we have no hope. Scripture says, "I tell you the truth, all the sins and blasphemies of men will be forgiven them" (Mark 3:28).

Is there a point at which God says, "That's it—no more forgiveness," or "Okay, I forgave your little sins, but that one is too bad to be forgiven"? No. *All* our sins have been forgiven—past, present and future. All of them have been placed on the Cross. When all our sins were nailed to that Cross, they were all future sins.

Will there be any difference in heaven between people who have committed horrible sins and those who have tried to live good moral lives? Is there any difference between you and Karla Faye Tucker, the ax murderer who threw herself on the mercy of God? No. We were all born dead in our trespasses and sins. Most of the differing degrees of observable sin in people can be explained by an act of natural birth. Somebody born in a wretched situation with no moral guidance is going to appear more sinful than one who was reared in a very supportive home with strict moral guidelines. Both need Christ. That is why the ground is level at the foot of the Cross, where all our sins were forgiven.

Probe

Have you ever thought your life was so messed up that you could never be of useful service to God? How could your testimony of failure be used as a source of blessing to others?

Journal

_____

_____

_____

_____

_____

DAY 36

Thought for Today: The sorrow of the world produces death, but the sorrow that comes from God leads to repentance and life without regret.

Blessed are they whose transgressions are forgiven, whose sins are covered.
Blessed is the man whose sin the Lord will never count against him.
ROMANS 4:7,8

Do you ever feel guilty? Most of us do when we sin, because sin violates our consciences and contradicts who we are in Christ. To sin is to go against our new nature as children of God. We're supposed to come under conviction when we sin, but the real question is, "Am I guilty?" Absolutely not! God has pronounced us "not guilty" because of the finished work of Christ on the Cross.

When I entered the Christian treatment center, I was really down. Julia had finally had all she could stand and had kicked me out of the house. I had to leave my job for two months in order to seek treatment for my addiction. Consequently, there was very little money coming in. I didn't see how we could keep from declaring bankruptcy and losing our house.

This was the second treatment center I had been to in three months. I got drunk within a few weeks after getting out of the first treatment center. Based on such overwhelming evidence, my friends were now convinced I was an irresponsible drunk. How could they not be convinced of that? I was a complete failure as a Christian.

I arrived at the center on a Friday afternoon, so I had to wait until Monday morning to meet with the director. I was just one of many older alcoholics mixed in with younger addicts, chronic offenders and street people. How could a seminary graduate and former pastor sink so low? How could I have failed so miserably? How could I still call myself a Christian?

When I met with the director for the intake interview, he found out that I had been in the pastorate. He brought up the possibility of going back into ministry. At the time, it seemed like a cruel joke. It was so painful that I couldn't even think about it. I begged him not to let any of the men know that I had been a pastor. I was so ashamed of myself and where I had ended up. We did keep it a secret, and during the two months I was there, none of the men found out. I was still trying to hide my shame and save my reputation.

I was convinced that God had given up on me. The idea of being in ministry again was inconceivable. I would have settled for just being normal, although I wasn't sure what that meant. If God had offered me the opportunity to leave the center, find a job (any job) where I could show up for work, come home at night and be a decent husband, I would have taken it in a heartbeat. I was completely defeated and full of self-pity. I was groveling in my guilt, trying to find some nobility in my life. But there's nothing noble about living in defeat and bondage.

Paul says, "For the sorrow that is according to the will of God produces a repentance without regret, leading to salvation; but the sorrow of the world produces death" (2 Cor. 7:10, *NASB*). I was experiencing the sorrow of the world and was slowly dying. I was sorry I got caught, sorry my reputation was soiled, sorry my wife had kicked me out. The conviction of God was present within me, but I was still trying to find my own way out. Judas betrayed Christ, came under the sorrow of the world and hung himself. Peter betrayed Christ three times, came under the conviction of God, repented and became the first spokesperson for the Church.

Repentance means a change of mind. It is turning away from the lies of the world and embracing the truth of God's Word. I was sorry for my sin and my failure but ignorant of God's covering. I didn't know the truth that would set me free. I knew what to turn from, but I didn't know what to turn to. I knew I was in bondage, but I didn't know the truth that would set me free.

I was begging God to forgive me when I was already forgiven. I was asking God to do something for me that He had already done. I was trying to become somebody I already was. I was looking for some purpose for groveling in my sin and wasn't finding any, because God wanted me to glorify Him by living free in Christ. We can't be a positive witness if we are living in defeat. Now that I have discovered the truth that sets us free, I'm a liberated witness of the resurrection power of God.

Probe

Have you ever felt the sorrow of the world, but it only made matters worse because it didn't result in genuine repentance? Have you ever felt the conviction of God that did lead to genuine repentance and life without regret? Can you articulate the difference?

Journal

_____

_____

_____

_____

_____

OVERCOMING THE BIGGEST BARRIER TO FREEDOM

DAY 37

Thought for Today: Only Christ can set you free.

What a wretched man I am! Who will rescue me from this body of death?
Thanks be to God—through Jesus Christ our Lord!
ROMANS 7:24,25

When I teach at Christian treatment centers, I always say, "If you work this program perfectly, but that's all you do, you will probably be back on drugs or alcohol, or both, shortly after you leave here." Many are surprised by the statement, but most know it's true because they see it happen on a regular basis.

When I struggled with my addiction to alcohol, I hated myself for what I was doing, and I hated alcohol for what it was doing to me, but I couldn't stop. I resolved to do whatever it took to beat my problem. I sought answers and pursued programs with all my being. I wasn't going to give up. For eight years I tried everything I knew and I tried to follow everyone's advice. My wife, Julia, says I earned a DD—a Doctorate in Drunkenness. Following are some of the things I tried:

1. Pastoral counselors
2. Christian 12-step program
3. Christian counselor
4. Secular counselor
5. Addictions counselor
6. Antabuse drug
7. Public confession
8. Reading (every book on addiction)
9. Christian psychiatrist
10. Secular psychiatrist
11. Healing-of-memories session
12. Deliverance session
13. Baptism of the Holy Spirit session

14. Christian psychologist
15. Secular psychologist
16. Church discipline committee
17. Secular treatment center
18. Accountability
19. Biblical confrontation
20. Group therapy
21. Christian treatment center
22. Willpower
23. AA meetings and five separate sponsors
24. Prayer
25. Promises to God and my wife
26. Bible study
27. Scripture memorization
28. Fasting
29. Evangelism
30. Discipleship

Nothing worked! Why? Because the above list only includes people, techniques, advice and self-help programs. Paul didn't ask, "What will set me free?" He asked, *"Who* will set me free?" There is only one "person" who can set you free: "Thanks be to God—through Jesus Christ our Lord!" We are saved and set free by the grace of God through faith in the finished work of Christ. It is not faith plus good works; it is faith that results in good works.

Jesus said, "I am the vine; you are the branches. If a man remains in me and I in him, he will bear much fruit; apart from me you can do nothing" (John 15:5). It's not that we're only limited in what we can do without Christ; apart from Christ we can do nothing that lasts for all eternity. We will not bear fruit if we put our confidence in people, programs and strategies instead of in Christ. But if our confidence is in Christ, then almost any program will bear fruit.

Why don't more Christians turn to Christ with their addictive problems? Perhaps they don't believe He can really set them free. Scripture is clear that freedom is our rightful inheritance as children of God. "It is for freedom that Christ has set us free. Stand firm, then, and do not let your-selves be burdened again by a yoke of slavery" (Gal. 5:1). "So if the Son sets you free, you will be free indeed" (John 8:36). "Because through Christ Jesus the law of the Spirit of life set me free from the law of sin and death" (Rom. 8:2).

Probe

Have you successfully put your confidence in Christ alone for your salva-tion and freedom? If you have, how and when did you do it? If you haven't, why not do it now?

Journal

_____

_____

_____

_____

_____

DAY 38

Thought for Today: The problem is not that we are too weak but that we are too strong.

But he said to me, "My grace is sufficient for you, for my power is made perfect in weakness." Therefore I will boast all the more gladly about my weaknesses, so that Christ's power may rest on me. That is why, for Christ's sake, I delight in weaknesses, in insults, in hardships, in persecutions, in difficulties. For when I am weak, then I am strong.

2 CORINTHIANS 12:9,10

Why is it so difficult for most Christians to live in freedom? Are people just too weak in character and commitment? Is the Christian life too hard? Does God demand too much?

When I was at the Christian treatment center, several of the men had come off the streets. During the free (smoking) times, I listened to some of the men criticize people in authority—those who ran the treatment center, the president of the United States, Congress and the whole government. It was amazing to me that those men, who couldn't manage their own lives, believed they could do a better job of managing the country than those in authority.

One morning I was talking to one of the chronic criticizers. I was complaining about my roommate's snoring, which kept me awake most of the night. His voice held contempt as he said, "You'd never make it in a flophouse." He looked down on me because he thought I was weak and wouldn't be able to make it on the streets like he had been able to do. He was right.

After going through treatment, many people who have lived on the streets choose to return there rather than keep a steady job or live with relatives. Why? Because living on the streets is the ultimate form of independence. They aren't responsible to anyone or anything. At Bethel these people looked at me with disdain. Their self-sufficiency was keeping them in their lowly state and they were proud of it! They rightly perceived that I couldn't survive on the streets because I wasn't strong enough.[1]

As long as we believe we can do it ourselves, we will keep trying to control our lives, and God will let us. After all, we're hard chargers, high achievers, go-getters. We can make it happen, get it done and overcome anything. Such foolish pride is not the Christian way. Paul had that kind of self-sufficiency until God struck him down. Then Paul was able to share the key to the abundant life—living in Christ's strength (see 2 Cor. 12:9,10). God has to bring us to the end of our resources so that we can discover His.

The biggest barrier to my own freedom was me—my pride, my strength, my plans, my goals, my agenda. Yet my only qualification for writing this devotional was my failure. Only then could I experience all that God had for me. If even one of the things I tried had worked, then I probably would have said, "I did it!" and my pride and stubborn self-will would still be intact.

The only way anyone can find freedom, peace, joy and fulfillment is through Christ. The temptation is to think we are too weak and then try harder. The real problem may be that we are too strong and prideful to surrender our wills to the only One who can set us free.

I grew up believing that "God helps those who help themselves." That famous quote, credited to Benjamin Franklin, is wrong. Scripture says that "No king is saved by the size of his army; no warrior escapes by his great strength. . . . But the eyes of the LORD are on those who fear him, on those whose hope is in his unfailing love" (Ps. 33:16,18). Jesus isn't our helper, He is our life.

Probe

Have you been, or are you still, prideful, strong-willed and self-sufficient? How has it helped or hindered your relationship with God and others?

Journal

Note
1. Neil T. Anderson and Mike and Julia Quarles, *Freedom from Addiction* (Ventura, Calif.: Regal Books, 1996), pp. 109, 110.

DAY 39

Thought for Today: Our relationship with God is our eternal foundation.

The words "once more" indicate the removing of what can be shaken—
that is, created things—so that what cannot be shaken may remain.
HEBREWS 12:27

My wife presented me with an ultimatum: "I can't continue living this way even one more day. If you ever drink again, you will have to leave." I respected her decision and promised to leave if I drank again. Within a few days, I was drunk, and Julia gave me a week to find a place to live. I made plans to go to a Christian treatment center in North Carolina that had accepted me for a 60-day program.

The night I left, Julia and I went out for ice cream after dinner. The last thing she said to me was, "I don't want you to call or write to me during these 60 days." I was at the lowest point in my life when I boarded that all-night bus in Atlanta. My marriage was over. I was on the verge of bankruptcy and facing 60 days without income. All my friends and relatives had given up on me.

I suppose every believer has experienced a crisis that precipitated the questions, Why? What's happening to me? Problems pile up, nothing seems to go right and no matter how hard you try, you can't seem to get it together. Have you misunderstood God's purpose for your life and what He is doing in you?

I believe most Christians would like to live a successful Christian life. We want to be strong, mature, and do the right thing. Usually the problem is not about motivation but about direction and understanding. Paul says in Romans 8:29 that God predestined us to be conformed to the likeness of Jesus Christ.

God says that He will shake the things in our lives that can be shaken so that what cannot be shaken will remain (see Heb. 12:26, 27). What can be shaken in our lives? Every temporal thing. It may be something very dear to us, such as a career, a relationship, home, marriage, finances, possessions and so on. It's not that God wants to make us miserable, but He is willing to shake and strip away the flimsy foundation upon which we have built our lives so that He can establish a new foundation that cannot be shaken—our relationship with Christ.

God understands that we will suffer loss in this world. "Therefore you too now have sorrow; but I will see you again, and your heart will rejoice, and no one takes your joy away from you" (John 16:22, *NASB*).

Consider some of the things on a worldwide scale that have been shaken and have fallen in recent years: The Berlin wall, Communism, the USSR as a nation, the savings and loan industry. The psalmist says, "They know nothing, they understand nothing. They walk about in darkness; all the foundations of the earth are shaken" (Ps. 82:5). God does not shake the foundations of this world because He is arbitrary or cruel. He just knows that everything we have in this temporal world will be lost, no matter what we do. He wants us to put our faith and confidence in that which is eternal and not in things we have no right or ability to control.

King David had the right foundation: "He alone is my rock and my salvation; he is my fortress, I will not be shaken" (Ps. 62:6). "Those who trust in the LORD are like Mount Zion, which cannot be shaken but endures forever" (Ps. 125:1).

Probe

Is there any relationship, possession or position you now have that you cannot lose? Is it more important to you than your eternal relationship with your heavenly Father? Why or why not? What will happen to you in the future when you lose all the temporal things you now possess?

Journal

_____

_____

_____

_____

_____

DAY 40

Thought for Today: You are not the problem, but you may have one.

I am not saying this because I am in need, for I have learned to be content whatever the circumstances. I know what it is to be in need, and I know what it is to have plenty. I have learned the secret of being content in any and every situation, whether well fed or hungry, whether living in plenty or in want. I can do everything through him who gives me strength.
PHILIPPIANS 4:11-13

During the spring blizzard of 1993, our house was without power for a day, so I went over to my son's house. I was watching the video *Beauty and the Beast* with my four-year-old granddaughter, Kaitlin. In one scene the beast was ranting and raving and breaking dishes and turning over furniture. Meanwhile, Beauty was sitting quietly and demurely at the table. Kaitlin turned to me and said, "Is it his problem or her problem?"

Good question. What is your problem? Is it sickness, addiction, your spouse (or lack of one), rebellious children, lack of finances, a tyrannical boss, a sorry job? Is it your problem or their problem? Do you have a problem or are you the problem?

The first 50 years of my life were a continual struggle. I thought after I became a Christian that all my problems would be over. That wasn't the case. I bombed out in the pastorate and went back into business. I blamed everyone else, including the church.

I thought one of my biggest problems was the church where I was the pastor. I went there with great anticipation. I was going to build that church into a vibrant, witnessing, life-changing force in the community. I had many plans, ideas and programs in mind, and most of them remained right there. Every direction I took I seemed to run into a brick wall in spite of my best efforts. I sarcastically described the church as having rampant apathy and unbridled lethargy. My last sermon was on Revelation 3:16 where Jesus said He would spit lukewarm Christians out of His mouth.

It took me some time to realize that I was trying to meet my needs for acceptance, security and significance in my role as a pastor. It was the same thing I did as a stockbroker before I became a Christian. I hung on to the same false belief. The only difference was that as a pastor I measured my success by how well the church seemed to be doing. I evaluated my success by tangible evidence, such as attendance and giving. I was not getting my needs met, because the members didn't respond the way I wanted them to. I wasn't ministering the love of Christ and the truth of the gospel to those people; I was trying to get them to perform so that I could feel good about myself.

Actually, I wasn't the problem; but I had a problem, and it was mine, not somebody else's. If we are the problem, then the only way to get rid of the problem is to get rid of ourselves. But if we *have* a problem, then we can seek God's answer to resolve it. I was trying to control and manipulate people and circumstances in order to meet my own needs. I now know that the fruit of the Spirit is self-control, not spouse- or church-control.

We cannot always control what happens to us, but we can determine what our responses will be. When someone hurts us, we can choose to forgive them or we can seek revenge in anger and bitterness. When things don't go our way we can try to control others or we can choose to believe, with self under control, that God is working all things together for our good. We can be anxious about everything or we can choose to cast all our anxiety on Him because He cares for us (see 1 Pet. 5:7).

Bad things happen to good people, but regardless of what happens, because of Christ's death and resurrection, you have been forgiven of all your sins, redeemed from your past, been reckoned dead to the power of sin, made alive to God and received the promise that God will meet all your needs. God has adopted you as His child. He will never leave you nor forsake you. You are in Christ and Christ is in you. You can't get any more secure than that.

The real issue isn't the good or bad circumstances of life. They are inevitable. The real issue is our relationship with Christ. It is the only constant in life. That knowledge will simplify your life and enable you to turn to Christ and trust Him in every situation. Paul learned how to be content no matter what the circumstances. So can we. It is time to stop casting blame and to start becoming the people God created us to be.

Probe

What, or who, can keep you from being the person God created you to be? How can you find contentment in your life?

Journal

_____

_____

_____

_____

_____

DAY 41

Thought for Today: The soul was never designed to be the master.

His divine power has given us everything we need for life and godliness through our knowledge of him who called us by his own glory and goodness.
2 PETER 1:3

When you were young, did you have dreams or aspirations for your life? I wanted to be successful so others would admire me. The dream began to fade with every successive failure. Eventually, I couldn't even plan for tomorrow because survival for the day was at the top of my list.

When I taught a Sunday School class at a large church in Atlanta, I remember a man in the class who was very intelligent and owned his own business, but he just couldn't get his life together. His problems always seemed to drag him down. If it wasn't trouble in his marriage, it was trouble with personal finances or his business.

One day in class, he said, "I know all this stuff you're teaching. I've read all the books you have referred to. I know about my identity in Christ, but it just doesn't work for me."

"Let me ask you a question," I said. "Have you ever given up the right not to succeed, and are you willing to fail in business if that is God's will?"

"Absolutely not," he replied.

"That's your problem," I said.

His dream wasn't God's dream. His idea of success wasn't God's idea of success. His will wasn't God's will. In fact, He probably didn't even consider God's will.

God has given us everything we need for life and godliness, but if we believe we need something else, we will probably live in defeat. We can know the fundamentals of Christian doctrine and still live as though we are our own god, reserving the right to decide what is good for us.

The truth is, we are bond servants who were bought at a price—the precious blood of Christ—and we don't have any rights except those we have as God's children. He has given us the right to be children of God, but not to be self-determining. Being a child of the King is a tremendous privilege, but it also has certain responsibilities. The primary responsibility is to do His will. Paul wrote, "Therefore also we have as our ambition, whether at home or absent, to be pleasing to Him" (2 Cor. 5:9, *NASB*).

I thought I needed to have a fruitful pastorate in order to be successful. That was easy to justify, since it was Christian work. I pursued my goal with all my strength but never attained it. When I finally gave up the right to be a pastor who was in charge, God gave me a fruitful ministry where He is in charge. Now I thoroughly enjoy the work of the Lord. But if I lost it tomorrow I would still be fulfilled. We will only be satisfied when we decide to become the people God created us to be. Ministry takes place when the Spirit flows out of who we are in Christ.

Ministries come and go, marriages fail, children rebel, and "secure" jobs are lost every day. Friends fail you, the stock market falls, health deteriorates, *but* "those who trust in the LORD are like Mount Zion, which cannot be shaken but endures forever" (Ps. 125:1).

It takes a lot of energy to control others and manipulate circumstances. The inevitable result is burnout. It also makes for frustrated and unhappy people. The soul was never designed by God to function as master. Our duty is to be filled (controlled) by the Holy Spirit. Self-control is the result of being filled with the Spirit.

Jesus modeled the Christian life when He took upon Himself the form of a man and dwelt among us, living in total dependence upon our heavenly Father. "'My teaching is not my own. It comes from him who sent me" (John 7:16). "For I did not speak of my own accord, but the Father who sent me commanded me what to say and how to say it" (John 12:49). "The words I say to you are not just my own. Rather, it is the Father, living in me, who is doing his work" (John 14:10).

The person who is holding on to his right for self-determination must bear the consequences of playing god. But those who have received Him and have been given the right to be children of God will find peace and contentment in doing His will. There is only one peaceful place to be, and that is in the center of God's will.

Probe

Have you ever tried to control others and manipulate circumstances in order to accomplish your will? How well did it work? What rights do you have as a child of God?

Journal

_____

_____

_____

_____

_____

DAY 42

Thought for Today: The way up is down.

I tell you the truth, unless a kernel of wheat falls to the ground and dies,
it remains only a single seed. But if it dies, it produces many seeds. The
man who loves his life will lose it, while the man who hates his life in this
world will keep it for eternal life.

JOHN 12:24,25

I woke up in a strange place. My pants were ripped and my shirt torn and
bloody. I bolted up in the bed only to be abruptly jerked back. There were
rigid leather straps binding my wrists. Through the doorway I could see
people moving around.

"Help! Somebody please help me!" I screamed.

Two women in white uniforms rushed into the room.

"Calm down," a nurse said to me.

"Where am I? What's going on?"

"You're in Cooper Green Hospital."

"How did I get here?"

"The police brought you," the nurse answered in a calm voice. "You
were arrested and had a bad cut on your chin. They brought you here for
treatment."

Cooper Green was the indigent hospital in Birmingham, Alabama.
Although my mind searched for a reason, I couldn't determine why I was
restrained. When I asked the nurse, she said, "You were brought in last
night and were thrashing violently. We couldn't do anything with you."

"Please take off these straps," I said. "I want to go home."

"You can't leave. The Birmingham police have a hold on you. You're
a prisoner in our custody."

I had been a Christian for 13 years. I had graduated from seminary,
been ordained for ministry and had served for several years in the pastorate. My consuming desire was to make my life count for Christ. For
more than a dozen years I had responded to my calling with all diligence.

Who was this forlorn person strapped to a bed reserved for drunken bums?

After being taken from the hospital to the jail, the assistant pastor at our church brought my wife down to pay my fine for public drunkenness. Many times he and I had shared with each other our excitement about serving the Lord. About 10 years earlier, we had attended the same seminary. We started a weekly discipleship group that included our wives. We looked to the Scriptures for God's best in our marriages and ministries. Many times we had prayed together and discussed our desire to serve God and make our lives count for Christ.

Now, with this same friend, I walked out of jail. Julia couldn't lift her head to look at me. My pastor friend, who is 10 years younger than I am, saw my pitiful state and shook his head in disbelief. He fell silent and offered neither words of encouragement nor rebuke. Both of them knew I had heard it all and nothing else could be said. In my entire life I had never felt so low. It all seemed like a bad dream.[1]

What went wrong? I had been striving with all my strength to be a successful Christian. I wanted to blow the roof off my church. I was going to bring about God's will if it was the last thing I did. It almost was! Can you imagine the audacity of thinking it was "my" church? The same one He purchased by the blood of the Lamb. It was my strength, my wisdom and my plans that were in the way. So God had to bring me to the point where I no longer had any confidence in myself. He had to bring me to the end of myself in order to discover who I really was.

Revival is not the roof blowing off; it is the floor caving in. When the floor falls on our own plans, resources and good intentions, we can begin to trust in God's resources. Grace flows downhill and meets us at our point of need.

Jesus said, he who loves his natural life will lose it, but he who loses his (natural) life for my sake will keep it for all eternity (see Matt. 10:39). In other words, if we try to find our identity and purpose for being here in our natural existence, we will lose it. But those who find their identity and purpose for being here in their spiritual and eternal life in Christ will keep it. All children of God have that seed of eternal life sown in them, but it will remain dormant if we go on living for ourselves.

Dr. Charles Stanley has said that the number-one requirement for a Christian leader is brokenness. If you are looking for a new pastor, pray for a broken one. If you are praying for a spouse, ask God for a broken one. If you are in need of Christian counsel, ask God to lead you to a broken counselor. If you want to experience all that God has prepared for you from the foundation of this world, then "humble yourselves before the Lord, and he will lift you up" (Jas. 4:10).

Probe

Why do we struggle so hard to keep from being broken? Can we choose to humble ourselves or does God have to do it?

Journal

_____

_____

_____

_____

_____

Note
  1. Neil T. Anderson and Mike and Julia Quarles, *Freedom from Addiction* (Ventura, Calif.: Regal Books, 1996), pp. 17, 18.

DAY 43

Thought for Today: You have to let go and let God be God.

We were under great pressure, far beyond our ability to endure,
so that we despaired even of life. Indeed, in our hearts we felt the
sentence of death. But this happened that we might not rely on
ourselves but on God, who raises the dead.
2 CORINTHIANS 1:8,9

I completed the 60-day program at the Christian treatment center, and six months later started a ministry to alcoholics and addicts. I had achieved some degree of sobriety, but every few months I would go out and have a few drinks.

One afternoon, while Julia was out of town, I stopped on the way home from the office to have a beer. Many beers later, I drove home in the early hours of the morning. I had a ministry to alcoholics and addicts, yet I was trapped in the same bondage as the people I counseled. I felt like the world's biggest hypocrite.

For the next few hours I slept fitfully. I woke up full of remorse and self-loathing. Something had to be done, and I knew what my next step must be. I would notify the Presbytery, the ministry I was with, and the little Presbyterian church where I preached on Sundays. The next day I completed my calls, and then plunged into a deep, dark depression. I didn't have a job or any prospects for one. I felt completely devastated and without hope.

Jerry Clower, the Mississippi comedian, tells a story about when he and his good buddy Marcel went coon hunting. They think they've treed this big she-coon, and Marcel shinnies up the tree to shake it out. But when he gets up there, he discovers it's not a she-coon, but a lynx—what Jerry calls a souped-up wildcat. The lynx attacks Marcel and is about to tear him up. Marcel hollers down at Jerry, "Shoot . . . shoot! This thang is killin' me!"

"I'm afraid to shoot, I might hit you," Jerry hollers.

Marcel hollers back, "Shoot up here amongst us. One of us has got to have some relief!"

Jerry's story described my situation perfectly. Like the prodigal son, I was tired of ruining my life and wanted out of the pigpen. God, however, had me right where He wanted me. I had exhausted all my resources and options. Spiritually bankrupt, I finally was ready to let God be God and do what He wanted me to do all along.

Not everyone has to become a drunk and lose everything in order to get free, but we all have to come to the end of ourselves. I know a physician who experienced a gradual decline of self-reliance. He quietly broke free from himself and found his sufficiency in Christ. On the other hand, his son was hooked on drugs and teetered on the verge of suicide before he came to the end of himself. My experience was full of failure, pain and public humiliation. Julia also experienced a lot of pain, but it wasn't open and public. God used my struggle to bring her to the end of herself.

As Christians we should be strong and able to do the right thing. But there is only one way to do that. We have to "be strong *in the Lord,* and in the strength of *His might*" (Eph. 6:10, *NASB,* emphasis added). You can't do that if you don't know who you are "in the Lord," and if you are trying to be strong in your own strength.

In our ministry, we talk to people every day who are looking for a method to try, a program to follow, a formula to work or steps to take. Many people prefer the law over grace. They would rather have someone tell them what to do and then try to do it. The only problem is, "The letter [of the law] kills, but the Spirit gives life" (2 Cor. 3:6).

Probe

What are you holding on to that you don't want to let go of? Do you have it or does it have you? What would it take for you to come to the end of yourself and let God take control?

Journal

_____

_____

_____

_____

DAY 44

Thought for Today: If there is no pain, there is probably no gain.

I am the vine; you are the branches. If a man remains in me and I in him,
he will bear much fruit; apart from me you can do nothing.
JOHN 15:5

After one of my many failures, I talked my situation over with my brother-in-law. He told me I was fortunate. He said, "If you get away from God, you fail badly and everyone else knows it." He said that because of his own God-given natural abilities and relative stability, he could slowly move away from God and neither I nor anyone else would be aware of it for months.

"You are more aware of your need for God than I am, and for that reason you are very fortunate," he said.

My brother-in-law is right about me. Any movement away from God is a prescription for disaster. An old Southern expression says, "He has been broken from sucking eggs." Behind the saying is a story about a young farm boy who for some reason enjoyed punching a hole in an egg and sucking out the inside. One day the egg he selected was rotten. It permanently broke his habit. In terms of living the Christian life out of my own resources, I have been broken from sucking eggs.

One time after I gave a message on brokenness, a woman told me she was having great difficulty with this concept. She said she could do many things without Christ.

"Are you saying that apart from Christ you are just limited in what you can do?" I asked.

"Yes, that's it," she said. "I'm limited without Christ."

It's true that we can do many things without Christ when we live according to the flesh, but none of it will last for eternity. Paul explains it in 1 Cor. 3:11-15:

> For no one can lay any foundation other than the one already
> laid, which is Jesus Christ. If any man builds on this foundation

using gold, silver, costly stones, wood, hay or straw, his work will be shown for what it is, because the Day will bring it to light. It will be revealed with fire, and the fire will test the quality of each man's work. If what he has built survives, he will receive his reward. If it is burned up, he will suffer loss; he himself will be saved, but only as one escaping through the flames.

The tragedy in life isn't the experience of pain and failure that leads to brokenness. (That was actually my salvation.) The real tragedy is to never see our need of God. We will never experience freedom in Christ without such an awareness.

I don't know any painless way to die to self, but I know it is necessary if we want to be alive and free in Christ. "For we who are alive are always being given over to death for Jesus' sake, so that His life may be revealed in our mortal body" (2 Cor. 4:11). All true believers desire their work of service to last, but those who are bearing fruit know that apart from Christ, nothing will.

Probe

Why has it been hard for you to come to the end of yourself? Would others see you as a self-made person or a God-made person? Why or why not?

Journal

_____

_____

_____

_____

_____

DAY 45

Thought for Today: There is a price to pay for freedom.

Whoever finds his life will lose it, and whoever
loses his life for my sake will find it.
MATTHEW 10:39

After I recognized my identity in Christ and began to walk in freedom, I met with my pastor and shared with him the new truth I had learned. He expressed concern that this teaching didn't agree with the doctrines of our denomination. He arranged a meeting with other pastors to discuss it. I shared my story of how I gained my freedom by listening to Bill Gillham's tapes, "Victorious Christian Living."

My pastor reached over and picked up a copy of Gillham's book *Lifetime Guarantee* that contained the same teaching as the tapes. Point by point he explained how Gillham was off in his theology and how, as a result of listening to him, I had fallen into the same error. I respected this pastor as my mentor more than anyone else I knew. If I could select someone to emulate as a godly example of a pastor, he would be the one. He had recommended me to the church where I pastored and was the most influential person in my life.

As I listened to him, I was surprised that his position didn't threaten or faze me. Although I respected and loved this man, I wasn't shaken. God had revealed to me the truth of my identity based on His Word. After years of pain and anguish, my life had been drastically altered, and I was now living in freedom and peace. Although our discussion remained friendly and I knew he had my best interest at heart, we could not agree about what the Word said concerning a believer's identity in Christ.

Finally, he said, "I don't think you can stay in our denomination, Mike, if you continue to hold this understanding of Scripture." Rather than be divisive, I thought it would be best if I left the denomination with which I had identified for 17 years. It was a sad day, but I could not deny the truth that had finally set me free. My identity was no longer in a denomination, it was in Christ.

When I first came to Christ, old friends and even my first wife left me. Every new believer experiences some separation from the world. Likewise, when we discover who we are in Christ, we may face opposition in our churches and friendships when they don't understand. Thankfully, nothing can threaten our position in Christ. There has always been a price to pay for freedom, but it will always be worth it.[1]

Our freedom comes with a huge price tag that Jesus willingly paid. The only price we pay is the loss of self-centered living. "You are not your own; you were bought at a price. Therefore honor God with your body" (1 Cor. 6:19,20). Only by losing do we win. Most of us are so stubborn and independent that the process is a painful one. We have to learn the hard way to "trust in the Lord with all your heart and lean not on your own understanding; in all your ways acknowledge him, and he will make your paths straight" (Prov. 3:5,6). I didn't learn that truth by reading the verse. I learned it by failing to live it. My own way was a highway to nowhere.

I learned a liberating truth from my defeat. I discovered that what I gave up—self-centered living—was the very thing that was keeping me in bondage.

Probe

Have you ever been afraid to buy into the Christian message completely for fear of losing something? What would you lose? Is that worth more to you than your freedom in Christ?

Journal

_____

_____

_____

_____

_____

Note
1. Neil T. Anderson and Mike and Julia Quarles, *Freedom from Addiction* (Ventura, Calif.: Regal Books, 1996), pp. 148, 149.

DAY 46

Thought for Today: Freedom is not determined by what you lose but by what you gain.

What is more, I consider everything a loss compared to the surpassing greatness of knowing Christ Jesus my Lord, for whose sake I have lost all things. I consider them rubbish, that I may gain Christ.

PHILIPPIANS 3:8

I counseled a man who had struggled with alcoholism for many years. Steve lived a shallow and empty life. He and his wife lived in the same house but he had no relationship with her, nor with his children. He had no close friends and seemed to have no hobbies or outside interests.

He did have one thing—money, and lots of it. He had inherited millions and had been able to retire at age 52. Every day his routine was the same. He would sleep until early afternoon. He would have lunch, then drive to his health club and enjoy the whirlpool, sauna and steam bath. After a massage, he would return home and start drinking. He continued to drink until after midnight, when he fell into bed in a drunken stupor and slept until the next afternoon.

He lived in a mansion on top of a mountain, drove a BMW and had the "finer things" of this world. He spent hundreds of thousands of dollars at secular treatment centers, trying to cure his alcoholism. He claimed to be a Christian, but his stubborn self-will kept him from totally trusting God. After one of our meetings, he said, "Mike, I guess I'm too weak to live the Christian life and trust God."

"You aren't too weak," I said. "You're too independent and self-sufficient."

Eventually, he left my counsel and searched for the program or treatment center that would finally rid him of his addiction. With his millions, he could afford the "best."

Before I met him, he had gone to Miami on a drunken binge with a couple of his cronies. At a fashionable restaurant, he almost choked to death on a piece of steak. His heart had stopped beating, and his doctor said it was a miracle he hadn't suffered brain damage. After that incident, Steve said, "I believe God was trying to get my attention." Unfortunately, God never really got his total attention. A few months later, he choked to death on a sandwich in his home.

Obviously, Steve wanted to get rid of his problem. He had spent almost half a million dollars trying to do so. But he had nothing to replace it with. If abstinence is the goal, then Ephesians 5:18 would read, "Do not get drunk on wine, which leads to debauchery. Therefore, stop drinking!" The answer is to be filled with the Spirit. "So I say, live by the Spirit, and you will not gratify the desires of the sinful nature" (Gal. 5:16).

I receive a number of calls from people who want us to help them stop drinking and drugging. I always tell them, "I don't have any interest in helping you do that, and I don't believe God does either." My ministry is to help people get radically right with God. When that happens, you can "live by the Spirit and not gratify the desires of the sinful nature."

God has much more in store for us than just our stopping a destructive habit. He has brought us into a loving relationship with Himself and He wants to bless us. Not only has He made us His children, but also His coheirs with Christ. "Now if we are children, then we are heirs—heirs of God and co-heirs with Christ, if indeed we share in his sufferings in order that we may also share in his glory" (Rom. 8:17).

We can't treat our problem like a haircut—just trim us up so we look better. That's not the "good news," that's window dressing. Paul would call all that rubbish. He lost all things to gain Christ. I did, too, and it was the best thing that ever happened to me. Now that I have Him, I just want to know Him and conform to His image. Maybe Steve would have come to know Him, too, if he had lost his millions.

Probe

What is the difference between knowing Christ and knowing all about Him? Have you ever solved a problem only to have one or more other problems surface the next day? How can you get beyond that?

Journal

_____

_____

_____

_____

_____

DAY 47

Thought for Today: We are following Jesus when we identify with Him and deny self-rule.

Then Jesus said to his disciples, "If anyone would come after me, he must deny himself and take up his cross and follow me. For whoever wants to save his life will lose it, but whoever loses his life for me will find it."
MATTHEW 16:24,25

Most Christians have read or heard Philippians 4:19, which tells us that Christ meets all our needs according to His riches in glory. But many people live as though they haven't gotten the message. They try to meet their needs for acceptance, security, and significance through appearance, performance or social status.

When I got out of the Christian treatment center, my first order of business was to secure a good job. In the middle of my worst drinking times, I had changed brokerage firms. My business fell sharply and my drinking escalated. I had worked for the new company less than a year. Three of those months I had been in two different treatment centers. The management was not impressed.

When I returned from the second treatment center, my boss and I met for breakfast. He told me, "Mike, the firm has given up on you. We no longer need your services." My years in the brokerage business had worn on me. I was ready for a complete change, but to what? I had no idea, and I was afraid to try anything different. I checked with some other brokerage companies, and one was willing to give me a chance.

I lasted less than four months. I had no enthusiasm or energy for the business. I lost almost all my clientele as they observed my whirl through two treatment centers and three brokerage firms in less than a year. I had no heart to solicit new clients. I couldn't even pick up the phone and call anyone, and when you can't pick up the phone in the brokerage business, you're out of business. I had no option but to face the facts and leave. For the next several months I tried financial planning, but it was similar to the brokerage business. I put little enthusiasm into what I was doing and didn't make any money.[1]

Here I was with no job, no money and no prospects. My career as a stockbroker, which had been successful at one time, was over. I really didn't have anything left. I didn't know it then, but I was now in a position to hear the truth that would set me free.

My situation was not unlike that of a story I once heard. A ship-wrecked man who managed to reach an uninhabited island decided to protect himself against the elements and to safeguard the few posses-sions he had salvaged by painstakingly building a little hut. Still, he con-stantly and prayerfully scanned the horizon for the approach of a ship. Returning to his makeshift shelter one evening after a search for food, the man was shocked to see his hut completely enveloped in flames. What a crushing disaster! The next morning he awoke to find a ship anchored off the island. When the captain stepped ashore, he said, "We saw your smoke signal and came." Everything the marooned man owned had to be destroyed before he could be rescued.

What do we need to give up in order to find freedom? The answer is found in what Neil refers to as "The Great Omission," found in Matthew 16:21-27. He calls it that because it is an often overlooked or misunder-stood Scripture passage, yet it is the central teaching of all four gospels and the ministry of Freedom in Christ. We will never be able to fulfill the Great Commission or be all that God created us to be unless we learn what it means to deny self, pick up our cross daily and follow Jesus.

Denying ourselves is not the same thing as denying ourselves certain pleasures. Many religions do that in order to live an austere life. The denial Scripture is talking about is saying no to self-rule. There is only one cross—the cross of Christ—and when we daily pick up the Cross and follow Him, we are denying self-rule and acknowledging Him as Lord. Whether it is in our own little kingdom or the kingdoms of this world, only one can rule. In the end, only One will: "That at the name of Jesus every knee will bow . . . and every tongue confess that Jesus Christ is Lord, to the glory of God the Father" (Phil. 2:10,11).

Probe

What is the difference between giving something up for God and giving ourselves up for God? Which is easier? Which one will have little impact? Why?

Journal

_____

_____

_____

_____

_____

Note
1. Neil T. Anderson and Mike and Julia Quarles, *Freedom from Addiction* (Ventura, Calif.: Regal Books, 1996), p. 98.

DAY 48

Thought for Today: The joy of the Lord is our strength.

*Now is your time of grief, but I will see you again and you will rejoice,
and no one will take away your joy.*
JOHN 16:22

A powerful tornado passed through Atlanta in the spring of 1998. It ripped up large trees, tossed cars around and destroyed homes and businesses. Several people were killed. Damage was in the millions of dollars. The governor of Georgia declared several counties disaster areas.

An older, affluent neighborhood was the worst hit. Most of the homes were destroyed and hundreds of huge trees were toppled. What was once one of the most beautiful neighborhoods in Atlanta was a scene of destruction. A family in our church lost their home in that neighborhood. The following Sunday they shared what had happened. The father made it to the basement with two grandchildren just before two large trees crashed through the house. One fell into the room where the baby had been moments before.

The mother said, "When you look at all the damaged furniture and other belongings and know that no one was hurt, and all your loved ones are safe, you realize that everything we lost was just stuff. That's all it is! Just stuff!" She and her husband manifested joy and peace in spite of their circumstances. Joy is a fruit of the Spirit, not dependent on good or bad circumstances.

After I found freedom from my alcoholism, I wondered, *Will my new-found freedom have any implications for daily living?* The circumstances surrounding my life hadn't changed. I had resigned from my ministry in disgrace. The presbytery was investigating me to determine what kind of disciplinary action should be taken. I had no income, no job and no prospects for a job. One morning, as I sat at my desk and reviewed all the facts of my current situation, for the first time in my life I sensed the peace of God and the joy of the Lord. Something internal had changed.

I was experiencing the fruit of the Spirit completely apart from my circumstances. The joy of Christ flooded my soul and I jumped up and shouted, "Hallelujah! Praise God!" Then I sat down and silently thanked God for a joy that no person could take away. Then I had one of my all-time weirdest thoughts: *I hope I don't get a job anytime soon. For a while, I want to enjoy just knowing I don't need anything but Christ for freedom, peace and joy.*

Nehemiah said, "Do not grieve, for the joy of the LORD is your strength" (Neh. 8:10). Joy reflects the character of God. We have become partakers of that divine nature. The joy that Jesus gives is the result of being at one with His own disposition.

The Bible contains more than 200 verses on joy. God wants us to experience His joy, which no one can take away. It comes from our relationship with God and God alone. Leonard Small said, "Joy is the standard that flies on the battlements of the heart when the king is in residence."[1] If we stake our joy on anything other than Christ, it can be changed in an instant. There is more joy in Jesus in one instant than there is in the world for a lifetime. I know, because I have tasted the fruit of both.

Where there is no joy, there is a lack of hope. The result can be depression, which has been called the "common cold" of mental illness. Never have people had so much material prosperity and been so depressed as they are right now. It has been said that you can live 40 days without food, seven days without water, and seven minutes without air, but you can't live a moment without hope. The antidote for lack of hope? The psalmist wrote, "Why are you in despair, O my soul? And why are you disturbed within me? Hope in God, for I shall again praise Him, the help of my countenance, and my God" (Ps. 43:5, *NASB*). Joylessness is the absence of God. Joy is found in relationship with Him.

Probe

Have you ever felt totally hopeless? Describe your relationship with God at that time. How can the joy of the Lord be your strength?

Journal

_____

_____

_____

_____

_____

Note

1. Sherwood Wirt and Kersten Beckstrom, eds., *Living Quotations for Christians* (New York: Harper & Row, 1974), p. 136.

BELOVED, NOW YOU ARE A CHILD OF GOD

DAY 49

**Thought for Today: The problem you think you
have is probably not your problem.**

*The acts of the sinful nature are obvious: sexual immorality, impurity and
debauchery; idolatry and witchcraft; hatred, discord, jealousy, fits of
rage, selfish ambition, dissensions, factions and envy; drunkenness,
orgies, and the like. I warn you, as I did before, that those who live like
this will not inherit the kingdom of God.*
GALATIANS 5:19-21

An old preacher once said, "Your problem is that you don't know what
your problem is. You think your problem is your problem, but that's not
the problem at all, and that's your main problem."

As I sought help for my alcoholism, people directed me to all sorts of
perceived solutions to do away with my problem drinking. With the best
of intentions, they wanted to explain to me the nature of alcoholism and
how to stop drinking. My pastor and assistant pastor tried to help me, as
did numerous Christian counselors. All of them pointed me toward a
variety of ways to deal with the problem of alcoholism.

I soon discovered that programs couldn't help me get to the root of
the problem. Alcoholism, anorexia, bulimia, sexual addiction, gambling,
perfectionism or workaholism are symptomatic of a far deeper problem.
What is the root problem of addiction? Paul explains habitual sin as an
act of the flesh, which includes drunkenness, sexual immorality, idolatry,
witchcraft, envy, jealousy, selfish ambition, anger, hatred and rage (see
Gal. 5:19-21). The basic problem is that we are living by the flesh instead
of by the Spirit.

Before I became a Christian, I had neither the presence of God in my
life nor the knowledge of His ways. So I learned how to live my life independent of Him. In other words, I learned to live according to the flesh—
to cope and survive independently of God. I had no choice, and neither
did you. I also had to establish my own identity and learn how to meet

my own needs for acceptance, security and significance. Of course we can't do that, so we turn to some other means to cope or cover the pain. For me it was alcohol, which became my dominant flesh pattern.

Many addicts have learned to cope by drinking and drugging, but they also have other patterns of the flesh, such as anger, envy, sexual immorality, perfectionism, jealousy, impurity, selfish ambition and so on. I would go for months without drinking, but my sexual lust would keep me in torment and I would go back to alcohol. Even if I controlled my lust, my anger would spill out and damage relationships and drive me back to drinking. I didn't have an alcohol problem, I had a life problem.

When well-intentioned friends tried to help me stop drinking, they were taking away my means of coping. That's one big reason why recidivism (going back to the addiction) is so high; people keep working on the symptom instead of the problem. I had legitimate needs that only Christ could meet.

To overcome an addiction, we must find a more satisfactory way of dealing with the pain and learn how our needs are met in Christ. We can't just take away the means of coping, even if it is destroying our lives. People reason that a failure identity is better than no identity, and drowning out their sorrows with chemicals is temporarily better than living in pain.

How do you get a filthy old bone away from a dog? If you try to take it away, you will have a dog fight. But throw the dog a steak and it will gladly spit out the old bone. Well, here's the good news: God has thrown us a steak. "God will meet all your needs according to his glorious riches in Christ Jesus" (Phil. 4:19). All we have to do is spit out the worthless old bone and take up the life-giving strength found in Christ.

I worked on my problem of alcoholism for eight years, trying anything and everything I could. Instead of overcoming the addiction, it grew worse. When I believed the gospel and learned who I was in Christ and what it meant to be a child of God, I started to walk in freedom by faith in the power of the Holy Spirit.

Probe

What success have you had by trying to abstain? Did your life improve or did other patterns of the flesh begin to surface? Did God tell us to change before we could receive the good news, or did we receive the good news and then slowly start to change?

Journal

_____

_____

_____

_____

_____

DAY 50

Thought for Today: No person can consistently behave in a way that is inconsistent with how he or she perceives himself or herself.

For you died, and your life is now hidden with Christ in God. When Christ, who is your life, appears, then you also will appear with him in glory.
COLOSSIANS 3:3,4

A defeated pastor made an appointment with Neil. "I've been struggling my whole Christian life," he said. "I think I finally know what the answer is. Recently, in my devotions, I read Colossians 3:3, 'For you died, and your life is now hidden with Christ in God.' I believe that is the key, but I don't think I know how to do it!"

"Dying is not your problem," Neil said. "Read the verse again."

"For you died, and your life is now hidden with Christ in God," the pastor quoted. He went on to say, "I know I need to die to myself and be alive in Christ, but I don't know how to do it."

"Read it once again," Neil persisted, "just a little bit slower."

"For you died—" he began again. Suddenly the light of understanding switched on. "I see what you're getting at . . . the verb is past tense, isn't it?"

"Indeed it is. Like many believers, you have been trying to accomplish something that has already been done, and you have been attempting to become someone you already are."

I (Mike) also did that for the first 15 years of my Christian experience. The death Paul talks about in Colossians 3:3 isn't something God expects you to do; it is something He expects you to know and believe. "For we know that our old self was [past tense] crucified with Him" (Rom. 6:6). We are no longer "in the flesh," we are "in Christ." Paul makes this clear in Roman 8:8,9 (*NASB*): "Those who are in the flesh cannot please God. However, you are not in the flesh but in the Spirit, if indeed the Spirit of God dwells in you. But if anyone does not have the Spirit of Christ, he does not belong to Him." The truth is, you can't do anything more to become what you already are.

Thanks to the incredible redemptive work of Christ, your old self "in Adam" has been replaced by a new self "in Christ." At the moment of salvation you became a new creation in Christ (2 Cor. 5:17). You are now identified with Christ in His death and in His resurrection (see 1 Cor. 15:20-22). The new life that characterizes your new self is nothing less than the life of Jesus implanted in you (see Gal. 2:20; Col. 3:3,4).[1]

As children, we all dreamed about becoming somebody special someday. The wonderful truth is, you're already somebody special. "Dear friends, *now* we are children of God" (1 John 3:2, emphasis added). We are not trying to become children of God, we *are* children of God, and we are becoming like Him as we mature in Christ. Therefore, "Count yourselves dead to sin but alive to God in Christ Jesus" (Rom. 6:11). We don't count ourselves dead to sin in order to be dead to sin, *we are dead to sin and alive in Christ.* Obviously sin is still present, and we can still choose to sin, but we don't have to.

You are not a human *doing*, you are a human *being*. Who we are always takes precedence over what we do. Who we are determines what we do. We cannot consistently behave in a way that is inconsistent with how we perceive ourselves. That's why it is so crucial to know who we are in Christ and what it means to be a child of God. After John's assertion that we are children of God, he says, "Everyone who has this hope in him purifies himself, just as he is pure" (1 John 3:3).

If we look at our past experiences and failures, it's easy to conclude that we are sinners. Those who believe they are sinners are driven to perform. They try to overcome what they believe about themselves, but they can't. Nobody can be anything other than what he or she really is without being a hypocrite. It is not hypocritical to believe the truth about who we really are in Christ, even though we don't feel like it at times. Hypocrisy does not mean living differently from what we feel, it means living differently from what we profess to believe.

Most addicts feel like no-good, dirty, rotten sinners. Defeated Christian addicts add the line, "saved by grace." What do sinners do? They sin! Everybody acts out what they really believe about themselves. They may not always live according to what they profess, but they will always live according to what they believe. God wants us to believe that we are children of God who are saved by grace through faith and are now alive in Christ and dead to sin.

Probe

Can you see the futility of trying to become somebody you already are? How can this truth change your life if you choose to believe it every day?

Journal

_____

_____

_____

_____

_____

Note
1. Neil T. Anderson, *Victory over the Darkness* (Ventura, Calif.: Regal Books, 1990), pp. 77, 78.

DAY 51

Thought for Today: Being alive and free in Christ is the birthright of every child of God.

How great is the love the Father has lavished on us, that we should be called children of God! And that is what we are!

1 JOHN 3:1

When you were a child, suppose your older brother had said, "You weren't born into this family. In fact, you weren't even legally adopted— we found you on the doorstep." As a result, you didn't know who you really were or where you came from.

One day you discovered your birth certificate. You were born into your family after all! Your older sibling hadn't told the truth. What a relief! Did that birth certificate make you part of your family? No, it just authenticated that you were born into that family and were now a part of it.

When I was growing up, my mom and dad didn't show any love for each other. They fought most of the time. My worst childhood memories were of lying in bed at night and listening to them having one of their violent arguments. Once my dad chased everyone out of the house with a loaded shotgun.

My father's insecurity was demonstrated by his anger and impatience. He abused alcohol and "disciplined" us in rage. We all lived in fear of his tirades and beatings. As we grew older, he withdrew from the family. He would come home from work, make a large drink, go into his bedroom, lock the door and take a nap. Mom served his meal in the bedroom. For the rest of the evening he would watch television and not come out of his room. We were forbidden to go near him. If anyone woke him from his nap or disturbed him, all hell would break loose. The message I learned was that I was unworthy and unacceptable.

My dad could do almost anything with his hands, but he was extremely impatient. If I ever attempted to fix anything he would say,

"You can't do anything right." He repeated the message so often that I believed him. After all, he was my father. I came to believe that I was inadequate.

I outperformed my brother and sister in most things, but trouble was my middle name. If something was done wrong, my parents looked for me. More often than not, I was guilty. My parents would say, "Why can't you do anything right like your brother and sister?" I grew up believing that I was guilty.

I didn't introduce myself to people by saying, "Hello, I'm Mike Quarles. I'm unacceptable, inadequate, insecure and guilty." But that was how I perceived myself. I lived with that identity for many years. When I understood and believed the truth that God loved me unconditionally and I was His child, everything changed. Discovering my "birth certificate" changed the way I saw myself, the way I behaved and the way I related to others. I finally understood that being a child of God was the birthright of every true believer. I began to live as though I was alive and free in Christ, because I really was.

The truth of how I had behaved in the past hadn't changed. I had behaved miserably as a Christian, a father, a husband, a pastor and a businessman. But even during that time, God loved me and accepted me unconditionally. I was a child of God and I was united with Christ. Choosing to believe it brought me great hope and tremendous encouragement. When I started to walk by faith, according to what God says is true, my life began to change. I grew excited about the Christian life and about being a husband, a father, a grandfather and a minister. I was enthusiastic about sharing with others the truth that sets us free. One of my closest friends told me he had never seen anyone change as much as I had.

There are times when I still feel unacceptable, insecure, inadequate and guilty. But I know I don't have to let those feelings determine who I am. They are just feelings that do not represent who I am in Christ.

Dear Christian, your birth certificate is clearly spelled out in the Word of God. Who does it say you are? "Yet to all who received him, to those who believed in his name, he gave the right to become children of

God—children born not of natural descent, nor of human decision or a husband's will, but born of God" (John 1:12,13).

We can never be alone, because He has promised never to leave us or forsake us (see Heb. 13:5). We are not inadequate, because we can do all things through Christ who strengthens us (see Phil. 4:13). We are not guilty, because there is no longer condemnation for those who are in Christ (see Rom. 8:1). We are not failures: "In all these things we are more than conquerors through him who loved us" (Rom. 8:37). We are not sinners, we are saints (see 2 Cor. 5:21). We are not addicts, we are children of God and deeply loved by the Father (see 1 John 3:1).

Probe

What self-perception did you get from your early childhood? How has that affected the way you live? How can your new identity in Christ change your perception of yourself and how you live?

Journal

DAY 52

**Thought for Today: We cannot be free from our past until
we know who we are in Christ.**

*For you know that it was not with perishable things such as silver
or gold that you were redeemed from the empty way of life handed
down to you from your forefathers, but with the precious blood
of Christ, a lamb without blemish or defect.*

1   PETER   1 : 18 , 19

As I struggled with my alcoholism, I tried a "geographical" cure—I left the
brokerage firm I had been with and went to work for another. It didn't
stop my life from spiraling out of control. I was with the new firm less
than six months, and three of those months I spent in two different alcoholism treatment centers. Needless to say, my new firm was not
impressed. I was fired.

A few years later I found my freedom in Christ and joined a counseling ministry in Atlanta. I met a couple who asked me to teach a Bible
study in their home, which I agreed to do. The first night they introduced
me to the group, one of the men said, "I know who you are; you were with
the brokerage firm I am with." Sure enough, he was an executive with the
firm that had fired me. *Oh no. This guy knows what a horrible alcoholic and a
colossal failure I was.*

Then I thought, *Wait a minute, that's not who I am. I'm a child of God who
is greatly loved, and I am free in Christ. I'm here to share about the grace of God
and the truth that sets you free.* That night I shared my testimony of how I
found my freedom. Guess who was the most responsive? We became
friends and he became a supporter of my ministry. When his son struggled with alcoholism, he referred him to me for counseling.

This incident showed me that we must do two things to be free of
our past. First, we must see the events of the past in the light of who we
now are in Christ. Second, we must forgive those who have hurt us. We'll
discuss this in greater detail later.

Christians can be emotionally tied to their past because of certain traumas they have experienced. It isn't the trauma that's keeping them emotionally bound, it's the lies they believe because of the trauma, such as: "I'm no good"; "God doesn't love me"; "I'll never amount to anything"; "I'm a failure"; "I can never get over this." Those lies are deeply embedded either because of the trauma or because they have been repeated so many times over a long period of time. When a present event reminds us of our past, it triggers those primary emotions. When I saw that man at the Bible study, old feelings immediately surfaced. At that moment it would have been easy to believe what I felt instead of believing what is true.

In a similar vein, people who have been abused by their fathers have a hard time believing they are unconditionally loved by their heavenly Father. Just mentioning the word "father" can trigger those primary emotions. Lies from our past carry a tremendous amount of emotional baggage. But now that we are alive and free in Christ, we can look at our past from the perspective of who we are today. When lies are replaced by the truth, the emotional baggage disappears. That is how the truth sets us free. Perceiving those events from the perspective of our new identity in Christ is what starts the process of healing damaged emotions.

A Christian missionary was facing an emotional breakdown. She attended one of Neil's conferences and found her freedom in Christ. Then she discovered that her father was having a homosexual affair. Neil asked her, "How has the knowledge of this truth about your father affected your heritage?" She started to respond in reference to her natural family; then suddenly she stopped and said with joy, "It hasn't."[1]

Do you see it, Christian? This woman's emotional state reflected the truth of who she really is. We are not just a product of our past; we are a product of Christ's work on the Cross. If this were not true, then all of us would be emotionally and spiritually bound to our past and we would remain victims for the rest of our natural days.

We have all done things we're ashamed of. That is why Christ died on the Cross. He has not only forgiven us and set us free from our past, He has made us a new creation in Christ. "Therefore, if anyone is in Christ, he is a new creation; old things have passed away; behold, all things have become new" (2 Cor. 5:17, *NKJV*).

Probe

In what way does your past still have a hold on you? How would you respond to someone who knew you and knew about some of your darkest deeds before Christ suddenly entered into your Christian experience?

Journal

_____

_____

_____

_____

_____

Note
1. Neil T. Anderson, *Victory over the Darkness* (Ventura, Calif.: Regal Books, 1990), pp. 199, 200.

DAY 53

Thought for Today: We live out our own self-perceptions.

For as he thinks in his heart, so is he.
PROVERBS 23:7, NKJV

Julia and I were preparing to teach our Freedom from Addiction workshop at a church in California. As we drove into the parking lot, a man on a motorcycle pulled in beside us. He had long hair, tattoos all over his body and the sleeves were cut off his T-shirt.

At the workshop he told me someone had been killed in a wreck he was involved in while under the influence of drugs. After his wife left him, he lay in his bed with a loaded gun, planning to kill himself, but he was so high on drugs he passed out before he could do it. He awoke to the screams of his daughter who was being chased through the house by her five-year-old brother holding the loaded gun. The man decided he had to somehow get sober.

How do you think this man perceived himself? Perhaps as a murderer, a felon, a biker, an addict, an outcast, a failure as a father and a husband? He shared with the group that he had recently gone to a Christian support group. He had been reading *Victory over the Darkness* and learning about his identity in Christ. At the beginning of the session, all participants introduced themselves in the usual way: "My name is John, and I am an addict (alcoholic)." When it was his turn, he said, "My name is Randy and I'm not an addict; I'm a child of God."

Later he told me, "The moment I publicly confessed that truth, God confirmed to my heart that I was indeed His child." He said he also knew he was free and didn't have to do drugs anymore. The shock of seeing his son chase his daughter with a loaded gun contributed to his sobriety, but he wasn't free until he understood the gospel and who he was in Christ. God is now using him to minister that truth to addicts and prisoners.

What do alcoholics do? They get drunk. What do addicts do? They do drugs. What do failures do? They fail. What do sinners do? They sin. What do Christians do? Better yet, what do saints do? They live righteous lives. What do Christians do who think they are alcoholics, addicts and failures? They probably continue to struggle with their habitual sins. People live according to what they believe: "For as he thinks in his heart, so is he."

If you have trusted Jesus Christ to be your Savior and Lord, you are not who you used to be. Being a Christian is not just about getting something, it is about *being someone* radically new who didn't exist before. It's about being a new creation. People don't stand up in a cancer ward and say, "Hello, my name is Sam and I'm cancerous." They may say correctly, "Hello, my name is Sam and I have cancer." I could stand up in a group and say, "Hello, my name is Mike and I am a child of God, and I have struggled for years with the temptation to drink alcohol."

Even though you are struggling with an addiction, that is not who you are. Even if you have failed greatly in your Christian life, you are not a failure. My friend Randy had failed more than most people have, but today he is an inspiration and an encouragement to many. I consider it a privilege to be his friend and am always blessed and encouraged when I'm around him. What changed him so drastically? The more appropriate question is, Who changed him? Jesus Christ changed him, and Randy's behavior began to change dramatically when he realized it.

We all establish some identity before we come to Christ. But God doesn't identify us according to who we were before salvation. He identifies us for who we now are in Christ. "Therefore from now on we recognize no man according to the flesh; even though we have known Christ according to the flesh, yet now we know Him [in this way] no longer. Therefore if any man is in Christ, he is a new creature; the old things passed away; behold, new things have come" (2 Cor. 5:16,17, NASB).

Probe

How do people, even Christians, identify themselves and others? According to the flesh or according to who they now are in Christ? How have you identified yourself? How has this affected your self-perception?

Journal

_____

_____

_____

_____

_____

DAY 54

**Thought for Today: We are not called to dispel the darkness;
we are called to turn on the light.**

*To them God willed to make known what are the riches of the glory of this
mystery among the Gentiles: which is Christ in you, the hope of glory.*
COLOSSIANS 1:27, NKJV

In his book *Spiritual Burnout*, Malcolm Smith tells the story of a drug
addict he ministered to. Hector had been a heavy drug abuser before he
came to know the Lord. But he had a marvelous conversion. He was
reunited with his wife and she, too, came to know the Lord.

Even though he was a new creation in Christ, it wasn't long before
Hector sensed he still had strong temptations to return to his old drug
habit. One morning at 4:00 A.M., his wife, greatly distressed, called
Malcolm Smith. Apparently Hector had been very upset the previous day.
He left the house and hadn't returned. Gloria was convinced he was look-
ing for a drug dealer.

In the gray dawn, Malcolm went to the area where Hector had spent
his days as an addict. After a few inquiries, he found Hector in a sleazy
pool hall. He took him aside, but Hector said, "Pastor, please leave me
alone! I have let God down. I have let you down and all the brothers and
sisters at the church. It's no use, I'm not worth bothering with anymore."

Malcolm looked Hector squarely in the eye and said, "God loved you
when you were a junkie and He saved you. Do you think now that you are
His child, He doesn't love you freely and unconditionally? He still loves
you, even though last night you hurt yourself and your family. He loves
you in exactly the same way at this moment as He did when you were
singing in the Spirit last week. God's love is not dependent on what you
do or don't do. He forgives you. Take His forgiveness and thank Him!"

Then Malcolm turned his attention to the question of how Hector
handled the temptation to return to drugs. Hector assured the minister
that he continually said no. This was Hector's problem. Just saying no to

any temptation is like trying to live under a law that says, "Thou shall not get high on drugs." Telling people what they are doing wrong does not give them the power to stop doing it. The law is powerless to give life; only by the life of Christ can we overcome sin. "For if a law had been given that could impart life, then righteousness would certainly have come by the law" (Gal. 3:21).

"Hector," the minister said, "you must understand that faith never says no to temptation—it says yes to Jesus." Malcolm went on to explain that Hector's sins had been nailed to the Cross with Jesus, and now the Spirit of Jesus lived within Him. Life was not a matter of Hector's trying to be good; it was a matter of admitting that on his own he could never be good! Once he understood this, he would never think that Christianity was a matter of adjusting his behavior, but rather of letting Christ live through him in His strength and power. "Faith is not collecting all my willpower into a mighty no!" Malcolm said. "It is recognition at the point of my weakness that, even though I do not feel it, Christ is my strength."

Some months later, pressures again developed in Hector's life. He fell back into the same old legalistic pattern of trying to say no. In the following weeks, his resistance became weaker and weaker. He had all but decided to get high and be a drug dealer. What little resistance was left screamed no as loudly as it could. As he got closer to making a deal, Hector cried out inside, *Please, God, help me!*

He remembered the conversation with Malcolm months before. *This desire for drugs is not the real me,* he told himself. *This Hector died with Christ, and I am now risen with Him. Now He is my life. I am trying to deal with this as though He were not inside me. Lord Jesus, I don't want to get high, but I am weak. You take over and live Your victory through me.*

Remember, we are not called to dispel the darkness; we are called to turn on the light. The way you overcome temptation is not by saying no or by rebuking the lie. You overcome temptation by saying yes to Jesus and by choosing the truth.

In that moment of conflict, Hector realized he was a branch in the Vine and the life of Christ was there for him. Faith united him with Christ who is his life. The Spirit of the Lord led him into that truth and he walked away from the temptation, praising God. That was many years ago, and Hector has never been seriously tempted to return to drugs again.[1]

The Christian life is not difficult to live; it is impossible to live. There really is only one Christian life and that is Christ's life. His life is the means by which we overcome temptation, because He is the way, the truth and the life (see John 14:6). Jesus didn't come to give us a new set of rules; He came to give us life. The answer for temptation is, "Christ in you, the hope of glory" (Col. 1:27).

Probe

What is the difference between saying "I'm not going to do something wrong" and saying "I'm going to do something right"? Why hasn't the "Just Say No" campaign against drugs worked?

Journal

_____

_____

_____

_____

_____

Note
1. Malcolm Smith, *Spiritual Burnout* (Tulsa, Okla.: Honor Books, 1988), pp. 100-103.

DAY 55

Thought for Today: What you do or what you have done does not determine who you are.

Nor thieves nor the greedy nor drunkards nor slanderers nor
swindlers will inherit the kingdom of God. And that is what some of you
were. But you were washed, you were sanctified, you were justified in the
name of the Lord Jesus Christ and by the Spirit of our God.
1 CORINTHIANS 6:10,11

If we as believers are alive and free in Christ, then why do so many of us struggle with bondage? One reason is that we've been deceived by the devil, who is the father of lies. Our true identity has been distorted by Satan, the deceiver. The last thing he wants us to know is who we are in Christ.

This deception was brought home to me a few years ago when I (Neil) was counseling a Christian girl who was the victim of satanic oppression.

"How do you perceive yourself?" I asked her.

"I'm evil," she said.

"You're not evil. How can a child of God be evil? Is that how you see yourself?"

She nodded in agreement.

This girl may have done some evil things, but she wasn't evil. She was basing her identity on what she had done, not on who she was in Christ. She was letting Satan's accusations influence her perception of herself and thus influence her behavior.

Many Christians are caught in this trap. When we fail, we see ourselves as failures, which only causes us to fail more. When we sin, we see ourselves as sinners, which only causes us to sin more. We have bought into Satan's futile equation: "What you do determines who you are." That false equation sends many into a tailspin of hopelessness and defeat.[1]

The reason secular treatment programs often don't have lasting results is because they only try to change the behavior, which is not the root problem. Jesus came to change us first, then He sent the Spirit of truth to lead us into all truth (see John 14:16,17). Even redeemed Christians will not change their behavior until they change their beliefs. We are saved and set free not by how we behave but by what we believe. Jesus said, "You will know the truth, and the truth will set you free" (John 8:32).

You can work a treatment program perfectly and do everything the counselors tell you to do; but if you don't change who you are and your beliefs, you will remain unchanged. You will walk out the door the same person who walked in, and you will continue to live according to what you have chosen to believe.

As long as a person believes he is a hopeless addict, he will never realize his freedom in Christ. He will be dependent upon some program to gain or maintain sobriety or some other behavioral goal. I did everything I knew to do and tried anything anyone told me to do. Nothing worked, because I believed these things:

1. I am an alcoholic.
2. I am helpless, it's hopeless, and I'm never going to change.
3. I am rejected, unloved and unaccepted.
4. I am different from others, and my problem is different.
5. I am a victim of family background, genetics and other influences.
6. I am insecure and need someone to validate me to be OK.
7. I am guilty and condemned because of my behavior.
8. I am a sorry, no-good sinner.
9. I am a failure, I am inadequate, and I will never measure up.
10. I am worthless and inferior to others.

Notice that only one of the above lies had anything to do with alcohol. Satan's grand scheme is deception. He is the father of lies. If he can get us to believe a lie, he can control our lives.

In 1 Corinthians 6:9-11, Paul lists those who will not inherit the kingdom of God. Then he says, "And such were some of you." That's who you *were,* not who you are now. Something dramatic happened to you at salvation. You were washed, justified and sanctified in the name of the Lord Jesus Christ and by the Spirit of our God (see 1 Cor. 6:11).

What does being washed, justified and sanctified mean? To be "washed" means that you have been regenerated. You have been born again, transformed into someone you weren't before. You are now a new creation in Christ. The word "justified" means that your sins have been forgiven and you have been made right with God, and you now have peace with Him.

The word "sanctified" means to be set apart. You have been set apart for God. The root of the word means "to make holy." You have been made holy not by what you have done but by what Christ has done. The word for "sanctified" is also the term from which we get the word "saint." You are no longer a sinner but a saint who sometimes sins. "God made him who had no sin to be sin for us, so that in him we might become the righteousness of God" (2 Cor. 5:21). "Anyone who has died has been freed from sin" (Rom. 6:7).

Probe

Have you ever struggled with condemning thoughts, finding yourself believing them? Why is it necessary to take every thought captive to the obedience of Christ (see 2 Cor. 10:5)? How can you do that?

Journal

_____

_____

_____

_____

_____

Note
  1. Neil T. Anderson, *Victory over the Darkness* (Ventura, Calif.: Regal Books, 1990), p. 21.

DAY 56

Thought for Today: We find rest for our souls in
the finished work of Christ.

It is because of him that you are in Christ Jesus, who has become for us
widsom from God—that is, our righteousness, holiness and redemption.
1 CORINTHIANS 1:30

Several years ago, Neil conducted some informal research to discover
what Christians were struggling with. He asked 50 counselees the same
question: "How many of the following characteristics describe your life:
inferiority, insecurity, inadequacy, guilt, worry and *doubt?*" Forty-nine said,
"All six!" One person could relate to only four of the characteristics.

All six characteristics were true of me when I struggled with alcoholism. Do any of these traits describe you? Read what Scripture says
about your feelings.

Do you feel *insecure?* Your God will never leave you nor forsake
you (see Heb. 13:5).

Inadequate? You can do all things through Christ (see Phil.
4:13).

Guilty? There is no condemnation for those who are in
Christ Jesus (see Rom. 8:1).

Worried? God has offered His peace for your anxiety (see
John 14:27; Phil. 4:7; 1 Pet. 5:7).

Do you *doubt?* God provides wisdom for those who ask (see
Jas. 1:5).

When talking to a Christian man who was struggling with alcoholism, I asked him what he thought his problem was. He replied, "I was
victimized by my dad, who physically and emotionally abused me. He
never gave me any love and acceptance." That describes most of the alco-

holics I have talked with. Trying to stop parental abuse and win their approval would prove futile in most cases, and yet that is what many of us try to do.

Your parents may never change, but you don't have to wait until they do. You have another parent who doesn't need to change and has already acted decisively and dramatically by sending His Son, Jesus Christ, to live, die and rise from the dead, just for you. The following benefits are just a few of the many you have received from your heavenly Father:

1. You have been forgiven and made righteous (see Rom. 5:1).
2. You died with Christ to the power of sin in your life (see Rom. 6:1-7).
3. You are free from condemnation (see Rom. 8:1).
4. You have become united with Christ by God's doing (see 1 Cor. 1:30).
5. You have received the Spirit of God into your life that you might know the things freely given to you by God (see 1 Cor. 2:12).
6. You have been given the mind of Christ (see 1 Cor. 2:16).
7. You have been bought with a price. You are not your own; you now belong to God (see 1 Cor. 6:19,20).
8. You have been established, anointed and sealed by God in Christ and have been given the Spirit as a pledge, guaranteeing your inheritance to come (see 2 Cor. 1:21,22; Eph. 1:13,14).
9. You have been crucified with Christ and it is no longer you who live, but Christ lives in you (see Gal. 2:20).
10. You have been made complete in Christ (see Col. 2:10).
11. You have been blessed with every spiritual blessing (see Eph. 1:3).
12. You have been redeemed and forgiven, and you are a recipient of His lavish grace (see Eph. 1:7,8).
13. You have been made alive together with Christ (see Eph. 2:5).
14. You have been raised up and seated with Christ in the heavenly places (see Eph. 2:6).
15. Your life is now hidden with Him in God, and Christ is now your life (see Col. 3:1-4).

There is nothing more joyful than to see a person resolve his or her personal and spiritual conflicts and find freedom in Christ. There is tremendous joy in being released from our past. In many cases it comes when we forgive our parents. Suddenly we are aware that we have a new and perfect Father!

> For you did not receive a spirit that makes you a slave again to fear, but you received the Spirit of sonship. And by him we cry, "Abba, Father." The Spirit himself testifies with our spirit that we are God's children. Now if we are children, then we are heirs—heirs of God and co-heirs with Christ, if indeed we share in his sufferings in order that we may also share in his glory (Rom. 8:15-17).

We don't have to plead for God to do something about our problem. God *has* done something. We can rest in the finished work of Christ. It is our choice to believe what He has done for us and start walking by faith according to what He says is true.

Probe

Have you ever lived with the hope that someone, such as your parents, would change and start acting on your behalf? Where did that get you? Which of the six negative characteristics listed in the beginning paragraph have you struggled with the most, and why?

Journal

DAY 57

Thought for Today: Positional truth is real truth.

Once you were not a people, but now you are the people of God; once you had not received mercy, but now you have received mercy.

1 PETER 2:10

I was attending the annual Christian Addiction Rehabilitation Association meeting. Most of those who were there are involved in long-term Christian treatment for addicts and alcoholics. The first speaker was a distinguished seminary professor who directs a large and well-respected counseling center. During his presentation, he said, "Abstention is a daily war." At the question-and-answer time, I asked about this statement and how it related to Paul's words, "It is for freedom that Christ has set us free" (Gal. 5:1). Abstention was not a daily war for me, just as it was not for others who have experienced their freedom in Christ. He told me this freedom was not the experience of most people.

Unfortunately, what he said is true. The experience of most Christians who struggle with addiction is a daily war. Why doesn't our experience line up with God's Word? Because we have based our theology on our experience. That's what I did at one time. When my experience didn't match the Word of God, I chose to believe my experience. I didn't believe, or know, that I was dead to sin; consequently, I didn't live as though I were. Scripture clearly teaches that we can be free in Christ and that we are dead to sin and alive in Christ (see Rom 6:2,6,11).

If you don't believe you can be liberated from addictive behaviors, then you probably can't be. In my struggle with addiction, I never considered that what I believed about myself was crucial. I just kept on trying to do what was right—and I kept failing and falling. No one ever said to me, "Mike, the problem is not you; the problem is based in the lies you believe." No one ever said to me, "Mike, you are a child of God. Overcoming your struggle with sin isn't found in what *you* do but in what Christ has already done." Now that would have been good news! Instead,

I heard, "Try this, do this, don't do that, refrain from that, abstain from that, attempt this," and so on.

I was taught, "Once an addict, always an addict." If that is true, then the best I could do was learn how to cope with the addiction I would always have. It's the same thing as saying, "Once a sinner, always a sinner." But that's not true. I was once a sinner, but now I am a saint, a born-again child of God. My theological training told me: It's just positional truth. The implication? It's not real truth. The real truth is your experience, and your experience is telling you that it really isn't true!

Another subtle lie I picked up from secular counselors: The addict is different, his problem is different, and therefore he needs a different solution from people who aren't addicted. In other words, Christ and His work on the Cross might work for the average person, but the addict needs something more. The same truth that liberates people-pleasers, workaholics, perfectionists, codependents, controllers, materialists, thieves, liars, murderers and adulterers is the same truth that sets the addict free. The finished work of Christ is sufficient to set *all* captives free. "So if the Son sets you free, you will be free indeed" (John 8:36).

I asked a man who he was, and he said, "I am loved by Christ." What a great answer! We are alive in Christ and dead to sin, and it doesn't make any difference what the sin is. We are not addicts trying to become children of God; we are children of God who are becoming like Christ. However, our position in Christ is realized only after we repent and believe.

The Steps to Freedom in Christ, found in our book *Freedom from Addiction,* will help you resolve your personal and spiritual conflicts. The process will help you appropriate your freedom and stand against any demonic influences that are trying to deceive you. Being a child of God and free in Christ is positional truth, but it is also real truth and must be appropriated before we can continue in Christ. "So then, just as you received Christ Jesus as Lord, continue to live *in him,* rooted and built up *in him,* strengthened in the faith as you were taught, and overflowing with thankfulness" (Col. 2:6,7, emphasis added).

There is no such thing as instant maturity. It will take the rest of our lives to renew our minds and conform to the image of God. But it won't take the rest of our lives to be children of God or to be free in Christ, because in both cases we already are.

Probe

Have you ever looked at the biblical statements declaring who we are in Christ and said, "I guess I believe that, but . . ."? But what? Was that truth for somebody else? Did you believe you were different? Was it just positional truth?

Journal

_____

_____

_____

_____

_____

DAY 58

Thought for Today: If you knew who you were in Christ, would your behavior change?

You, dear children, are from God and have overcome them, because the one who is in you is greater than the one who is in the world.
1 JOHN 4:4

I was in Los Gatos, California, teaching a Freedom from Addiction workshop. In one of the sessions I noticed a young lady sitting in the back row. I could tell by her body language and facial expressions that she was having a lot of difficulty with what I was saying. Finally, at one of the question-and-answer sessions, she asked, "Do you mean to tell me that if I just believe who I am in Christ—that I'm dead to sin and alive to God—it will change my behavior?"

"If the Bible is true," I told her, "and if you really believed that you are a child of God and therefore dead to sin and alive in Christ, of course it would change your behavior."

This is not the power of positive thinking. It is the power of truth believing. I'm not trying to get you to believe that you're someone you're not. Knowing who you are as a child of God is the fundamental truth that sets you free.

The truth that we are dead to sin and alive to God is not the problem. The problem is that we don't really believe it. For most people it seems too simple. We think we have to go through some incredible ordeal to attain the freedom we so desperately want. The only ordeal we have to go through is a crisis of faith. We have to give up trying to find the freedom we already have and start trusting God to be our salvation and life. We are not saved by how we behave but by what we believe.

Consider whether your behavior would change if you believed the facts on the following list:

1. God has so worked in your life that you are dead to sin and alive to Christ (see Rom. 6:2,3).
2. God is for you and nothing can stand against you (see Rom. 8:31).
3. You have been given the wisdom, righteousness, sanctification and redemption of Christ (see 1 Cor. 1:30).
4. You have been given everything you need for life and godliness (see 2 Pet. 1:3).
5. You have been blessed with every spiritual blessing in the heavenlies in Christ (see Eph. 1:3).
6. God is meeting all your needs according to His glorious riches in Christ Jesus (see Phil. 4:19).
7. You are a child of God and the evil one can't touch you (see 1 John 5:18).
8. Christ in you is greater than Satan, your enemy in the world (see 1 John 4:4).
9. God has given you authority over Satan (see Eph. 1:19-23; 2:6).
10. God is working all things together for your good (see Rom 8:28).

11. Satan is a defeated foe (see Col. 2:15).
12. God has given you the victory (see 1 Cor. 15:57).
13. You are more than a conqueror (see Rom. 8:37).
14. God always leads you in triumph (see 2 Cor. 2:14).
15. Nothing can separate you from the love of God (see Rom. 8:39).

If you are not experiencing your freedom in Christ, the problem is not your evil sin nature, your immorality, your lack of commitment, your lack of character, your weakness, your environment or your heredity. The problem is that you don't believe the truth. If you believe you are an unredeemable and incurable addict, then you will strive to overcome in your own strength what Christ has already accomplished for you. If you know who you are in Christ and what God has already done for you, you will know that you are a new creation in Christ and have already been set free. Will you ever be tempted again? Sure! We will all experience temptation every day of our lives. But when we know who we are, we have the option of choosing to believe the truth that we are alive in Christ and dead to sin.

In 1996, Freedom in Christ Ministries had a staff meeting in Denver at a beautiful country club. Our meeting room was next to a well-stocked and attractive bar. On the third day of the retreat, one of the staff asked me if it bothered me to be meeting next to the bar. I realized at the time that it hadn't even crossed my mind. It just wasn't an issue. That doesn't mean I'll never be tempted. But if I walk by faith according to what God says is true, I will remain free.

Perhaps you're thinking, *That sounds great, but I just don't feel dead to sin. In fact, I feel very much alive to sin.* You're no different from any other Christian. We all have to choose to believe the truth, regardless of our feelings. If you choose to live by your feelings, you will have an up-and-down Christian experience—mostly down. But if you choose to live by faith, according to what God says is true in the power of the Holy Spirit, you will not carry out the desires of the flesh and you will continue to live as a liberated child of God.

Probe

Are you a hypocrite if you choose to live contrary to how you feel, or are you a hypocrite if you choose to live contrary to what you profess to believe? What kind of a day would you have if you got up in the morning and chose to believe only what you felt? What kind of a day would you have if you got up in the morning and said, "Thank You, Lord. I deserved eternal damnation, but You have given me eternal life, and I choose to live today by faith according to what You said is true in the power of the Holy Spirit"?

Journal

_____

_____

_____

_____

_____

DAY 59

**Thought for Today: Who you are and how you perceive yourself
determines what you do.**

_For you were once darkness, but now you are light in the Lord.
Live as children of light._
EPHESIANS 5:8

It's not often that you read an article in the newspaper's sports section that has redeeming value. Usually you read about the latest arrest of a professional athlete or the nasty dispute over his multimillion-dollar contract. A few years ago, a different kind of sports piece appeared in the _Birmingham News_. It was a column about Ed Murphy, the University of

Mississippi basketball coach. He had had a losing record for the few years he had been there, and it was a foregone conclusion that he would be fired after the next game. His response to this tough situation was interesting.

The columnist reported that while Murphy had another season left on his contract, his career at Ole Miss was likely to end during the Southeast Conference tournament. The game against Georgia could be his last one. The columnist wrote:

> Murphy stood in the bleak concrete corridor of the Birmingham-Jefferson Civic Center and reflected on the ways of basketball and that other globe, the world. In a profession overrun with zanies, Murphy is refreshingly sane. "The season has been tough," he reflected on the year of rumor and uncertainty, "but a lot of people have had harder seasons. People have had trouble with their kids. People have had trouble with their families. Don't put me high on your list to feel sorry for. Coaching is my living, but it's not my life. It's not even second or third or fourth. You can't be what you do. If you are, you're a pretty shallow person."[1]

I don't know where Ed Murphy stands with the Lord, but it's obvious that he understands a fundamental truth about living: It's not what we do that determines who we are; who we are determines what we do. Ask the average person, "Who are you?" and most would answer by describing what they *do*—"I'm a doctor, a lawyer, a pastor, a housewife, a businessman, a student, a plumber." Is that who they are? Surely not.

If you're a baseball player who gets paid $5 million a year for hitting home runs, you may be rich and famous, but you're a pretty shallow person if that's all you are. Your behavior will often reflect how you perceive yourself, but it does not determine who you are.

People have been labeled alcoholics and sex addicts because of what they've learned to habitually do. Unfortunately, they continue to wear that label when they become Christians. Well-meaning counselors and self-help programs even insist that they do so. They falsely believe the adage "Once an addict, always an addict." What kind of hope is that? The good news is that you are a new creation in Christ.

In order to be free, God had to change who we are. Now we must change what we believe. If you want to change your behavior, don't focus on what you are doing or not doing. Instead, look at the belief (or rather misbelief) behind the behavior that causes you to act the way you do. Misbeliefs will always manifest themselves in sinful and irresponsible behavior. We don't do anything without first thinking it. The key is to change the way we think.

Although irresponsible and sinful behavior will cause a lot of problems, trying to change a person's behavior without changing what he believes can only lead to legalism or rebellion. Some try desperately to work the program and change their behavior. In order to do so they need continuous external accountability and support. Most will end up as dry drunks because nothing has really changed internally. Others rebel against the program because rules without a relationship lead to rebellion or burnout.

Why is it that the only problem people say they are recovering from is an addiction? You never hear anyone say, "I'm a recovering gossip" or "I'm a recovering liar." Was Paul a recovering legalist? Was David a recovering adulterer? Was Abraham a recovering womanizer? All of us have a failure identity that is rooted in our flesh, but that's not who we are. All of us have sinned, fallen short and failed (see Rom. 3:23), but that doesn't define who we presently are in Christ. Our flesh is simply the way we attempted to meet our needs apart from God. Our flesh patterns reveal the direction we took when we attempted to live our lives independently of God. If we are still deriving our identity from who we were "in Adam" and from our learned flesh patterns, we have no hope of being free from our failure identity.

Probe

Think of all the self-help programs that have tried to get you to change how you behave. How successful has that approach been? How is that approach substantially different from what the gospel is offering (changing who we are and then how we believe)?

Journal

_____

_____

_____

_____

_____

Note
1. Clyde Bolton, "Basketball Needs a Guy Like Ed Murphy," *Birmingham News*, March 12, 1992, n.p.

DAY 60

Thought for Today: You are a spiritual being who lives in a physical body.

But anyone united to the Lord becomes one spirit with him.
1 CORINTHIANS 6:17, NRSV

Claire attended a church college ministry. On a physical and material level, she had very little going for her. She had a dumpy figure and a poor complexion; her father was a drunk who had deserted his family; her mother worked two menial jobs just to make ends meet; her older brother was addicted to drugs and on the run from the law.

There was no way she could compete in a young adult society attracted to physical beauty and material success. I was surprised and delighted to learn that everybody in the group liked Claire and loved to be around her. She had lots of friends. Eventually she married the nicest guy in the college department. What was Claire's secret? She simply believed what she perceived herself to be: a child of God. She accepted herself for who God said she was in Christ.[1]

Claire knew she couldn't compete on the physical plane. Most of us can't. Actually, nobody can. Somebody will always come along and do it better. Our beauty will fade, our talents will diminish and we will no longer have the energy to keep up with the upcoming young stars of tomorrow. But we can all be better people than we were yesterday.

We are spiritual beings who live in bodies that are destined to die. Jesus tells us that "whoever lives and believes in me will never die" (John 11:26). Even though physical death is inevitable, we will continue to live spiritually in the presence of God. Our bodies are just earth suits we are wearing until we go to be with Jesus. To be absent from the body is to be present with the Lord (see 2 Cor. 5:6-9).

If we lack spiritual life, we will try to find our identity in our performance and appearance. Many movie stars and professional athletes struggle when they are past their prime. They have made their living and established their identity and sense of worth from their ability to perform and look good. Life becomes shallow when we build our lives around our physical existence. We have nothing to look forward to but diminishing status.

Many people go through a midlife crisis when they realize the decline of their physical prowess and realize that life is passing them by. As we continue to get older, being successful in a materialistic world can only get harder. Perhaps a midlife crisis could more accurately be called an identity crisis.

I had a midlife crisis when I struggled with alcoholism. One of my most vulnerable times for getting drunk was after a tennis match. Why? I realized that my body just wouldn't perform the way it used to. Tennis reminded me that I was getting older, slower, weaker; and I was not going to get any better physically. If my self-perception was based on my performance in tennis, I had nothing positive to look forward to.

I am 61 years old at the time of this writing. I have made peace with my deteriorating body. After all, that's not who I am, and one day I'm going to get a resurrected and perfect body. By the grace of God, I am a better person than I was before I knew Christ. Actually, I'm getting better every day, and that is a great source of encouragement to me and all those who know me. With the apostle Paul, we should all be able to say, "Therefore we do not lose heart. Though outwardly we are wasting away, yet inwardly we are being renewed day by day" (2 Cor. 4:16).

I once took an attractive lady through the Steps to Freedom in Christ. She had a poor sense of self-worth and was very codependent. She had struggled with anorexia for over 15 years. She said that the only time her father ever complimented her was on her appearance. If she gained a few pounds, he brought it to her attention. She learned to get her acceptance and sense of worth from how she looked. She believed the lie that many others believe: "You can't be too thin."

Approximately 10 years ago, newspapers carried the story of the death of Christy Heinrich, Olympic gymnast. At the height of her career she weighed 98 pounds. There wasn't an ounce of fat on her body. But she believed she was fat, so she starved herself down to 56 pounds and died. She believed the lie that her identity, acceptance and sense of worth were found in her body.

We are far more than our bodies; we are children of God.

Probe

What do you have to look forward to as you get older? Has appearance, performance and social status been more important to you than developing the inner person? Why or why not?

Journal

_____

_____

_____

_____

_____

Note
1. Neil T. Anderson, *Victory over the Darkness* (Ventura, Calif.: Regal Books, 1990), p. 51.

THE CHAINS OF BONDAGE HAVE BEEN BROKEN

DAY 61

Thought for Today: Those who have died with Christ are free from sin.

For we know that our old self was crucified with him so that the body of sin might be done away with, that we should no longer be slaves to sin—because anyone who has died has been freed from sin.
ROMANS 6:6,7

I had been struggling with alcoholism for eight years and was drunk as recently as the night before. Julia suggested I get out of her face and give her some space. I headed to Lookout Mountain, Tennessee, to visit some friends.

I started listening to the "Victorious Christian Living" audiotapes by Bill and Anabel Gillham. I was listening to the third tape, "Co-crucifixion Is Past Tense." Bill Gillham was teaching on our death with Christ, from Romans 6:6: "Our old self was crucified with [Christ]." Bill pointed out that most Christians don't understand what actually happened at the Cross. If they did, they wouldn't live in such defeat. We understand that Christ died for our sins, but few of us understand that we also died with Christ. Therefore, the old self, the person we used to be, is no more; we are now "in Christ." "In Christ" is one of the most repeated prepositional phrases in the New Testament.[1]

Paul says that anyone who has died with Christ has been freed from sin (see Rom. 6:6,7). I knew that was what I needed. But how could I make that true in my life?

Gillham goes on to say that "it isn't something you do, it's something that has been done; our death with Christ is past tense; the old person that we were 'was crucified,' and anyone who has died has been freed from sin." Then he said, "You 'died to sin' (Rom. 6:2); you are 'dead to sin' (v. 11). You don't act dead to sin; you don't feel dead to sin; you don't even look dead to sin. You think that's just a 'positional truth.' You think that's just what God says about you. Listen: If that's what God says about you, that's the truth about you."[2]

At that moment, I finally believed the truth. I knew I had died with Christ. The old sin-loving sinner had died and was no more. For many years I believed I was a sinner and I acted like it. Now I knew that I was dead to sin, whether I acted like it, felt like it, looked like it or anyone else believed I was. It was true because God said it was true. I also knew the truth that I was free: "Because anyone who has died has been freed from sin" (v. 7).

Jesus said, "Then you will know the truth, and the truth will set you free" (John 8:32). I had believed I was a hopeless, helpless alcoholic. For years I lived in bondage. But now, less than 24 hours removed from being drunk, I knew without any doubt that I was a child of God who was a new creation in Christ. I had died with Christ, I was dead to sin, and I had been freed from sin. At last I was free. Praise God, I was free at last![3]

The solution to my years of addiction may seem too simple. How could I be released from bondage by listening to a tape? That's not what set me free. I believed the truth that was taught on the tape and, just as Jesus promised in John 8:32, the truth set me free.

In our conferences, we often ask, "How many of you have died with Christ?" Almost everyone raises their hands. Then we ask, "How many are free from sin?" It had better be the same hands, because the Scripture clearly states in Romans 6:7 that anyone who has died with Christ has been freed from sin.

Every born-again Christian has died with Christ, so every Christian has been freed from sin. If they don't believe they are free from sin, they won't live like they are, because we live according to what we believe. The central issue is always identity. If you don't know the truth about your identity in Christ, you will not be able to experience freedom through a program or through spiritual disciplines.

Even our freedom in Christ is an accomplished fact, but many are not living like children of God and free in Christ. Should they try harder? Does something more need to be done or added to the finished work of Christ? Absolutely not! The apostle Paul tells us: "Now if we died with Christ, we believe that we will also live with him" (Rom. 6:8). We simply need to believe the truth that sets us free.

Probe

Is our salvation and freedom in Christ a matter of human effort? Of faith? Of faith plus works? Why do you think this simple truth has been so hard for people to accept? Why is the message so confused in our churches? Why isn't it being taught in recovery programs?

Journal

_____

_____

_____

_____

_____

Notes
1. Bill and Anabel Gillham, "Co-crucifixion Is Past Tense," *Victorious Christian Life* tape series (Fort Worth, Tex.: Lifetime Guarantee, n.y.), audiocassette.
2. Ibid.
3. Neil T. Anderson and Mike and Julia Quarles, *Freedom from Addiction* (Ventura, Calif.: Regal Books, 1996), pp. 124, 125.

DAY 62

**Thought for Today: God is not trying to improve your old nature—
He is giving you a new nature.**

I have been crucified with Christ and I no longer live, but Christ lives in me. The life I live in the body, I live by faith in the Son of God, who loved me and gave himself for me.

GALATIANS 2:20

I can vividly remember a scene that was repeated countless times during my years of struggling with alcoholism. I would wake up in the morning and think, *Oh no, I can't believe it. I got drunk again last night. My situation is hopeless because I'm helpless and I'm never going to change.* Then the waves of guilt, remorse and despair would flood over me.

I hated what I was doing and what I had become, but I didn't know a way out. I was living a nightmare from hell with no end to the dream. I didn't know it at the time, but I was right where Satan wanted me—believing exactly what he wanted me to believe. As long as I believed the lie that I was helpless and hopeless and that I could never change, I would stay in bondage.

From the time I became a Christian, my consuming desire was for my life to count for Christ. I knew that I had a problem and would have to change drastically. I had been a selfish, greedy person who lived to satisfy my own desires. I had been a womanizer and an alcoholic. After my conversion, a friend told me that I had been one of the most obnoxious and arrogant persons he had ever known. I definitely had my work cut out for me if I wanted to change and become the person the Lord wanted me to be. How would I do that?

I received plenty of advice and instruction. There is certainly no shortage of information about what you need to do to live the Christian life. There are sermons, books, seminars, conferences, audiotapes and videotapes. There are more programs for improvement than any one person could ever begin to hope to complete in one lifetime.

There is a strange and puzzling paradox in the Church today. We tell Christians they are sinners saved by grace, but if they don't act like saints, then we'll have to discipline them. How can somebody act consistently in a way that is inconsistent with who they are? For me it became very confusing and frustrating. I had to confess that I was an alcoholic, but somehow I wasn't supposed to live like one. I was trying as hard as I could, yet I couldn't seem to get it together. I might do okay for a week or so, and sometimes longer, but sooner or later I would blow it.

After trying and failing so many times, I gave up on the notion that there even was an abundant and victorious Christian life. I could not deny that I was living in bondage to alcohol. So how could I be free and at the same time be in bondage? I didn't need anyone to tell me to stop sinning. I knew better than anyone else that what I was doing was sinful, and I wanted to stop more than they wanted to see me stop. I just didn't have a clue how to do that. Being told what to do (and many people tried) just set me up for greater failure, frustration and condemnation.

Most of this well-meaning advice required me to free myself. But I couldn't change who I really was, and my advice givers were telling me that I was a sinner and an alcoholic. I worked diligently to try to change myself. But God has made no provision for us to save ourselves or change ourselves. I was trying to improve the flesh—a synonym for self-rule. But the flesh is hostile to God and cannot please Him (see Rom. 8:7,8). It cannot be changed; it must be put to death.

Many of us have embarked on self-improvement programs to change ourselves, but self-improvement is an oxymoron because you can't improve self or the flesh. I had spent most of my Christian life trying to get my act together. When I finally learned the truth, it was as if God were saying to me, "I don't want you to change yourself and get your act together. Your act is no good. It was so bad that I had to include you in Christ's death on the cross and crucify it. I don't want you to change yourself. I want you to give up on your old self-centered and self-sufficient ways and exchange your old self-life for Christ's life. I want you to trust Him to live in you and be your life."

The Christian life is lived not by sincere human effort but by faith in Christ and in His life and His resources. There is only one Christian life, and that is Christ's life. If you are a Christian, then you have the life of Christ in you. God wants us to (1) admit that we can't free or save ourselves, (2) confess that apart from Christ we can do nothing, and (3) give up our self-centered living and live in total dependence on Christ and His resources.

Probe

What improvement have you seen in your old nature since you have become a Christian? Why is any self-help program nothing more than an attempt to live according to the flesh?

Journal

_____

_____

_____

_____

_____

DAY 63

Thought for Today: Believing the truth doesn't make it true; God's Word is true; therefore, we believe it.

Likewise you also, reckon yourselves to be dead indeed to sin, but alive to God in Christ Jesus our Lord.
ROMANS 6:11, NKJV

If you find it hard to believe the fact that you were "crucified with Christ" (Rom 6:6), you are not alone. The great Chinese Christian leader, Watchman Nee, also struggled to believe this truth. He wrote:

For years after my conversion I had been taught to reckon. I reckoned from 1920 until 1927. The more I reckoned that I was dead to sin, the more alive I clearly was. I simply could not believe myself dead, and I could not produce the death. Whenever I sought help from others I was told to read Romans 6:11 and the more I read Romans 6:11, and tried to reckon, the further away death was: I could not get at it. I fully appreciated the teaching that I must reckon, but I could not make out why nothing resulted from it. I have to confess that for months I was troubled. I said to the Lord, "If this is not clear, if I cannot be brought to see this which is so very fundamental, I will cease to do anything. I will not preach any more; I will not go out to serve Thee any more; I want first of all to get thoroughly clear here." For months I was seeking and at times I fasted, but nothing came through.

I remember one morning—that morning was a real morning and one I can never forget—I was upstairs sitting at my desk reading the Word and praying, and I said, "Lord, open my eyes!" And then in a flash I saw it. I saw my oneness with Christ. I saw that I was in Him, and that when He died I died. I saw that the question of my death was a matter of the past and not of the future, and that I was just as truly dead as He was because I was in Him when He died. The whole thing had dawned upon me. I was carried away with such joy at this great discovery that I jumped from my chair and cried, "Praise the Lord, I am dead!" I ran downstairs and met one of the brothers helping in the kitchen and laid hold of him. "Brother," I said, "do you know that I have died?" I must admit he looked puzzled. "What do you mean?" he said, so I went on: "Do you not know that Christ has died? Do you not know that I died with Him? Do you not know that my death is no less truly a fact than His?"[1]

Many of us try to "reckon" something to make it true when it is already true. If we do this we will reckon ourselves into a wreck. In the South we say, "I reckon it might rain tomorrow," but that's not the kind of reckoning the Bible is talking about. The word "reckon" in Romans 6:11 (*NKJV*) is a precise, mathematical term that was used in bookkeeping. But why does God say we are to reckon ourselves dead? Because we are dead! God never tells us to reckon on what is not a fact.

Do you believe Christ died for your sins on the Cross? "Of course I believe," you say. But why do you believe it? You weren't there; you don't know anybody who was there, so why would you believe it? "Because," you say, "the Word of God tells me so." Good answer. The Word of God also tells you that you were crucified with Him (see Rom. 6:6). You have the same proof that you died as you have proof that Christ died. If you know that your old self was crucified with Christ, you will be free. Why? Because you are free.

The only experience necessary for you to be free was Christ's experience on the Cross 2,000 years ago. Our identity in Christ and the fact that we are dead to sin and alive to God is based on the historical fact of Christ's death and resurrection. It is futile and frustrating to try to make something that is already true, more true.

Probe

We consider ourselves to be dead to sin and alive to God because it is so. It is not a matter of whether we feel like it or whether we act like it but whether we believe it. Death is the end of a relationship, not the end of existence. Sin is still present, still powerful and still appealing; but whenever we are tempted to sin, we can say no to it because we are alive in Christ and dead to sin. How can this truth benefit you on a daily basis?

Journal

_____

_____

_____

_____

_____

Note
1. Watchman Nee, *The Normal Christian Life* (Wheaton, Ill.: Tyndale House Publishers, 1977), pp. 64, 65.

DAY 64

**Thought for Today: We are identified with Christ in His death
and in His resurrection.**

Now if we died with Christ, we believe that we will also live with him.
ROMANS 6:8

Watchman Nee describes what it is to believe: "There are some yellow
flowers on my desk. I did not enter the room and repeat, 'There are some
yellow flowers here, there must be some yellow flowers here,' and by some
kind of auto-suggestion bring them magically into being! No, they were
there all the time. I just opened my eyes and looked."[1]

Many Christians think it's too simple to just believe. They want to do
something. But if God has done it—and He has—then our faith response
should be, "Thank You, Lord, for including me in Christ's death and
making me dead to sin and alive to God."

"How do I do that? How do I die to sin?" you ask. The answer is, you
can't! Why not? Because you have already died to sin. The phrase "we
died to sin" (Rom. 6:2) is past tense. You can't do what has already been
done. If you're thinking that you don't feel dead to sin, and besides,
you're still sinning, remember, it is not what you do that determines who
you are. You will have to set your feelings aside. It is not what you feel, it
is what you believe that is going to set you free. God's Word is true
whether you and I choose to believe it or not.

Perhaps you're thinking, *I can't believe that I don't have to do anything.*
Can you believe that you didn't have to do anything when you were physically born the first time? You had nothing to do with your conception,
and your mother bore all the labor pains. Your heavenly Father knew you
from the foundation of the world, and Christ suffered for your sins and
was resurrected so that you would have new life in Him. How can you add
to that? Why would you want to, and why would you need to?

When we choose to believe the truth, we step out of the darkness of
deception into the light. We can't identify with Christ in His death with-

out also identifying with His resurrection. Thank God for Good Friday, when Jesus died for our sins; but thank Him even more for Easter, when He was resurrected so that we would have new life in Him. "Now if we died with Christ, we believe that we will also live with him" (Rom. 6:8). Do you believe it?

One night, while teaching at a Christian treatment center, I needed more light. During a break I noticed a ceiling fan that had a light on it, but it wasn't on. I was trying to figure out how to turn it on, looking all around the fan, when suddenly someone flipped the wall switch and the light came on. Isn't that the way it is with us? We can look inside ourselves all day to try to make ourselves dead to sin and what we find just gets worse. But if we turn our attention to the source of power, the light will come on. Belief is the switch that activates the truth.

Scripture tells us that people love darkness (see John 3:19). Why? Because what they are doing is evil and they don't want to be exposed (see John 3:20). But those who live by the truth come into the light (see John 3:21). Someone has said: The truth will set you free, but first it will make you miserable.

It is not a good feeling to face our sins and take responsibility for our wrongdoing, but it is the only way to come out of darkness into light and out of bondage into freedom. Just knowing the truth as information doesn't change anyone. Many people hear the gospel and choose not to believe it. Many people hear the truth of their death with Christ and choose not to believe that. Now that you've heard it, you can choose to dismiss it or believe it. You can wait until your feelings measure up with the truth, but that will never happen. You can excuse yourself by saying, "It doesn't apply to me; my problem is different and it won't work for me."

The only proper response to a scriptural truth is to believe it. "Now if we died with Christ, we believe that we will also live with him" (Rom. 6:8).

Probe

Why are we inclined to believe only half the gospel—that He died for our sins—but then fail to grasp that He came to give us life? Can you be a forgiven sinner in Christ and not be a redeemed saint?

Journal

_____

_____

_____

_____

_____

Note
1. Watchman Nee, *A Table in the Wilderness* (Wheaton, Ill.: Tyndale House Publishers, 1988), p. 47.

DAY 65

Thought for Today: You cannot do for yourself what Christ has already done for you.

You have been set free from sin and have become slaves to righteousness.
ROMANS 6:18

In the book *Spiritual Strongholds,* Don McMinn records a story told by Zig Ziglar—an incident that illustrates how a wrong perspective can prohibit freedom:

> Harry Houdini, the famed escape artist, issued a challenge wherever he went. He could be locked in any jail cell in the country, he claimed, and set himself free in short order. Always he kept his promise, but one time something went wrong. Houdini entered the jail in his street clothes; the heavy metal doors clanged shut behind him. He took from his belt a concealed piece of metal, strong and flexible. He set to work immediately, but something seemed unusual about this lock. For thirty minutes he worked and got nowhere. An hour passed, and still he

had not opened the door. By now he was bathed in sweat and panting in exasperation, but he still could not pick the lock. Finally after laboring for two hours, Harry Houdini collapsed in frustration and failure against the door he could not unlock. But when he fell against the door, it swung open! It had never been locked at all! But in his mind it was locked and that was all it took to keep him from opening the door and walking out of the jail cell.[1]

Many Christians are trying to open the door that Christ has already unlocked. "It is for freedom that Christ has set us free. Stand firm, then, and do not let yourselves be burdened again by a yoke of slavery" (Gal. 5:1). Legalism is the yoke of slavery. Trying to live righteously by the law, in our own efforts, will only cause us to return to the yoke of slavery. The door to freedom was opened wide when Christ died on the Cross. In fact, Jesus said, "I am the door; if anyone enters through Me, he shall be saved, and shall go in and out, and find pasture" (John 10:9, *NASB*).

How can we walk through that wide-open door to freedom? Simply by believing the truth. As Watchman Nee writes, "Oh, it is a great thing to see that we are in Christ! Think of the bewilderment of trying to get into a room in which you already are! Think of the absurdity of asking to be put in! If we recognize the fact that we are in, we make no effort to enter."[2]

Freedom in Christ is not something to work for and attain by our own achievement. It is part of the death, burial and resurrected life we receive in Christ. It is our inheritance as children of God. It is our birthright. Dr. D. Martyn Lloyd-Jones sums it up well:

Understand that the old man is not there. The only way to stop living as if he were still there is to realize that he is not there. That is the New Testament method of teaching sanctification. The whole trouble with us, says the New Testament, is that we do not realize who we are, that we go on thinking we are the old man and trying to do things to the old man. That has been done;

the old man was crucified with Christ. He is nonexistent, he is no longer there. . . . If we but saw this as we should, we would really begin to live as Christians in this world.[3]

Putting off the old self is putting off the effects of the old self. You learned how to live under the rule and authority of the old man; now you need to learn to live in your newfound freedom. God is telling us that we are dead to sin, alive to God and free in Christ. When we believe the truth of who we are, our behavior will begin to match up with our identity.

Probe

If God has done everything for you to be free, what must you do to experience it? Read through Romans 6:1-11 and learn again what God has already done for you; then choose to believe that truth and let it work out in your experience.

Journal

_____

_____

_____

_____

_____

Notes
1. Don McMinn, *Spiritual Strongholds* (Oklahoma City: NCM Press, 1993), pp. 73, 74.
2. Watchman Nee, *The Normal Christian Life* (Wheaton, Ill.: Tyndale House Publishers, 1977), pp. 64, 65.
3. D. Martyn Lloyd-Jones, *Romans, The New Man* (Grand Rapids, Mich.: Zondervan Publishing House, 1973), p. 62.

DAY 66

Thought for Today: We have a choice.

What then? Shall we sin because we are not under law
but under grace? By no means!
ROMANS 6:15

I scheduled an appointment to take a young woman through the Steps
to Freedom in Christ. Then I learned that she was a victim of satanic ritual abuse. I had never worked with someone like that, so I was apprehen-
sive. When the young lady showed up, she looked and acted normal. She
was a guidance counselor in a high school and seemed very pleasant. She
told my wife and me that the last time she had tried to address her problem she turned over furniture and chased the people around the room
who were trying to help her.

As I started to take her through the Steps, I did something we advise
people not to do: I confronted the demonic spirit prematurely. She let
out the loudest, most ungodly, bloodcurdling scream I have ever heard in
my life. After I rebuked the demon and led the young woman to regain
control, she settled down.

"You knew that was coming, didn't you?" I asked her.

"Yes, I did," she said.

"You don't have to give in to that. You have a choice not to surrender
to those demonic thoughts and let him have control."

After working through the Steps, the woman walked out a free
person. As she was leaving, she said, "No one ever told me before that
I didn't have to give in to that." She had always had a "no button," but
she had never exercised her will by pushing it. No one told her that
she could.

The greatest power we have is the power to choose. We can choose to
believe or not to believe; we can choose to read our Bibles or not read
them. We can choose to live according to the flesh or according to the
Spirit.

Satan will use intimidation tactics to make us think we don't have a choice. If we are trapped by that snare, we are fearing Satan more than we're fearing God, thereby elevating Satan above our heavenly Father. Satan wants to be feared because he wants to be worshiped.

People in bondage believe the lie that they are powerless to make a choice. A dedicated Christian couldn't bring herself to forgive her husband for something he had done to her. She would get so angry that her anger would consume her. She would actually lose control and have a psychotic break. When this happened, her husband would have to take her to a mental hospital. After a few days, she would realize that if she wanted to get out of there, she would have to start acting rationally again. So she did. She knew when she was losing touch with reality, and she could stop it if she wanted to. If that is true, then doesn't she have the same power to choose forgiveness over bitterness?

Earl Jabay, a Christian author who was a chaplain in a neuropsychiatric hospital in New Jersey, told me an interesting story. He got to know a patient well enough to tell him, "If you would be willing to admit that you are wrong on this one particular issue you are obsessed with, I believe you could get out of here and live a productive life."

"Let me think about that," the man said. A few days later he came up to Earl and said, "I've thought it over and I'm not willing to admit that I'm wrong and get out of here. I'd rather be right."

He is certainly not the only one. When Jesus came, His first message was "Repent and believe the good news" (Mark 1:15). "Repent" means to change your mind. If you have a life-controlling problem or a besetting sin, or if you're in the bondage of addiction, you will have to change your mind if you are going to get free. You will have to make some hard choices, but you can do it by the grace of God. You made choices that led you to bondage; now you have to make choices that will set you free.

To continue doing the same things over and over again and expect different results is insanity. One of the most liberating things you will ever do is to admit your wrongdoing and acknowledge your weaknesses. It's called repentance. You can choose to do that and then make the choice to believe the truth that sets you free.

Probe

Why is it so hard to admit when we are wrong and to acknowledge our weaknesses? If you had the choice to sin, do you also have the choice not to sin?

Journal

_____

_____

_____

_____

_____

DAY 67

Thought for Today: We live under the authority of a new Commander in Chief.

So then, brethren, we are under obligation, not to the flesh, to live according to the flesh—for if you are living according to the flesh, you must die; but if by the Spirit you are putting to death the deeds of the body, you will live.

ROMANS 8:12,13, NASB

When Neil was in the Navy, they called the captain of the ship the "Old Man." His first Old Man was tough and crusty and nobody liked him. When in port, he drank every night with the chief petty officers and belittled the other officers. He was not a good example of a naval officer. When that Old Man got transferred to another ship, everybody rejoiced.

They got a new skipper—a New Man. The Old Man no longer had any authority over them; he was gone and completely out of the picture. But the crew was trained under the Old Man. So how do you think they related to the new skipper? At first they tiptoed around him, expecting him to bite their heads off, because that's how they had lived under the authority of their previous Old Man.

When Neil got to know the new skipper, he realized he wasn't a crusty old tyrant like the previous Old Man. He wasn't out to harass his crew; he was a good guy and was really concerned about them. Although Neil's mind had been programmed to react a certain way when he saw a captain's braids, he eventually realized he didn't need to react that way any longer.

You once served under a cruel, self-serving Old Man—your old sinful self under the authority of the god of this world. The admiral of that fleet is Satan himself, the prince of darkness. But by God's grace you have been delivered "from the dominion of darkness and brought . . . into the kingdom of the Son he loves" (Col. 1:13). Your new self is infused with the divine nature of Jesus Christ, your new admiral. As a child of God, a saint, you are no longer under the authority of your Old Man. He is dead, buried and gone forever.

So why do you still react as though your old skipper is still in control of your behavior? Because of the way your old self was conditioned and trained under the old skipper. Your old actions, reactions, emotional responses, thought patterns, memories and habits are ingrained in a part of your brain called "the flesh." The flesh is that tendency within each person to operate independently of God and to center a person's interests on himself. An unsaved person functions totally in the flesh (see Rom. 8:7,8), worshiping and serving the creature rather than the creator (see Rom. 1:25). Such persons "live for themselves" (2 Cor. 5:15), even though many of their activities may appear to be motivated by selflessness and concern for others.

When you were born again, your old self in Adam died and your new self in Christ came to life. You were made a partaker of Christ's divine nature. But you brought to your Christian commitment a fully conditioned mind-set and lifestyle developed apart from God and centered on yourself. Since you were born physically alive but spiritually dead, you had neither the presence of God in you nor the knowledge of His ways. So you learned to live your life independently of God. It is this learned independence that makes the flesh hostile toward God.

During the years you spent separated from God, your worldly experiences thoroughly programmed your brain with thought patterns, memory traces, responses and habits that are alien to God. So even though your old skipper is gone, your flesh remains in opposition to God as a preprogrammed propensity for sin, which is living independently of God.

A careful distinction must be made concerning your relationship to the flesh as a Christian. There is a difference in Scripture between being in the flesh and walking according to the flesh. As a Christian, you are no longer "in the flesh." That phrase describes people who are still spiritually dead (see Rom. 8:8), those who live independently of God. Everything they do, whether morally good or bad, is in the flesh.

But you are not in the flesh, you are in Christ. You have declared your dependence upon Him by placing your faith in Christ. But even though you are not in the flesh, you may still choose to walk according to the flesh (see Rom. 8:12,13), responding to the old mind-sets, patterns and habits ingrained in you by the world you lived in.

Getting rid of the old self was God's responsibility, but rendering the flesh and its deeds inoperative is your responsibility (see Rom. 8:12). God has changed your nature, but it's your responsibility to change your behavior by putting "to death the misdeeds of the body" (Rom. 8:13). How do you do that? There are two elements involved in getting victory over the flesh.

First you must learn to condition your behavior after your new skipper—your new self that is infused by the nature of Christ. Paul promised: "Walk by the Spirit and you will not carry out the desire of the flesh" (Gal. 5:16, NASB). Second, your old pattern of thinking and responding to your sin-trained flesh must be transformed by the "renewing of your mind" (Rom. 12:2).[1] (The process of renewing your mind is the topic of Section 10 in this devotional book.)

Probe
Think back to your days before Christ. How were you trained and what were you told to believe? How does this still have an effect on you today?

Read Romans 8:1-17. What has God done so that you can have victory over the flesh? What are you exhorted to do as a result of what God has done?

Journal

_____

_____

_____

_____

_____

Note
1. Neil T. Anderson, *Victory over the Darkness* (Ventura, Calif.: Regal Books, 1990), pp. 78-81.

DAY 68

Thought for Today: You are not the problem, but you will have one if you believe a lie.

They exchanged the truth of God for a lie, and worshiped and served creat-ed things rather than the Creator—who is forever praised. Amen.
ROMANS 1:25

Jenny was a beautiful and talented woman in her mid-20s. As an active Christian for 13 years, she sang in a professional singing group, wrote music, led worship at her church and oversaw a discipleship group. She attended one of our conferences and gave no indication that she had been struggling with bulimia for 11 years.

Jenny was captivated by Satan's lies about her appearance and sense of worth for hours at a time. In addition, a childhood trauma had left her fearful. When her husband was gone at night, she slept on the couch with all the house lights on. She had submitted to counseling without success and believed the thoughts that prompted her to induce vomiting were her own.

During the conference, I (Neil) said, "Every person I know with an eating disorder has been the victim of a stronghold based on the lies of Satan." The next morning Jenny told me, "You have no idea how that statement impacted my life. I have been battling myself all these years, and I suddenly understood that my enemy was not myself but Satan. That was the most profound truth I have ever heard. It was like I had been blind for 11 years and could suddenly see. I cried all the way home. When the old thoughts came back last night, I simply rejected them for the truth. For the first time in years I was able to go to sleep without vomiting."[1]

When I (Mike) struggled with my own addiction, no one ever said to me, "The problem is not you but the lies you believe." Even if people didn't come right out and say it, the implication was you aren't trying hard enough . . . you're not committed enough . . . you're weak . . . you have bad character . . . you have low morals . . . you're an addict, and so on. Such advice is like telling parents they have a problem child. If that were true, then the only way to get rid of the problem is to get rid of the child. The truth is, they have a child who has a problem.

The gospel became "good news" when I learned that my problem was the lies I was believing. I could do something about that. But if the problem was me—if I was born an addict and would always be one—then the best I could expect was to learn to cope with my problem.

Jesus said, "You will know the truth, and the truth will set you free" (John 8:32). If truth sets us free, then what keeps us in bondage? Lies! And who is the father of lies (see John 8:44)? If the devil can get you to believe a lie, he can control your life. We have been clearly warned about such a possibility. "The Spirit clearly says that in later times some will abandon the faith and follow deceiving spirits and things taught by demons" (1 Tim. 4:1).

I (Neil) was counseling a young lady who was struggling with anorexia. To keep her weight down she was taking 50 laxatives a day. Was she simply stupid? No, she had graduated from a top Christian university. But she was deceived. I asked her to repeat after me, "I renounce the lie that defecating is a means of cleansing myself. I trust only in the cleansing work of Christ." As soon as she said that, she broke down and cried. When she regained her composure, I asked her, "What were you thinking during that time?" She said, "I can't believe the lies I've believed."

What lies have you believed? Have you believed the lie that your problem defines who you are?

What do alcoholics, addicts, gamblers, overeaters and bulimics do? They get drunk, do drugs, gamble, overeat, binge and purge. Or they spend the rest of their lives trying not to do those things. Just trying to change behavior will not result in lasting change. The problem is not the behavior, but the misbelief behind the behavior. People will not change until they change their beliefs. Most of the lies we believe about ourselves are rooted in early childhood experiences that are burned into our minds over time or by the intensity of the experiences. The trauma itself does not keep us in bondage; it is the lies we believe about ourselves, God and life in general that keep us in bondage.

Probe

What early childhood experiences caused you to think negatively about yourself? How did that precipitate your addictive behavior?

Journal

Note
  1. Neil T. Anderson, *Victory over the Darkness* (Ventura, Calif.: Regal Books, 1990), pp. 171, 172.

DAY 69

Thought for Today: You cannot do for yourself what God has already done for you.

His divine power has given us everything we need for life and godliness through our knowledge of him who called us by his own glory and goodness. Through these he has given us his very great and precious promises, so that through them you may participate in the divine nature and escape the corruption in the world caused by evil desires.

2   PETER   1 : 3 , 4

When it was painfully obvious to me that I was addicted to alcohol, I resolved to do whatever it took to beat my problem. I had been taught that the secret to the abundant life was "doing the right thing." The key was to spend time with God in Bible study and prayer. Through this time I could learn what God wanted me to do and receive strength for action.

The idea was, if I spent enough time in the Scriptures I would know what God's will is and somehow be able to do it. I would often spend two hours in "quiet time," then be drunk before dark. I was living proof that having an intellectual knowledge of the Bible was not enough.

As I studied the Bible for hundreds of hours, I looked for scriptural principles of deliverance. I tried the gamut of spiritual activities such as fasting, praying, Bible reading and studying, Scripture memory and so on. I tried discipleship groups, charismatic meetings, revivals, prayer meetings and praise gatherings. I went to a healing-of-memories session and two sessions for casting out demons.

I went to a variety of Christian counselors, psychologists and psychiatrists. Like Naaman the leper in the Old Testament (see 2 Kings 5), if someone had told me to wash in the Jordan River seven times, I gladly would have done it.

I was told that I needed accountability. Accountability is good, but it doesn't give freedom. On a Christian radio program, a man told how he overcame a problem with lust and pornography when he traveled. His solution was to take someone with him on each trip to hold him accountable. Now this was a creative solution, but all it proved was that the man was not free. It may have kept him from acting out, but external accountability will never transform the inner person.

I tried a Christian 12-step program and went to hundreds of AA meetings. I went through five sponsors at AA before I finally realized they couldn't tell me how to get free. I never heard anyone involved with AA say he or she was free.

I believed the lie that I could live the Christian life through determination and resolve. I believed that if I just had enough commitment, then I could make it work. But I found myself in a deep pit of bondage and I didn't know how to get out. It was a sad day when I was forced to admit that all I had learned about living the Christian life didn't work.

All of the advice and counseling I received (and I believe it was all sincere) did accomplish one thing. It proved conclusively to me that I couldn't free myself, no matter what I did. When I learned the truth that I was dead to sin, alive to God and had been freed from sin, what did I do? I didn't do anything. I simply accepted the truth of what God had done for me and I placed my faith in Him. Two decades of trying to do my best accomplished nothing; one act of believing the truth of what God had done set me free.

What has God done? Reread 2 Peter 1:3,4, above. God "has given us everything we need for life and godliness." He has placed us in Christ, and Christ now lives in us (see John 14:20). He not only delivered us from the penalty of sin, He delivered us from the power of sin (see Rom. 6:11).

The Christian life is not achieved by pulling yourself up by your bootstraps and doing the best you can. Thanks be to God! He gives us the victory through our Lord Jesus Christ (see 1 Cor. 15:57). He "always leads us in His triumph in Christ" (2 Cor. 2:14, NASB).

Romans 8:31-39 asks some important questions and makes some incredible declarations of fact:

> What, then, shall we say in response to this? If God is for us, who can be against us? He who did not spare his own Son, but gave

him up for us all—how will he not also, along with him, graciously give us all things? Who will bring any charge against those whom God has chosen? It is God who justifies. Who is he that condemns? Christ Jesus, who died—more than that, who was raised to life—is at the right hand of God and is also interceding for us. Who shall separate us from the love of Christ? Shall trouble or hardship or persecution or famine or nakedness or danger or sword? As it is written: "For your sake we face death all day long; we are considered as sheep to be slaughtered." No, in all these things we are more than conquerors through him who loved us. For I am convinced that neither death nor life, neither angels nor demons, neither the present nor the future, nor any powers, neither height nor depth, nor anything else in all creation, will be able to separate us from the love of God that is in Christ Jesus our Lord.

Probe

Do you believe, as someone once said, that "doing your best is just another definition of sin"? Distinguish between "doing your best to do for yourself what God has already done for you" and "doing your best to be all that God has created you to be in Christ."

Journal

_____

_____

_____

_____

_____

DAY 70

**Thought for Today: You have to be filled with the Spirit
in order to fulfill your purpose.**

*Therefore do not let sin reign in your mortal body so that you obey
its evil desires. Do not offer the parts of your body to sin, as
instruments of wickedness, but rather offer yourselves to God,
as those who have been brought from death to life; and offer the
parts of your body to him as instruments of righteousness.*

ROMANS 6:12,13

Suppose we flew an Aborigine from the outback of Australia to Detroit, Michigan. There we showed him a brand-new Lincoln just off the assembly line. The battery gives it a spark of life, but the gas tank is empty. We ask the Aborigine, "What do you think the purpose is for the automobile?" He has never seen or heard of a car before. He only knows it is the prettiest object he has ever seen.

His original thought might be that the car's purpose must be found in its appearance. But when he sits in the leather seats that move up and down, he decides that maybe its purpose is to provide comfort. Somebody switches on the stereo with quadraphonic sound. Now he thinks the car's real purpose is to make music. When he honks the horn, the Aborigine becomes convinced that this is a noise machine. Suddenly someone turns on the lights, and the visitor wonders if the purpose of this machine is to provide light.

An automobile has only one real purpose—to provide transportation. But a car can never fulfill its purpose without gasoline. And we can never fulfill our purpose without the presence of God in our lives. Without Christ, we try to fulfill our purpose by trying to look good, by seeking man-made comforts, by making a lot of noise and creating our own light. What a shallow pursuit! It's a great day when we finally admit something is missing.

The world suggests that something is wrong with our "car," or our way of traveling through life. So we try harder, but our increased efforts don't work. Finally, we admit we need some help. Well-meaning people come alongside to offer their assistance.

One group, who believes something is still wrong with your car, strives to fix it for you. Another group doesn't want to hurt your feelings by suggesting your car is no good. They use the nonthreatening approach. They see that your purpose for living has been misguided, so they attempt to help you get back on track by teaching you how to push your car. Still another group rescues cars that have been traveling on the wrong track for a long time. They have a towing service. They pull you out of the muck, then help you wash your car.

All these attempts to fix your "car" won't work if you are on the wrong road. If your self-imposed purpose for being here has been world-centered or self-centered, trying to change it won't be enough. Unless your car is filled with gasoline and traveling on the right road, it will never fulfill its created purpose.

Our purpose is to glorify God in our bodies (see 1 Cor. 6:20). The glory of God is a manifestation of His presence. "By this is My father glorified, that you bear much fruit, and so prove to be My disciples" (John 15:8, *NASB*). We can only do this if we abide in Christ. We cannot do for ourselves what Christ has already done for us. But we can choose to repent of our self-centered ways, choose the right way, start living by faith according to what God says is true and receive the very life of Christ within us. He alone is "the way and the truth and the life" (John 14:6).

Whose responsibility is it—ours or God's—to keep sin from reigning in our bodies? We will not be able to do what Romans 6:12,13 says unless we first believe what Romans 6:1-11 says—that through God's grace we are dead to sin. It is that truth that sets us free and keeps us free. Believing the truth is what must precede and determine responsible behavior.

Clearly it is our responsibility not to let sin reign in our mortal bodies. We are responsible for our own attitudes and actions. As Paul says in verse 13, "Do not offer the parts of your body to sin, as instruments of wickedness, but rather offer yourselves to God, as those who have been brought from death to life; and offer the parts of your body to him as instruments of righteousness."

Notice that we must take only one negative action, but two positive actions. On the negative side, we are not to use our bodies in ways that would serve sin. If we do, we allow sin to reign (rule) in our physical bodies. On the positive side, we are to (1) offer ourselves to God and (2) offer our bodies to Him. We are told to consciously present "ourselves" to God because we belong to Him. Then we are to present "our bodies" to God. Why does Paul separate "ourselves" from "our bodies"?

The self is who we essentially are. Our culture promotes the belief that our identities are derived from the things we do, and individually we tend to identify one another by our physical bodies. As natural people, this is our only means of identification. However, as children of God, we have new identities. Our hope does not rest in the eternal preservation of the outer man but in the fact that though our outer man is decaying, our inner man is being renewed day by day (see 2 Cor. 4:16). Our inner man will live forever with our heavenly Father, but our bodies won't.

That which is mortal is also corruptible. Are our physical bodies evil? No, they are amoral or neutral. So what are we to do about the neutral disposition of our bodies? We are told to present them as instruments of righteousness. "Present" means to put at the disposal of. An instrument can be anything the Lord has entrusted to us. The Lord is commanding us to be good stewards of our bodies and to use them only as instruments of righteousness.[1]

Probe

How would you describe your purpose for being here? Can you fulfill that purpose by hard work or human ingenuity?

Journal

_____

_____

_____

_____

Note
1. Neil T. Anderson and Mike and Julia Quarles, *Freedom from Addiction* (Ventura, Calif.: Regal Books, 1996), pp. 253-57.

DAY 71

Thought for Today: Satan blinds the minds of the unbelieving.

Don't you know that when you offer yourselves to someone to obey him as slaves, you are slaves to the one whom you obey—whether you are slaves to sin, which leads to death, or to obedience, which leads to righteousness?

ROMANS 6:16

Slavery in the United States was abolished by the 13th Amendment on December 18, 1865. How many slaves were there on December 19th? In reality, none. Yet many still lived like slaves because they had not learned the truth. Others knew and even believed they were free but chose to live as they had been taught.

Imagine a fictitious conversation between some plantation owners and their chief spokesman, Satan.

"We're ruined!" the plantation owners cried out. "We've lost the battle to keep our slaves."

"Not necessarily," Satan said. "As long as these people think they're still slaves, the Emancipation Proclamation will have no practical effect. We don't have a legal right over them anymore, but many of them don't know it. Keep your slaves from learning the truth and your control over them won't even be challenged."

"But what if the news spreads?"

"Don't panic," Satan replied. "We have another bullet in our gun. We may not be able to keep them from hearing the news, but we can still keep them from understanding it. They don't call me the 'father of lies' for nothing. We still have the potential to deceive the whole world. Just tell the slaves that they misunderstood the 13th Amendment. Tell them they are *going* to be free, not that they are free already. The truth they heard is just positional truth. Someday they may receive the benefits, but not now."

"But my slaves will expect me to say that," the plantation owner said. "They won't believe me."

"Then pick out a few persuasive ones who are convinced they are still slaves, and let them do the talking for you. Remember, most of these free people were born as slaves. All we have to do is deceive them into thinking they still are slaves. As long as they continue to do what slaves do, they will maintain their slave identity. The moment they try to profess they are no longer slaves, just whisper in their ears, 'How can you think you're no longer a slave when you're still doing the things that slaves do?'"

Long before 1865, Jesus made another Emancipation Proclamation: "You will know the truth, and the truth will set you free" (John 8:32). Yet all these years later, many people still enslaved by addictions have not heard that wonderful news. Quite naturally they continue to live the way they have always lived. Others have heard the good news, but they evaluate it by what they are presently doing and feeling. They reason, "I'm still living in bondage, doing the same things I have always done. I'm feeling the same way I did before the proclamation, so it must not be true." They continue to live according to how they feel, not wanting to be hypocrites!

One former slave hears the good news and receives it with great joy. He checks out the validity of the proclamation and discovers that the highest of all authorities has originated the decree. Not only that, but it personally cost the authority a tremendous price, which He willingly paid so the former slave could be free. The slave's life is transformed. He correctly reasons that it would be hypocritical to believe his feelings instead of the truth stated by the authority. Determined to live by what he knows to be true, his experiences begin to change rather dramatically. He realizes that his old master has no authority over him and does not need to be obeyed. The former slave gladly serves the one who set him free.[1]

According to Paul, we are "freed from sin" (Rom. 6:7). *Wait a minute*, you may be thinking. *Are you telling me I don't have to sin?* My answer is, "Where did you get the idea that you have to sin?" John wrote, "My dear children, I write this to you so that you will not sin. But if anybody does sin, we have one who speaks to the Father in our defense—Jesus Christ, the Righteous One" (1 John 2:1). Obviously, Christian maturity is a factor in our ability to stand against temptation. But what an incredible sense of defeat we would have if we believed that we had to sin while at the same time being commanded by God not to sin. "For you were once darkness, but now you are light in the Lord. Live as children of light (for the fruit of the light consists in all goodness, righteousness and truth)" (Eph. 5:8,9).

People who live in bondage are caught in a web of faulty thinking: *God, you made me this way and now you condemn me for it! The Christian life is impossible.* Then when they fall, they protest, "I'm only human!" Those who struggle with chemical and sexual addictions lead this parade of despair. They constantly entertain such thoughts as the following: *Christianity works for others but it doesn't work for me. Maybe I'm not a Christian. God doesn't love me. How could He? I'm such a failure. I'm just a miserable sinner with no hope of breaking the chains of addiction.*[2]

Lies! All lies! These people are still living like slaves because they're still thinking like slaves. The truth? You have been crucified with Christ so that you should no longer be a slave to sin (see Rom. 6:6); you have died to sin (see 6:7); you have been raised up with Christ and seated with Him (see Eph. 2:6), and you have been freed from sin (see Rom 6:7).

Probe

Can you see why people who have been enslaved to sin would have trouble accepting their newfound freedom? In what way has it been difficult for you to accept the truth that would set you free?

Journal

_____

_____

_____

_____

_____

Notes
1. Neil T. Anderson and Mike and Julia Quarles, *Freedom from Addiction* (Ventura, Calif.: Regal Books, 1996), pp. 239-241.
2. Ibid., pp. 241, 242.

DAY 72

Thought for Today: Victory is not found in striving but in resting in the finished work of Christ.

It is because of him that you are in Christ Jesus, who has become for us wisdom from God—that is, our righteousness, holiness and redemption.

1 CORINTHIANS 1:30

With the exception of the apostle Paul, Hudson Taylor just might be the greatest missionary who ever lived. Like all of us though, Taylor had his struggles and failures. He had been a Christian for 20 years and lived in China for 16 years before he learned the truth that set him free and enabled him to enter into what he called "the exchanged life." He told of his struggles and his experience in a letter to his sister:

> I felt the ingratitude, the danger, the sin of not living nearer to God. I prayed, agonized, fasted, strove, made resolutions, read the Word more diligently, sought more time for meditation— but all without avail. Every day, almost every hour, the consciousness of sin oppressed me.
>
> I knew that if only I could abide in Christ all would be well, but I could not. . . . Each day brought its register of sin and failure, of lack of power. To will was indeed present within me, but how to perform I found not. . . . Then came the question, Is there no rescue? Must it be thus to the end—constant conflict, and too often defeat . . . ? I hated myself, my sin, yet gained no strength against it. . . . I felt I was a child of God. . . . But to rise to my privileges as a child, I was utterly powerless.
>
> All the time I felt assured that there was in Christ all I needed, but the practical question was—how to get it out. . . . I strove for faith, but it would not come: I tried to exercise it, but in vain. . . . I prayed for faith, but it came not. What was I to do?

When my agony of soul was at its height, a sentence in a letter from dear McCarthy was used to remove the scales from my
eyes, and the Spirit of God revealed to me the truth of our oneness with Jesus as I had never known it before. (I quote from
memory): "But how to get faith strengthened? Not by striving
after faith, but by resting on the Faithful One."

As I read, I saw it all! "If we believe not, he abideth faithful."
I looked to Jesus and saw (and when I saw, oh, how the joy
flowed!) that He had said, "I will never leave thee." I thought, "I
have striven in vain to rest in Him. I'll strive no more. . . ."

I am no better than before. In a sense I do not wish to be.
But I am dead, buried with Christ—aye, and risen too! And now
Christ lives in me and "the life that I now live in the flesh, I live
by the faith of the Son of God, who loved me and gave Himself
for me." . . . Do not let us consider Him as far off, when God has
made us one with Him, members of His very body. Nor should
we look upon this experience, these truths, as for the few. They
are the birthright of every child of God . . . the only power for
deliverance from sin or for true service is Christ.[1]

Are you, like Hudson Taylor, striving for holiness and freedom from
sin, trying to do right but not experiencing victory? Striving isn't the
answer. Taylor also wrote,

Striving, longing, hoping for better days to come is not the true
way to holiness, happiness or usefulness. . . . How then to have
faith increased? . . . Not a striving to have faith . . . but a looking
off to the Faithful One seems all we need; a resting in the Loved
One entirely, for time and eternity.[2]

Christ is in us (see Col. 1:27). We are one with Him (see Rom. 6:5). He
is our life (see Col. 3:4). We are dead, buried, raised with Him, united to
Him in His resurrection and freed from sin (see Rom. 6:4-7). When we
realize these truths and we stop striving and struggling, we rest in Him

and begin to trust Him to be our life—our holiness, our peace, our patience, our love. It's called living by faith. It is trusting Christ to be all that we need.

John 15 tells us that Christ is the Vine and we are the branches. As branches attached to the Vine, our responsibility is to abide in Him, to remain in Him, to rest in Him, to trust Him, to rely on Him and to depend on Him to fulfill His promises and be all that we need. "By His doing you are in Christ Jesus, who became to us wisdom from God, and righteousness and sanctification, and redemption" (1 Cor. 1:30, *NASB*).

In order to have our sins forgiven and go to heaven, we have to rely on what another Person has done. In order to live free from sin, we have to rely on what another Person will do in us and through us. "God has chosen to make known among the Gentiles the glorious riches of this mystery, which is Christ in you, the hope of glory" (Col. 1:27).

Probe

One way to stop striving and start resting in the finished work of Christ is to pray as Paul did in Ephesians 1:17-23. Make this your daily prayer for the next week.

Journal

_____

_____

_____

_____

_____

Notes
1. Dr. and Mrs. Howard Taylor, *Hudson Taylor's Spiritual Secret* (Chicago: Moody Press, 1990), pp. 158-164.
2. Ibid., pp. 155, 156.

DISCOVERING
THE GRACE
OF GOD

DAY 73

Thought for Today: The Christian is not governed by a set of rules but by a relationship.

For you did not receive a spirit that makes you a slave again to fear, but you received the Spirit of sonship. And by him we cry, "Abba, Father." The Spirit himself testifies with our spirit that we are God's children.

ROMANS 8:15,16

David Seamands tells a story about a young man in India, when David served there as pastor of an English-speaking church. He said that Devedas was one of the finest young adults in the congregation. He was a deeply committed, Spirit-filled believer from a family who had long been Christians. The name Devedas means "servant of God," and the young man lived up to his name. Although he had to ride a bicycle for several miles to get to church, he attended every service. He was a good Bible student and a faithful witness among his Hindu friends, despite the fact that they ridiculed his faith. "If necessary," Seamands wrote, "Devedas would have died for his Christianity—no doubt about that. The real question, just now, was why he seemed to be almost dying from it."

The young man shared what Seamands called "his never-ending battle with the tyranny of the oughts." He had a pervasive sense of guilt, condemnation, acute anxiety and low self-esteem from constant self-belittling. Yet he seemed to live in denial, repressing negative emotions such as anger and depression. His overscrupulous conscience tended to make him legalistic.

Devedas had summed up his feelings by saying, "I ought to, I should, I could, I try, but I never seem to be able to do enough." As Seamands observed, "That's the inescapable bondage, the vicious circle from which there is no escape through bigger and better performance." Such guilt is the "core of the curse, the horrible hub from which all the spokes emanate to hold the wheel of the treadmill in place."[1]

While people have varying degrees of this "performance concentration," Seamands believes that the syndrome itself is a kind of disease, a malignant virus that lies at the heart of all of us, the ultimate lie behind a myriad of ordinary lies, persuading us that every relationship in life is based on performance—on what we do.

> The lie insists that everything depends on how well we perform—our salvation and status; our relationship with God; our sense of self-worth; our relationship with ourselves; our sense of security and belongingness; our relationship with others; our sense of achievement and success; our relationship with society around us.[2]

A Muslim was talking to a Christian missionary about the Koran. He said it was their book of rules to live by. The missionary replied, "You have your Koran, which gives you your rules to live by, and we Christians have our Bible, which gives us our rules to live by."

That is a popular misconception, but it is far from the truth. We do learn how to live from the Bible, but the Bible is not a rule book. The Bible points to Christ and His redemptive work, and to our relationship with Him.

I once counseled a young man in his 20s. "Whenever I get close to the Lord, I have a psychotic break," he told me. As he told his story, I understood what he meant. To get close to the Lord he would spend a lot of time in the Bible. The problem wasn't that he was getting close to the Lord. The problem was that he saw the Bible as a rule book. The more he read it, the more he saw what he ought to be doing. The more he saw how far short he was falling, the greater the condemnation he felt.

Most Christians don't have psychotic breaks, but if they see the Bible as a rule book, they live in defeat and condemnation. If the Christian life is just rules, we are really no better off (in practice) than the Muslims. We may be worse off, because the Bible sets forth a high standard. We are told to "be perfect, therefore, as your heavenly Father is perfect" (Matt. 5:48). How can we do that? We can only live the Christian life by faith, which means that we depend on Christ's life in us.

We are also told that "apart from [Christ] you can do nothing" (John 15:5). It doesn't mean that apart from Christ we are just limited or handicapped; it means that we really can do nothing that lasts for eternity. God wants us to know the truth that says, "I can do everything through him who gives me strength" (Phil. 4:13).

The greatest day of any Christian's life is when he learns there is nothing he can do to make God love him more, and nothing he can do to make God love him less. David Seamands says, "I am convinced that the basic cause of some of the most disturbing emotional/spiritual problems which trouble evangelical Christians is the failure to receive and live out of God's unconditional grace, and the corresponding failure to offer that grace to others."[3]

God is love, and it is His nature to love us. He has adopted you as His son or His daughter. Your relationship with Him doesn't depend on what you do but on what He has done.

Probe

Do you have a case of the "oughts"? What are driven people trying to achieve? What is the motivation behind all their efforts?

Journal

_____

_____

_____

_____

_____

Notes
1. David Seamands, *Healing Grace* (Wheaton, Ill.: Victor Books, 1988), pp. 12, 13.
2. Ibid., p. 13.
3. Ibid., p. 14.

DAY 74

Thought for Today: Self-help is no help at all.

Watch and pray so that you will not fall into temptation. The spirit is willing, but the body is weak.
MATTHEW 26:41

At the end of the summer of 1984, I was called before our church discipline committee for my drinking. It was the same church from which I had been called into the ministry in 1972. The promising preacher had become the prodigal son.

I considered killing myself. I also considered leaving town or turning my back on the church and not attending their meeting. In the end I submitted to what I thought God wanted me to do, so I showed up. They recommended that I enter a secular treatment center. They told me it was my best option. I wasn't convinced, but I had no other options. The last thing I wanted to do was go to a secular treatment center for 30 days. The treatment would involve a large sum of money that we didn't have, and my insurance didn't cover treatment for alcoholism.

I was convinced that I didn't need to go into treatment. I would do whatever else it took to stay close to the Lord and not drink. On a Wednesday morning I met with our pastor and presented my case with all the eloquence and force I could muster. He shared his doubts about what I was saying. He knew that for the last five years I had tried every other option. He listened attentively but remained neutral. Like everyone else, he wanted me to be free from alcohol. I left our meeting encouraged and determined to change my behavior.

Before sundown of that same day, I was thoroughly drunk. It was another classic example of "the spirit is willing, but the flesh is weak" (Matt. 26:41, *NASB*). The Bible says "the righteous will live by faith" (Rom. 1:17). Somehow I believed the lie that I could live the Christian life through determination and resolve. If I just had enough commitment, I could make it work.[1]

The stronghold of self-help—believing we can do it ourselves—possibly keeps more people in bondage than any other factor. In Christianity, it's nothing but bootstrap religion and positive legalism. It's just another version of "God helps those who help themselves." Most people believe that if they can change their behavior, they can change themselves. This is simply untrue.

Alcoholics and addicts know they can enter a treatment center and be fine and have little struggle while they are there. If they don't change their beliefs, though, they will quickly go back to their old way of living.

When it comes to self-help, I was the world's worst. If, as Paul said, he was the Pharisee of Pharisees, I was the legalist of legalists. Every week or so I came up with another scheme. Countless times I ran to Julia or my minister and told them about a wonderful new plan to solve my problem. Within a week (and sometimes sooner) my plan was shattered and in ruins. The greater my hopes rose, the harder I fell.

God doesn't expect us to shape up the old person in an all-out spiritual boot camp. That isn't Christianity, and it will only bring despair and grief. Self-help—hoping for self-improvement—is motivated by self-centered living. It is nothing more than a flesh improvement program. Secular programs are designed to strengthen the old nature and modify behavior. But God isn't interested in trying to improve the flesh; He wants us to crucify it (see Gal. 5:24).

It is difficult to give up on our beliefs and devices. But God only responds to faith, not our empty promises and futile strivings. Isaiah 50:11 tells us what happens to those who depend on themselves: "But now, all you who light fires and provide yourselves with flaming torches, go, walk in the light of your fires and of the torches you have set ablaze. This is what you shall receive from my hand: You will lie down in torment."

We believe that if we can do the right things, all will be well. Paul addressed this false belief in his letter to the Galatians. He said he was amazed that the Galatians would return to their own pitiful efforts. Eugene Peterson's THE MESSAGE vividly captures his words:

Let me put this question to you: How did your new life begin? Was it by working your heads off to please God? Or was it by responding to God's Message to you? Are you going to continue this craziness? For only crazy people would think they could complete by their own efforts what was begun by God. If you weren't smart enough or strong enough to begin it, how do you suppose you could perfect it? Did you go through this whole painful learning process for nothing? . . . Answer this question: Does the God who lavishly provides you with his own presence, his Holy Spirit, working things in your lives you could never do for yourselves, does he do these things because of your strenuous moral striving or because you trust him to do them in you? (Gal. 3:2-5).

Probe

If we are saved by the grace of God through faith and faith alone, then how are we perfected?

Journal

_____

_____

_____

_____

_____

Note
1. Neil T. Anderson and Mike and Julia Quarles, *Freedom from Addiction* (Ventura, Calif.: Regal Books, 1996), pp. 76, 77.

DAY 75

Thought for Today: Your failure cannot overcome the grace of God.

The law was added so that the trespass might increase. But where sin increased, grace increased all the more.
ROMANS 5:20

David Seamands tells a story that illustrates the point Paul made in the passage for today. It's about a turning point in the spiritual life of a teenager in his church. The young man had already made a personal commitment to Christ. He tried hard, but like most adolescents, he was plagued by ups and downs in his Christian life. It wasn't uncommon to find him coming forward when an invitation was given after a church service. After one evening service, Rev. Seamands prayed with the young man once again. The young man's face was sober as he affirmed his determination "to make it this time." Then he asked, "But what if I fail? What happens if I fall?"

Seamands replied, "Steve, I've come to know you pretty well. Probably better than anyone in the church. So I think I can guarantee one thing—you will fail, you will fall. So what?"

The young man looked up at the minister a bit shocked. He had expected assurance that he would never fail again. He turned Seamand's response over in his mind. Then a light dawned on the young man's face. He began to smile and nod his head. "Hmmm," he said, finally. "I think I see what you mean. I think I'm catching on. Of course I'm going to fail; sure I'll fall. But that really doesn't make any difference, does it?" And then the smile lit up his whole face.

Rev. Seamands said that although the young man subsequently showed significant growth, that moment proved to be his initial discovery of the grace of God. Discovering the truth that failure isn't the end changed his life. Seamands later wrote that it was a joy to watch the young man grow in grace. "He became a dispenser of grace as a pastor for eleven years, and now teaches about grace as a professor of systematic theology in a seminary. Are you wondering about my strange reply that I was sure he would fail because I knew him so well? That's because I happen to be his dad!"[1]

Is there a limit to God's grace? Is there a point at which God says, "All right, that's enough, no more"? God will never give up on us, although He will discipline us and allow us to suffer the natural consequences of our own sin and irresponsibility. He may even call some of us home if the course of life we are pursuing is self-destructive and damaging to ourselves and others. But He does call us home to be with Him (see 1 Cor. 11:30).

Is God surprised when you sin? Does He look down from heaven and say, "I can't believe he did it again?" No. How could He be surprised if He has nailed all our sins on the Cross? But it grieves God to see us sin again and again, because He knows what that will lead to in our lives. God will never say, "Look, we need to talk. Some of the sins you committed were so bad we didn't put them on the Cross." His grace is sufficient for all we have done and will do.

Paul writes, "Therefore, there is now no condemnation for those who are in Christ Jesus" (Rom. 8:1). The Greek word for condemnation carries with it a sense of judgment. There is no more judgment for the Christian. Why? Because we have already been judged when Christ paid the penalty for all our sins. He took all our punishment on Himself.

If we're still not convinced, Paul raises the question again in Romans:

What, then, shall we say in response to this? If God is for us, who can be against us? He who did not spare his own Son, but gave him up for us all—how will he not also, along with him, graciously give us all things? Who will bring any charge against those whom God has chosen? It is God who justifies. Who is he that condemns? Christ Jesus, who died—more than that, who was raised to life—is at the right hand of God and is also interceding for us (Rom. 8:31-34).

The point that God is hammering home is that if He has done everything necessary to acquit us, justify us and make us right with Him, who is qualified to bring further charges? Who is going to condemn?

"No one!" God thunders to us.

So who is bringing the charges? Who is accusing and condemning? "Satan, who leads the whole world astray. . . . who accuses [the brethren] before our God day and night" (Rev. 12:9,10).

The old hymn says it well: "Grace, grace, God's grace, grace that will pardon and cleanse within; grace, grace, God's grace, grace that is greater than all our sin."[2] The grace of God is not a license to sin, it actually is a gracious means not to sin. Paul later says, "What shall we say then? Are we to continue in sin so that grace may abound? May it never be! How shall we who died to sin still live in it" (Rom. 6:1,2, NASB)? By the grace of God we don't have to sin. We can live righteous lives in Christ.

Probe

Have you believed the lie that your failure and sin can overcome the grace of God? Has that belief caused you to doubt God's love, so you live in condemnation and defeat? Have you ever believed that you were unredeemable? Renounce that lie and affirm the truth with the following affirmation: I renounce the lie that my failure and sin can overcome the grace of God. I announce the truth that Christ died for all my sins, past, present and future, and that all my sins have been placed on the Cross, and I am forgiven. I now choose to believe there is no more condemnation because I am in Christ.

Journal

_____

_____

_____

_____

_____

Notes
1. David Seamands, *Healing Grace* (Wheaton, Ill.: Victor Books, 1988), pp. 116, 117.
2. Julia H. Johnston, "Grace Greater Than Our Sin," *Worship and Service Hymnal* (Chicago: Hope Publishing Co., 1968), p. 197.

DAY 76

Thought for Today: The problem with pride is that it has "I" in the middle.

But he gives us more grace. That is why Scripture says: "God opposes the proud but gives grace to the humble."

JAMES 4:6

When I was counseling with Grace Ministries in Atlanta, one of the other counselors asked me to talk with a counselee who was struggling with alcoholism. The counselee spent the whole session telling us about his plans to solve his problem. Although his wife may have been encouraged to hear these plans—get up early, read his Bible, pray, go to church—I explained that I had tried these things and more, all to no avail. But the man would not hear me. After the session, I told the counselor, "I seriously doubt if he lasts a month." He didn't; and the next time he got drunk, he landed in jail.

During my ministry to alcoholics and addicts in Birmingham, Alabama, one young woman came up with a unique solution. She said, "Because I always get drunk on either Friday or Saturday night, I have solved my problem. I'll start my Sabbath early by attending a messianic worship service on Friday night, then another one on Saturday night." I attempted to point out that she was setting herself up for a fall. But I didn't dampen her enthusiasm a bit. What happened? She didn't last till Friday. Instead, she got drunk on Thursday—two days after telling me her plan.[1]

Whenever people say, "Just tell me what to do and I'll do it," they are not yet ready for God's plan. They still believe they can do for themselves what God has already done for them. Those who are ready for God's help know they can do nothing. The most difficult people to help are those who think they can do it, are willing to do it and are determined to do it. We may have to step back and let these people give it their best shot. Many people have to learn the hard way, as I did, that we can't free ourselves before we are ready to receive the good news that Christ has already done it for us.

What stands in the way of receiving God's grace and help? Only ourselves! It is our self-sufficient pride that is the obstacle. Such foolishness will not win God's favor, because God resists the proud but gives grace to the humble (see Jas. 4:6).

Why is it so difficult to give up and let someone else do it for us? Because then we have to admit we can't do it ourselves. Scripture tells us that the Cross is an offense (see 1 Cor. 1:23). The Cross says that apart from Christ we are nothing and can do nothing. The Cross is an indictment that says man apart from God is judged and found guilty and is inadequate to do anything about it.

The Cross says that we were so bad that God had to include us with Christ on the cross, crucify us with Christ, raise up a new person and start all over again. The Cross is meant for those who are willing to admit their way doesn't work and they don't have another way to try. When we get to that point, we are ready to receive the grace of God.

I visit and teach in a lot of Christian treatment centers. I meet and talk with a lot of men who have struggled with addiction most of their lives. Many have been treated in numerous treatment centers. The one characteristic I continually see keeping these men from experiencing their freedom is not bad character, weak resolve, a dysfunctional family, lack of education or poor role models. It is the unwillingness to give up; it is the deep-seated pride that won't bend.

The majority of addicted people I talk to don't necessarily want to know what I've learned; they want to tell me what they have learned and what their plans are. We recently received a letter from a man in prison telling us where we were wrong in our book *Freedom from Addiction.* He said he would appreciate it if we would straighten it out. Obviously he speaks from a position of authority!

So what's the problem? It's pride—the belief that we can figure it out by ourselves and that we can do it by ourselves. It's your problem and it's my problem. "There is a way which seems right to a man, but its end is the way of death" (Prov. 14:12, *NASB*).

You can't earn the grace of God and you don't deserve it. You can't scheme for it or manipulate it. You can't figure it out or design a program to get more. All you can do is come to the end of your resources and discover His. When we have given up a way that seems right to us, we are ready to receive the grace of God.

Probe

Why do we cling to our own way of doing things? How does pride manifest itself in your life?

Journal

_____

_____

_____

_____

_____

Note
1. Neil T. Anderson and Mike and Julia Quarles, *Freedom from Addiction* (Ventura, Calif.: Regal Books, 1996), pp. 180, 181.

DAY 77

Thought for Today: We are free to believe, but we won't be free if we fail to believe the truth.

Then they asked him, "What must we do to do the works God requires?"
Jesus answered, "The work of God is this: to believe in the one he has sent."
JOHN 6:28,29

I started my Christian life with great zeal and commitment. I believed that nothing could stop me. I wanted to become everything the Lord wanted me to be and to faithfully serve Him in ministry. I pursued education and preparation for ministry, attended seminars and read literally hundreds of books about the Christian life and ministry. I was a diligent student of the Bible and memorized entire chapters of it. I spent at least one hour daily in the Word and in prayer. On my wall was the motto by the great missionary to Africa, C. T. Studd: "Only one life, 'twill soon be past; only what's done for Christ will last." I would never have believed I could become an alcoholic.

I concluded that the Christian life was not working for me. The church where I was the pastor was going nowhere fast. If my wife, Julia, had not been married to the preacher, she would have attended another church. Let's face it: If I had not been the pastor, I would not have attended my own church. I had become a harsh and legalistic person. I demanded that Julia and the children attend every church function, and I didn't want them to do anything to embarrass me.

My formula for living the Christian life didn't work. I believed I had failed God, my family, my church and anyone who believed in me. Finally I came to grips with reality and admitted that I was unfit for ministry. In 1979, I resigned my pastorate. My vision had died along with my dream to make my life count for Christ.[1]

As I look back over all the things I tried to do to live the Christian life, none of them were wrong. Why, then, did I fail so miserably? Because the Christian life is not lived by the works of the flesh but by faith. There really is only one Christian life, and that life is in Christ (see Col. 3:4). If we try to live the Christian life by our own strength and resources, we will crash and burn.

The key to victorious Christian living is "Christ in you, the hope of glory" (Col. 1:27). The Christian life is a supernatural life that enables us to do all things through Christ (see Phil. 4:13). Apart from him, we can do nothing (see John 15:5). We may generate a lot of heat and smoke, but as Armin Gesswein said when he spoke to a Freedom in Christ staff retreat in 1998, "If the Holy Spirit doesn't do it, there's nothing to it."

Most of us enter the Christian life thinking that we will do whatever it takes to live it. We exert a lot of energy and follow all the formulas, but we always come up short. Why? Because all that our flesh can do is fail. The Bible says "the flesh counts for nothing" (John 6:63). God had to strike down the overzealous Paul in order for him to finally say, "We are the true circumcision, who worship in the Spirit of God and glory in Christ Jesus and put no confidence in the flesh" (Phil. 3:3, *NASB*). When the disciples asked Jesus what it took to do the works of God (or to live the Christian life), He gave them a startling answer: "The work of God is this: to believe in the one he has sent" (John 6:29).

Don't let the simplicity and profundity of Jesus' words escape you. He is saying that the work of God is done by believing in Jesus. If you truly live by faith in all that Jesus is and all that He has done, you will live a liberated life in Christ.

If we could do it on our own, we would take credit for it and say, "Look what I did!" Hannah Whitall Smith says, "Rather than admit helplessness, men will undergo many painful sacrifices, if only self may share the glory. A religion of bondage always exalts self. It is what I do— my efforts, my fasting, my sacrifice, my prayers. But a religion of freedom leaves nothing for self to glory in: it is all Christ and what He does."[2]

It's humbling to admit that there isn't another program, a better method, a conference, a counselor or a self-help book that will allow us to live the Christian life. I just read an e-mail from a person with a long-standing problem that has brought him incredible grief. He said his response was to "redouble his efforts." That is the definition of a fanatic.

Probe

What would you think of a person who had lost his way and then decided to double his efforts to get "unlost"? What would you advise him to do? If you could step back and take a look at all you have tried to do, how would you advise yourself?

Journal

_____

_____

_____

_____

_____

Notes

1. Neil T. Anderson and Mike and Julia Quarles, *Freedom from Addiction* (Ventura, Calif.: Regal Books, 1996), pp. 55, 56.
2. Hannah Whitall Smith, *The Christian's Secret of a Happy Life* (Old Tappan, N.J.: Fleming H. Revell, 1952), p. 169.

DAY 78

Thought for Today: You are a child of God, not a hired servant in His household.

But when the time had fully come, God sent his Son, born of a woman, born under law, to redeem those under law, that we might receive the full rights of sons.

GALATIANS 4:4,5

Do you recall the story of Devedas, the dedicated young man in India? David Seamands said that Devedas became excited after hearing him refer to John Wesley in a sermon. He quoted Wesley as saying that he became "an altogether Christian," and that while he had earlier had the religion of a servant, now he had the religion of a "son."

Devedas, whose name means "servant of God," came to see Rev. Seamands and said that he had never realized that he had literally been living up to his name, "servant of God." "I have been thinking, feeling and living not like a family member should, but like a servant does."[1]

Because everyone in India clearly understands the difference between a servant and a son, Seamands said to him, "Devedas, let's do some role-playing. You be the servant in the family and I'll be the son. Let's live out a day in their lives from morning to bedtime and see what the differences are." Devedas agreed, and soon the two were really getting into it, putting into words the differences between their roles. Seamands wrote:

> The servant is accepted and appreciated on the basis of what he does, the child on the basis of who he is. The servant starts the day anxious and worried, wondering if his work will really please his master. The child rests in the secure love of his family. The servant is accepted because of his productivity and performance. The child belongs because of his position as a person. At the end of the day, the servant has peace of mind only if he is sure he has proven his worth by his work. The next morning his anxiety begins again. The child can be secure all day, and know that tomorrow won't change his status. When a servant fails, his whole position is at stake; he might lose his job. When a child fails, he will be grieved because he has hurt his parents, and he will be corrected and disciplined. But he is not afraid of being thrown out. His basic confidence is in belonging and being loved, and his performance does not change the stability of his position.[2]

Jesus said, "I no longer call you servants, because a servant does not know his master's business. Instead, I have called you friends, for everything that I learned from my Father I have made known to you" (John 15:15). First John 3:2 says, "Now we are children of God," and 1 John 5:19 says, "We know that we are children of God." If we could see ourselves as God sees us—as His dearly loved children—everything would change.

The Bible does say that we are bond servants of God, but we are to be bonded to Him as sons who serve their parents. Like the older brother of the prodigal son in Luke 15, we often see ourselves only as servants. He said to his father, "Look! All these years I've been slaving for you and never disobeyed your orders" (v. 29). On the other hand, the prodigal son had "squandered [his father's] property with prostitutes" (Luke 15:30), so he had no good deeds to rely on. All he had was his relationship with his father—his status as a son. Which brother received what the father had for him? Both did, because they were both sons.

While it is true that the prodigal son performed badly and failed miserably, his status as a son wasn't affected. What did he do to enjoy the benefits of being his father's son? He simply admitted his wrong and went back to his father, who willingly received him.

We have all failed our heavenly Father and will likely fail again. We are growing Christians, not perfect Christians. The question is, How are we going to handle our mistakes and failures? You could blame somebody else or rationalize the mistake in order to keep your job as a servant. You could deny your failure and try to hide it, hoping God won't find out! Or you could admit it openly to your heavenly Father, who is "faithful and just and will forgive us our sins and purify us from all unrighteousness" (1 John 1:9).

Don't we need to do anything to live the Christian life, you ask? Yes, but whether you do it or not, or how you do it, doesn't affect whether you will remain a child of God. If you fail to be a good steward of what God has entrusted to you, you may end up feeding the hogs, but you would still be His child.

The son serves willingly and gladly, not because he must or ought or should, but because it is his delight to do so. King David, the psalmist of Israel, said, "Your commands are my delight" (Ps. 119:143), and "Your law is my delight" (119:174). The apostle Paul said, "For in my inner being I delight in God's law" (Rom. 7:22).

Probe

Read over the parable of the prodigal son in Luke 15:11-32. Which son do you identify with? What can you learn about God from this? About yourself?

Journal

_____
_____
_____
_____
_____

Notes

1. David Seamands, *Healing Grace* (Wheaton, Ill.: Victor Books, 1988), pp. 22, 23.
2. Ibid.

DAY 79

Thought for Today: We are what we are by the grace of God.

For sin shall not be your master, because you are
not under law, but under grace.
ROMANS 6:14

As I struggled to live the Christian life and find freedom, I sought to apply what I learned. I had been taught, and I believed, that the key was to spend daily quiet times with God in Bible study and prayer. I didn't view these times with God as opportunities to be with my loving heavenly Father. They were a duty I performed to get something from God that enabled me to do what I should (or wanted). Discipleship certainly does include Bible study, and prayer is essential for the growing Christian. But I mistakenly believed that it was my discipline of prayer and study that would change me.

One of the formulas I used for my quiet time was called "The Nine Ps." I selected a Bible passage, and then I went through it nine times. First I perused it; then I pondered it. Then I pushed it, pulled it, penetrated it, pounded it, pulverized it and so on. As I did this, I thought I would get from God what I needed. The late Jack Miller, past president of World Harvest Mission and a proponent of sanctification by faith, calls this method "sanctification by osmosis."

Now, I would be the first to admit there is nothing more encouraging and rewarding than spending time in the Word of God. But just spending time in it won't do it. Neither will gaining an intellectual knowledge of what the Word says. The truth has to penetrate our hearts and be incarnated. You can read the Bible and know all about God, and not know Him at all. The truth has to be appropriated and believed. Just reading and studying the Bible, or even memorizing it, won't necessarily transform our lives.

Born-again believers know that salvation is by grace through faith (see Eph. 2:8,9). God is the initiator and provider; all we have to do is believe and receive. What do we have to do to be saved? We place our faith in what someone else has done. But when it comes to sanctification, for some unknown reason we believe that living the Christian life is up to us. We are saved by faith and we are sanctified by faith. Our walk and our talk only reveal what we have chosen to believe. James says, "I will show you my faith by what I do" (2:18).

A fiery preacher who said that sanctification was not just by faith, was asked, "If it's not by faith, then how is it?" He replied, "You wrestle, fight and pray." The Christian life certainly includes wrestling, fighting and praying, but is that what sanctifies us? Or is the wrestling, fighting and praying a result of our faith? Paul said that we are to fight, but he said the fight was a fight of faith (see 1 Tim. 6:12). In 2 Timothy 4:7 he says, "I have fought the good fight, I have finished the race." How did Paul do that? The rest of the verse reads, "I have kept the faith."

Reading through the book of Acts and Paul's letters, it is amazing to see what he went through and what he accomplished. How did he survive all that persecution and still be able to write to and strengthen the churches? Paul said, "But by the grace of God I am what I am, and his grace to me was not without effect. No, I worked harder than all of them—yet not I, but the grace of God that was with me" (1 Cor. 15:10). Paul gave credit to the grace of God for all He did and all he was.

The issue of grace always takes us back to the Cross. In Galatians 1:6,7, Paul brings a scathing indictment against the Church: "I am astonished that you are so quickly deserting the one who called you by the grace of Christ and are turning to a different gospel—which is really no gospel at all."

How much of your daily life is based on a law or principle that causes you to respond in obedience? How much of your daily life is based on the life of Christ that causes you to respond by faith, according to what God says is true, and then live by the power of the Holy Spirit? The first question relates to living under the law and the second question relates to living under grace. To live by grace through faith requires the life of Christ within us. "For if a law had been given that could impart life, then righteousness would certainly have come by the law" (Gal. 3:21).

To live the Christian life we need to be empowered by the Spirit of God. The Holy Spirit is the Spirit of truth and will lead us into all truth (see John 14:17; 16:13). The Holy Spirit can only function in a dependent way with our heavenly Father, "For He will not speak on His own initiative" (John 16:13, *NASB*). He will lead us into a dependent relationship with our heavenly Father as well. Then we will live a victorious Christian life.

Probe

Being filled with the Spirit of God is a conscious choice we make. For the next week, try starting your day by declaring your dependency upon God and then asking Him to fill you with His Holy Spirit. Possibly you may need to do that several times a day when you are tempted or find yourself slipping back into your old patterns of the flesh.

Journal

_____

_____

_____

_____

_____

DAY 80

Thought for Today: Life is a gift.

How much more will those who receive God's abundant provision of grace and of the gift of righteousness reign in life through the one man, Jesus Christ.
ROMANS 5:17

After we moved to Atlanta in 1990, our desire was to purchase a house. However, I had poor credit and an inconsistent record of employment. I had been with Grace Ministries for only one year and had to raise my own support.

We signed a lease-purchase agreement on a house and moved in. We had to make a substantial down payment and spend several thousand dollars to fix up the house. At the end of the year we applied for a loan. While Julia and I sat in an office, talking to the mortgage-loan people, they discovered that a judgment had been filed against me seven years earlier, although I knew nothing about it. The people who filed it had also forgotten it, but it was still on my record. To make matters worse, the judgment had been accumulating interest at 12 percent a year. I had no earthly hope of paying it off.

I felt crushed. Now I couldn't get a loan, and we would lose all the money we had put into the house. We would have to move again. I walked out of the office in a state of shock. Julia turned to me and said, "There was a picture of a ship, the USS Victory, on the wall in that office. I kept looking at it and thinking, *Victory.*"

I said, "Yeah, sure, some victory." I was willing to do practically anything to get a loan, but what could I do?

As I drove back to the office, a Bible verse came to mind: "But thanks be to God! He gives us the victory through our Lord Jesus Christ" (1 Cor. 15:57). Then, in my mind, I heard God say, "Mike, I have given you the victory. Who are you going to believe—Me or your circumstances?"

My thought response was, *OK, God, I'm going to believe You. You say that You have given me the victory, so I receive it right now. Thank You for it.*

Then I had a peace about the situation and never worried about it again.

Later, with the help of an attorney friend, I was able to pay off the judgment at a fraction of the original amount, without any interest, and to have it removed from my record. We secured our loan and closed when interest rates were the lowest in many years. I experienced victory not when we signed the new loan but when I believed God and received His promise. Even if we hadn't acquired the loan and had lost the house, God had given me the victory.

Your situation may not look like victory, and you may not feel victorious. But God's Word is clear: He has given us the victory. It is up to us to believe it.[1]

I suppose most of us would like to have a simple formula for living the Christian life—something we can control. That is essentially what we had under the law. Under God's grace we have something far better. We are "servants of a new covenant, not of the letter, but of the Spirit; for the letter kills, but the Spirit gives life" (2 Cor. 3:6, *NASB*).

Many people in counseling say, "Just tell me what to do and I'll do it." They want somebody to tell them what is right and what is wrong and then they will try to do it. They want to say, "I earned it." God gave us an opportunity to earn it under the law, but nobody could. Now He has given us everything we need for life and godliness (see 2 Pet. 1:3). All we have to do is receive it by faith. He says that He has blessed us with every spiritual blessing in Christ (see Eph 1:3). If we are not experiencing those blessings, maybe we haven't swallowed our pride and gratefully received what we could not earn.

When I turned 61, I sent out a newsletter titled "Reflections from a Man Who Has Lived Half a Century Plus a Decade, or The Ramblings of an Old Man." I said this was the greatest time of my life because I had finally learned that the Christian life is not up to me. From beginning to end, from salvation to glorification and everything in between, the Christian life is up to God. If that is true, then my responsibility is to trust Him to do in and through me what He wants to do.

One of the most difficult but rewarding lessons we will ever learn is how to receive.

Probe

Why is it so hard to receive a free gift from God? Choose which category would most describe you:

1. I didn't know there was anything to receive.
2. It was too good to be true.
3. I didn't deserve it.
4. Nothing of value ever comes freely.

Journal

_____

_____

_____

_____

_____

Note

1. Neil T. Anderson and Mike and Julia Quarles, *Freedom from Addiction* (Ventura, Calif.: Regal Books, 1996), pp. 155, 156.

DAY 81

Thought for Today: A mistake is never a failure unless you fail to learn from it.

I well remember them, and my soul is downcast within me. Yet this I call to mind and therefore I have hope: Because of the Lord's great love we are not consumed, for his compassions never fail. They are new every morning; great is your faithfulness.
LAMENTATIONS 3:20-23

One of the biggest barriers in my life was the fear of failure. I did everything I could to not fail, which only made failure more imminent. It's true that we are free to fail, but there's a distinction between being free to fail and being a failure.

In October 1988, I found my freedom in Christ, but I had to face the ongoing discipline proceedings of the presbytery. The assistant pastor, a caring person, was also chairman of the ministers' committee. One of his duties was to inform me that I would face discipline. When he gave me the bad news, I had some unusual thoughts: *It looks as though I'm in for more disgrace and public humiliation. I don't want that, but it's OK. No matter what they do or think, I'm still a child of God and I'm alive and free in Christ. Nothing can change that.* Ordinarily such a meeting would have devastated me, but I walked away with an unusual joy and peace in my heart.

Many would consider me a colossal failure because of my alcoholic past. But my identity and my sense of worth no longer come from my performance and the opinion of others. My identity comes from God. He said that I am His dearly loved child. In addition, I am a saint, Christ's friend, God's workmanship and complete in Christ. My life is now hidden with Christ in God.[1]

Before I could appropriate my identity in Christ and find my freedom in Him, I had to admit that in and of myself I was a complete failure. That is the last thing we want to admit, isn't it? Our self-respect and sense of worth are hanging by a single thread, and we will do anything to keep from breaking it. But God slowly unravels that thread of self-sufficiency until it snaps and we fall gently into the arms of Jesus.

G. K. Chesterton said, "There is nothing that fails like success."[2] Why? Because the world's definition of success is impersonal and abstract and is usually measured by money, possessions, status, fame and/or acclaim. That kind of success misses the most important elements: people and relationships. Many successful people have sacrificed their families on the altar of success. Now that is true failure!

The best thing that can happen to us is to realize that in and of ourselves, all we can do is fail. Everything we accomplish will one day be left behind. We cannot appropriate our identity in Christ and receive the grace of God if we don't perceive the need. That is probably the reason the Lord said, "It is easier for a camel to go through the eye of a needle than for a rich man to enter the kingdom of God" (Matt. 19:24). If we are self-righteous and self-sufficient as was the rich young ruler (see Matt. 19:16-24), we too would probably walk away from the Lord.

Liberated Christians have given up on finding *self*-worth and *self*-acceptance. They have found their identity and worth in being children of God. They are free to fail. They simply live their lives by faith in the power of the Holy Spirit and leave the results to God. Such knowledge brings an incredible sense of peace and freedom. Dr. Neil Anderson has said repeatedly that Freedom in Christ Ministries was born out of brokenness. Our lives are filled with daily mistakes, but a mistake is never a failure unless you fail to learn from it.

Probe
As a Christian, how would you define failure? How would you define success?

Journal

_____

_____

_____

_____

_____

Notes
1. Neil T. Anderson and Mike and Julia Quarles, *Freedom from Addiction* (Ventura, Calif.: Regal Books, 1996), pp. 146, 147.
2. G. K. Chesterton, *Heretics* (London: Bodley Head, 1960), p. 13.

DAY 82

Thought for Today: Defeat is when we say, "My will be done." Victory is when we say, "Thy will be done."

Peter declared, "Even if all fall away, I will not." "I tell you the truth," Jesus answered, "today—yes, tonight—before the rooster crows twice you yourself will disown me three times." But Peter insisted emphatically, "Even if I have to die with you, I will never disown you." And all the others said the same.

MARK 14:29-31

I had no clue how to solve my problem. I was hopelessly ensnared in the bondage of defeat. I had exhausted all my resources and there was nothing left for me to try.

As I sat in my chair in a deep depression, I realized that everyone had given up on me. My pastor had said, "I don't know anything else to tell you." Even my closest friend gave up trying to help me. As a last-ditch effort, he gave me a set of tapes.

I looked at the label on the album: "Victorious Christian Living" by Dr. Bill and Anabel Gillham. About a year earlier I had purchased the advanced set. After listening to one tape, I hadn't listened to any more. These tapes were the basic set in the same series. Immediately I thought, *I don't want to listen to these. His theology doesn't agree with mine.*

Then another thought came: *Your theology is not doing you much good!* I decided to listen to the tapes with an open mind.[1] It was a turning point in my recovery.

How could anyone who started out with such zeal, commitment and determination end up like I had? Because the Christian life is not lived by even the most sincere efforts. The Christian life is not just difficult to live by our own strength, it's downright impossible. It's a supernatural life that can only be lived by faith in the power of the Holy Spirit.

Peter found this out when he told Jesus that even if all the other disciples fell away, he would not. He was willing to go to prison and lay down his very life for Jesus. But that wasn't enough. We know the outcome;

Peter not only didn't lay down his life, he denied that he even knew Jesus.

Let's not be too hard on Peter, because you and I have done the same thing. If we haven't done it in words, we've done it with our actions. We start off with such good intentions of serving God and living for Him. Why do so many of us end up in abject failure? How can Christians degenerate into drunks, druggies, adulterers, thieves and worse?

Was Peter sincere when he made his declaration? Of course he was. He wept bitterly when he failed to stand up for Jesus. Before he boastfully proclaimed his loyalty, Satan had demanded the right to sift Peter like wheat (see Luke 22:31). Jesus didn't stop him. He only instructed Peter by saying, "I have prayed for you, that your faith may not fail; and you, when once you have turned again, strengthen your brothers" (Luke 22:32, *NASB*). What right did Satan have to sift Peter like wheat, and what did Peter have to turn from? The context reveals a dispute among the brothers as to who was the greatest among them (see Luke 22:24). Pride is a killer!

When I was at a Christian treatment center, the director told me, "You need to make a commitment that you will never take another drink, no matter what happens. If someone comes in and beats you within an inch of your life, trying to force you to take a drink, you won't do it, no matter what." I don't believe that's good advice. I have seen too many people who struggle with addiction make the same basic commitment and end up failing just as badly as Peter did. The idea and the desired result are good, but the dependence on the person's resolve and commitment sets them up for a colossal failure.

Instead, we would encourage you to say: I place all my trust and confidence in the Lord. I put no confidence in the flesh and I declare myself to be dependent upon God. I know that I cannot save myself or set myself free by my own efforts and resources. I know that apart from Christ I can do nothing (see John 15:5). I know that all temptation is an attempt to get me to live my life independently of God. But God has provided a way of escape (see 1 Cor. 10:13). That is the first declaration of "The Overcomer's Covenant in Christ," (found at the back of this book).

Jesus said: "You will know the truth, and the truth will set you free" (John 8:32). We are set free not by how we behave or even what we profess, but by what we believe. People do not always live according to what they profess, but they always live according to what they truly believe. We would encourage you to begin each day by declaring the truth that sets you free in The Overcomer's Covenant in Christ, by affirming who you are in Christ and by reading through the "Who I Am in Christ" section found at the back of this book.

God has not called us to live up to an impossible standard in our own strength. He has placed us in Christ, and Christ lives in us. In Him we have everything we need to live victoriously. We put no confidence in the flesh but gladly live dependent upon Him.

Probe

Read "The Overcomer's Covenant in Christ" out loud. What new insights have you gleaned since the first time you read it?

Journal

_____

_____

_____

_____

_____

Note
1. Neil T. Anderson and Mike and Julia Quarles, *Freedom from Addiction* (Ventura, Calif.: Regal Books, 1996), pp. 119, 120.

DAY 83

Thought for Today: Our service for God may be the greatest enemy of our devotion to Him.

I have been crucified with Christ and I no longer live, but Christ lives in me. The life I live in the body, I live by faith in the Son of God, who loved me and gave himself for me.

GALATIANS 2:20

In his book *Grace Walk*, my good friend Steve McVey tells how he learned to trust Christ to be his life.

It was 1:00 A.M. on October 6, 1990, that I lay on my face in my office, crying. The previous year had brought me to a place of absolute brokenness. I had prayed for God to make me stronger, but He had a different plan. He was making me weaker. So there I lay, broken and hopeless. In seventeen hours I would have to stand in my pulpit on Sunday evening and deliver a "State of the Church Address." Either I could build a straw man of success or I could tell the truth. I didn't have the strength to pretend or the courage to be honest, so I prayed and cried. When I finished, I prayed and cried some more.

It didn't make sense. Had God brought me to this church only to set me up for failure? Couldn't He see I was doing every-thing I knew how for Him? I couldn't imagine what more He expected from me than my best. And I had done my best. *God, what more do You want from me?* Silence. At this moment He seemed light-years away. The weight of failure was suffocating, and not just my failure as a pastor. I felt like a failure as a Christian. I dedicated my whole adult life to God to do His work. If that wasn't enough, what more did He want?

I had left a church in Alabama where I felt very successful, where people loved and affirmed me. Our church was recognized for its numerical growth, and we led the denomination in baptisms in our county. I received recognition from the Jaycees for being an "outstanding religious leader." I served on various denominational committees and held office in our ministers' conference. For five years I believed I was a successful pastor.

I had moved from the small town to the big city (Atlanta) and there were lots of people just waiting to be reached! I pulled out my box of sugar-stick sermons and previously proven programs and went to work for God. But nothing happened. This was a new experience and I was puzzled. I reassessed the situation, prayed harder for God's help, took a deep breath and launched a second wave of church growth plans. We had sanctified pep rallies with our Sunday School teachers, strategy discussions with our newly formed Dream Team. But as the months passed, the dream began to look more like a nightmare. I knew that our church was in a sorry state. For the first time in my seventeen years of ministry, a church I served had declined in attendance in my first year. I was appalled![1]

Steve goes on to share how God used this experience to bring him to the end of himself and his self-sufficiency. He found out who he was in Christ and discovered the peace of God, the joy of the Lord and his freedom in Christ. One day he told me, "I had spent all my Christian life trying to make Jesus my Lord, and then I learned that I could just trust Him to be my life."

So what's the difference? A short answer would be, "Everything." We are trying to make Jesus our Lord when He already is. We just need to know it and choose to believe it. No matter how hard we try, we can't make Jesus our Lord by our own efforts. It is the difference between grace and law, between resting and striving. We are not driven to the Lord; we are called. Driven people have a hard time hearing the call. Those who trust Him to be their life are living by faith in His resources.

Here's what Steve said he learned:

God's purpose is not that we should rededicate our self with all
its abilities, but that we should give up all hope in self. We sometimes try to live for Him when He wants to live His life through
us. It is important to see the distinction here. To ask God to help
us live for Him is to request some sort of divine blessing on our
effort to "do what He wants us to do." But that isn't what God
desires. He isn't interested in what we can do for Him. Christ is
interested in living His life through us.[2]

That's good news! We trust in Him and He furnishes all the
resources and does all the work. Now, it wouldn't be such good news if
someone said to you, "Good news! I'm going to let you come over to my
house and paint it for me." But that's the way a lot of us view living the
Christian life. We're saved by grace, but now we've really got to get to
work and try to live the Christian life.

Christianity is not an act; it is a real thing. If we really believe that
Christ is our life (see Col. 3:4) and if it is no longer we who live but Christ
who lives in us (see Gal. 2:20), we will live real Christian lives and won't
be struggling, striving, straining and stewing.

Our service for God may be the greatest enemy of our devotion to
Him. Jesus said, "Come to me, all you who are weary and burdened, and
I will give you rest. Take my yoke upon you and learn from me, for I am
gentle and humble in heart, and you will find rest for your souls. For my
yoke is easy and my burden is light" (Matt. 11:28-30). Jesus is telling us
that the real Christian life is characterized by rest and is easy. He also said
that His burden is light.

Probe

Have you ever considered the possibility that your service for God is the
greatest barrier to your devotion to Him? Does God need us to serve
Him, or do we need to relate intimately with Him, which leads to a Spirit-
filled life of service to others?

Journal

_____

_____

_____

_____

_____

Notes
1. Steve McVey, *Grace Walk* (Eugene, Ore.: Harvest House Publishers, 1995), pp. 11-13. Used by permission.
2. Ibid., pp. 34, 35.

DAY 84

Thought for Today: If you're struggling to live the Christian life, it's not the Christian life.

Christ means the end of the struggle for righteousness-by-the-law.
ROMANS 10:4, PHILLIPS

In the summer of 1983, I seemed to have gone down as far as I could. That was when I woke up from a blackout and found myself handcuffed to a hospital bed and arrested for public drunkenness.

But I was mistaken; my life spiraled from bad to worse. As I continued to try to work as a stockbroker, I would often leave my office discouraged and full of self-loathing. I would drive around aimlessly and drink. Julia lived in fear that I would kill someone. She prayed that if I had a wreck I would be the one killed, and no one else. She prayed this way because she believed that as a Christian I would go to heaven. As my drinking continued to drag on, she and a lot of my friends began to doubt that I was even a Christian.

As much self-hatred as I felt, I never doubted my relationship with Christ. I knew that God loved me and accepted me. I expected to slip into heaven by the skin of my teeth. If I had doubted my salvation, I probably would have had nothing to live for. But I knew the Lord had an answer and maybe one day I would find it. For months I hung on to a single verse from the Bible, Ecclesiastes 9:4, which says: "Anyone who is among the living has hope—even a live dog is better off than a dead lion!"

Some may have thought my many disasters would bring me to my senses. Addiction, however, doesn't respond to common sense, logic or clear thinking. Alcoholics Anonymous calls it insanity, which they define as "continuing to do the same thing while expecting different results." It is insanity; and everyone struggling with an addiction has experienced it. However, it would be more accurate to call it spiritual bondage.

The year after my jail experience, the church discipline committee called me before them for my continued drunkenness. They sent me to a secular treatment center, but I was drunk within a week after I got out. I eventually lost my job and all our money and savings. I lost the respect of my wife, my family and my friends.

When Julia kicked me out of the house, I was almost glad, because I was consumed with guilt and despair. Her rejection was easier for me to handle than her love. Ironically, kicking me out was the most loving and redemptive thing she could have done. It paved the way for healing and restoration.[1]

I had become a Christian in 1970, yet I struggled to live the Christian life for 18 years. I was told many different things to do, and I tried most of them. I can honestly say that I don't know of one thing I tried that actually helped me. Most of the time I lived in defeat and bondage. The staff of Freedom in Christ Ministries estimates that only about 15 percent of Bible-believing Christians are living in freedom. What a tragedy!

Romans 6 tells us over and over again that we have been set free from sin (see vv. 2,3,8,11,14,17,18,22). Romans 10:4 says that "Christ is the end of the law so that there may be righteousness for everyone who believes." *Phillips* translates it this way: "Christ means the end of the struggle for righteousness-by-the-Law." What does that mean? It means that we can give up struggling, striving, straining and failing. It means that we have been given the perfect righteousness of Christ as a gift (see Rom. 5:17). It means that we are no longer under law to struggle to attain, to keep our reputation, to maintain an appearance or to do whatever we believe we need to be doing. Christ has redeemed us from the curse of the law (see Gal. 3:13).

According to Paul, as soon as we put ourselves under law (taking upon ourselves the responsibility for doing something in our own strength and wisdom), we cut ourselves off from Christ and His grace: "All who rely on observing the law are under a curse, for it is written: 'Cursed is everyone who does not continue to do everything written in the Book of the Law'" (Gal. 3:10). When we live by the law, we are still Christians, but we are living as though we aren't.

We are living under the law when we try harder to do God's will in our own strength and resources. This makes for go-getters, high achievers, hard chargers, perfectionists, type A personalities, driven people, workaholics and supermoms, who eventually burn up, blow out or go into full-blown sin and rebellion. Who can live the perfect life? Sooner or later we hit the wall. Fortunately, it is when we come to the end of ourselves that we begin to learn that we are not under law but under grace.

Probe

Does Bible study, prayer and church attendance seem like a duty to you? Do you have an inward desire to practice those Christian disciplines or do you feel you have to practice them in order to be a good Christian? What do you think Martin Luther meant when he said, "The law says 'Do this,' and never is it done. Grace says 'Believe in this one and it is already done'"?

Journal

_____

_____

_____

_____

_____

Note
  1. Neil T. Anderson and Mike and Julia Quarles, *Freedom from Addiction* (Ventura, Calif.: Regal Books, 1996), pp. 27, 28.

LIVING FREE IN CHRIST BY FAITH

DAY 85

**Thought for Today: Power for the Christian is in the truth,
but power for the devil is in the lie.**

*It has often thrown him into fire or water to kill him. But if you can do
anything, take pity on us and help us. "If you can?" said Jesus.
"Everything is possible for him who believes."*

MARK 9:22,23

One of the most dramatic turnarounds I (Neil) have witnessed in someone with a belief crisis over spiritual identity occurred in Jenny. I met
her during a conference I was presenting in a church. The church leaders had set up a series of counseling appointments for me between conference sessions, and Jenny was one of those appointments.

Twenty-three-year-old Jenny was a pretty girl with a seemingly
pleasant personality. She had loving parents and came from a good
church. But she was torn up inside, having never experienced anything
but a depressive life. She had bombed out of college and was on the
verge of being fired from her job. She had suffered from eating disorders for several years. Medical treatment for her problems seemed
futile.

Jenny and I sat together for almost two hours at that first meeting.
She claimed to be a Christian, so I challenged her with the biblical truth
of who she was in Christ. I couldn't tell if she was tracking with me or
not, but I kept sharing with her the good news of her spiritual identity.
Finally she said, "Are you always this positive?"

"It's not a matter of being positive, Jenny," I said. "It's a matter of
believing the truth. Because of your spiritual union with God, this is
who you are in Christ." She left the meeting with a glimmer of hope.

Later I had an opportunity to sit down with Jenny privately. "I am
not going to try to get you to change your behavior, Jenny," I said. "Your
behavior isn't your problem."

"I've always been told that my behavior is my problem," she said, looking a little surprised at my statement. "Everyone is trying to change my behavior."

"I'm not worried about your behavior," I replied. "It's your beliefs I'm interested in. I want you to consider changing your beliefs about who God is and who you are in Christ. You're not a failure. You're not a sick individual who is a problem to your parents and to your church. You are a child of God, no better or worse than any other person at this conference. I want you to start believing it, because it's the truth."

For the first time in her life, Jenny had been affirmed as the person of value to God that she truly was. And she began to believe it. After our time together, she studied the Word of God and prayed and interacted with supportive people. A dramatic transformation took place in her. In fact, the changes were nothing less than miraculous.

When Jenny visited her father, he beamed as he said, "I've never seen Jenny this happy and content. She's a different person."

She was also a completely different employee. After two weeks, her boss called her in and showed her the performance review he had prepared while she was gone. It was so bad that she deserved to be terminated. "But you've changed, Jenny," he said. "I'm not going to fire you; I'm going to give you a raise."

The change in Jenny was the result of her changed beliefs about God and herself. She was a child of God before I met her, but she had never heard it in a way that caused her to believe the truth of who she really is. The transformation took place when she started walking by faith according to the truth. Her behavior began to conform to the truth of her spiritual identity. Will Jenny's behavior continue to improve? Yes, as long as she continues to believe God and live in harmony with Him by obeying His commandments. Can she resort to old habits if she stops believing and obeying God? Sadly, yes. We all can.[1]

As people hear the truth of who they are in Christ, many have the same reaction Jenny did. "This is like the power of positive thinking. I just have to make myself believe it." No! And again I say, no! This is not like the power of positive thinking. Just thinking positive thoughts can lead one astray, because those thoughts may not be based on the truth.

The power of positive thinking might make you feel better about yourself for a while, but if that thinking is not based on truth, it is just another form of deception. The power of believing the truth is based on God's eternal and unchanging Word. That is what will set you free.

Probe
How can the "self-esteem" and the "power of positive thinking" movements be nothing more than a humanistic approach to picking ourselves up by our own bootstraps? What is the inevitable result if we try to change someone's behavior without changing what they believe?

Journal
_____

_____

_____

_____

_____

Note
1. Neil T. Anderson, *Victory over the Darkness* (Ventura, Calif.: Regal Books, 1990), pp. 64-67.

DAY 86

Thought for Today: The fruit of the Spirit is self-control.

While Jesus was still speaking, some men came from the house of Jairus, the synagogue ruler. "Your daughter is dead," they said. "Why bother the teacher any more?" Ignoring what they said, Jesus told the synagogue ruler, "Don't be afraid; just believe."
MARK 5:35,36

In 1994, my precious 16-month-old granddaughter, Aryele, was in intensive care at a hospital. She had several seizures and her condition didn't look good. Aryele was in one of the best children's hospitals in the world, but the doctors didn't know what was wrong. Her parents, grandparents, uncles and aunts would have done anything for her, but we were helpless. All we could do was cry out to God and confess our total dependence on Him. Audrey, her mother, said, "She's in God's hands." It was a good place to be.

On Saturday, Aryele lay limp and listless. By Monday afternoon we took turns being the designated "chaser" to follow her around the hospital halls. That night she was released after a "miraculous" recovery. Our hope and trust was in God. As Ephesians 2:4-7 says,

> But because of his great love for us, God, who is rich in mercy, made us alive with Christ even when we were dead in transgressions—it is by grace you have been saved. And God raised us up with Christ and seated us with him in the heavenly realms in Christ Jesus, in order that in the coming ages he might show the incomparable riches of his grace, expressed in his kindness to us in Christ Jesus.

A wonderful benefit of being free in Christ is rest—not passivity, but rest—from the struggles of life. If you live by faith, you will be active, but the striving will be over. The responsibility to make things happen isn't yours, it is God's. Hannah Whitall Smith said that our responsibility is to trust; God's responsibility is to work.

Many Christian workers and pastors are facing spiritual burnout. Perhaps they're trying to carry a responsibility that isn't theirs. After all, sheep are not burden-bearing animals. Hebrews 4:10 says: "For anyone who enters God's rest also rests from his own work, just as God did from his." Working in our own strength prevents us from finding God's rest. Hebrews 3:19 sums it up: "So we see that they were not able to enter, because of their unbelief."

Many people believe the way to find rest is to be in control of their circumstances and other people. Yet, controllers seldom find rest for their souls or have any lasting peace. If you are trying to control people and events, then guess who's not in control? The fruit of the Spirit is not spouse control, child control or staff control. It is self-control, which only comes when we are filled with the Spirit.

Bill Gillham says that controlling things is God's job description. If you're trying to do God's job, you are going to be at cross-purposes with Him. Each of us has areas in our lives that frustrate us because they are not under our control—children, health, finances, job security, the future. We might have some input in these matters, but we definitely aren't in control. The good news is that God is in control, and He "works for the good of those who love him" (Rom. 8:28).

My friend Ray Alton says, "The best way to lose your mind is to concentrate on not losing it." And the best way to be out of control is to concentrate on being in control. Trusting God takes the control out of our hands and puts it where it belongs. Trusting God to work everything for good can test our faith when a granddaughter is in ICU after her fifth seizure.

Jairus faced this problem when he came to Jesus. Jairus fell at Jesus' feet and told Him that his daughter was dying. "Please come and put your hands on her so that she will be healed and live," he said (Mark 5:23). So Jesus went with him, and a large crowd followed. But while Jesus was still speaking, some men came from Jairus's house and told him, "Your daughter is dead. . . . Why bother the teacher any more?" (v. 35).

Jairus could have taken these men at their word, returned home and made preparations to bury his daughter. But Scripture says, "Ignoring what they said, Jesus told the synagogue ruler, 'Don't be afraid; just believe'" (v. 36). Sometimes a crisis like that helps us to see the need to trust in a supreme being. The life of my granddaughter, like Jairus's daughter's life, was taken out of my hands. Thank God we had Jesus to turn to.

When we hear the voice of the enemy say, "Don't bother Jesus, you can handle this yourself," we need to do what Jairus did: "Ignoring what they said . . . ," and then follow Jesus' instructions, "Don't be afraid; just believe." We will have to ignore the advice of experts, professionals, newspapers, TV personalities and even our own feelings when they run contrary to Scripture.

Faith is never tested in a vacuum. It is tested the most during a crisis, which reveals who we really are. We exercise our faith in the hard-core, everyday circumstances of life. Jesus arrived at the house of Jairus where people were already crying and wailing in mourning. He asked what all the commotion was about, then told them the child wasn't dead, but asleep. "But they laughed at him. After he put them all out, he . . . went in where the child was. He took her by the hand and said to her, . . . 'Little girl, I say to you, get up!' Immediately the girl stood up and walked around" (vv. 40-42).

Never doubt the word of God. When He is in control, we are free to rest in Christ.[1]

Probe

Have you been more inclined to control others or to find self-control? What is the false belief that motivates people to become controllers?

Journal

_____

_____

_____

_____

_____

Note
1. Neil T. Anderson and Mike and Julia Quarles, *Freedom from Addiction*, (Ventura, Calif.: Regal Books, 1996), pp. 157-160.

DAY 87

Thought for Today: We don't have to bear fruit; we have to abide in Christ, and then we will bear fruit.

I am the vine, you are the branches; he who abides in Me, and I in him, he bears much fruit; for apart from Me you can do nothing.
JOHN 15:5, NASB

A Christian counselor who uses our resources in working with addicts shared a letter with me that one of his counselees wrote to her pastor. The following is an excerpt from her letter:

I have fought alcoholism off and on for the past twenty years—with little success and much unhappiness. I have honestly tried every available avenue I knew of and have continually failed at sobriety. I had given up on ever being obedient to God in this area. Richard began counseling me several months ago when I was at yet another low in my life. Through prayer, genuine concern and a gentle spirit, Richard has utilized several Christian books and studies that have helped to change my heart and life. First he had me read *The Bondage Breaker* by Neil Anderson to show me how spiritual conflicts played a part in my alcoholism. We then worked through a study called *Freedom from Addiction Workbook* by Anderson and Quarles, which has taken two and a half months to complete. Other study books he provided me are: *Victory over the Darkness* and *Tired of Trying to Measure Up.* Richard has honed in on specific issues, such as my identity in Christ, security, self-esteem and performance issues. Primarily, the Holy Spirit has worked through Richard to show me that a "works" oriented approach (I have striven to be sober through the years) will always fail. It has been through surrender, God's grace and realizing my position as a child of God that has truly freed me at last from the obsession to drink or use drugs.

This young woman discovered exactly what I and many others have found: a works-oriented approach to freedom will always fail. Why? Because we are set free not by how we behave but by what we believe.

There were many days when I would spend an hour reading my Bible and praying, then be drunk before dark. I talked to a man struggling with addiction who told me he worked through the *Freedom from Addiction Workbook* in two weeks. He is still struggling. He was approaching it as some magic exercise or quick fix to solve his problem. But the purpose of the workbook is to help people renew their minds with the truth that sets them free.

We need to fix in our minds that nothing *we* do will help us or change us. We are set free not by how we behave but by what we believe. Many Christians sit in church every Sunday and hear the truth, then walk out the door completely unchanged. Going to church and listening to sermons won't change you. Believing the truth will. Jesus said, "Then you will know the truth, and the truth will set you free" (John 8:32).

Suppose we took all the Christian books ever written on how to live the Christian life and listed everything they told us to do. How long would that list be? Could anyone do all the things listed in all the books? So what does it take to live the Christian life? More than 400 years ago, Martin Luther wrote:

> It ought to be the first concern of every Christian to lay aside all confidence in works and, increasingly, to strengthen faith alone, and through faith to grow in the knowledge, not of works, but of Christ alone. . . . Thus, when the Jews asked Christ as related in John 6:28 what they must do "to be doing the works of God," He brushed aside the multitude of works which he saw they did in great profusion and suggested one work, saying, "This is the work of God that you believe in him whom he has sent" (John 6:29).[1]

Jesus said there is one work that works: "Believe in Him." What's wrong with doing good works? There is nothing wrong with it; and if you know and believe the truth, you will do many good works. In fact, "We are His workmanship, created in Christ Jesus for good works, which God prepared beforehand, that we should walk in them" (Eph. 2:10, *NASB*).

Behaving a certain way because we think that's what we should be doing is like tying plastic apples on an apple tree. They lack life and substance and are good for nothing. Jesus was very clear about what it took to produce life:

> Remain in me, and I will remain in you. No branch can bear fruit by itself; it must remain in the vine. Neither can you bear fruit unless you remain in me. I am the vine; you are the branches. If a man remains in me and I in him, he will bear much fruit; apart from me you can do nothing (John 15:4,5).

Bob George said, "Finally I learned that Christ did not come to help me serve God. He came to live His life through me!"[2] All Christians have the life of Christ in them, and they are united with Him in one Spirit with the Lord (see 1 Cor. 6:17). The fruit we bear is just the result of abiding in Christ. We don't have to bear fruit, we have to abide in Christ and then we will bear fruit.

Probe

Why do we spend so much time trying to bear fruit (do good works) and so little time learning to abide in Christ? If mankind is able to accomplish something without Christ, how long will it last?

Journal

_____

_____

_____

_____

_____

Notes
1. Harold J. Grimm, ed., *Christian Liberty* (Philadelphia: Fortress Press, 1957), p. 10.
2. Bob George, *Classic Christianity* (Eugene, Ore.: Harvest House Publishers, 1989), p. 52.

DAY 88

Thought for Today: Our feelings are essentially a product of our thought life.

To the Jews who had believed him, Jesus said, "If you hold to my teaching, you are really my disciples. Then you will know the truth, and the truth will set you free."

JOHN 8:31,32

The key to victorious Christian living is believing the truth, regardless of your feelings. Bob George tells a story that vividly illustrates this truth.

Bob had worked with an alcoholic named Pete, who called him one night nearly three years after they had last talked. Pete had been unwilling to take responsibility for his problem and finally stopped seeing Bob.

"It wasn't a very pleasant conversation," Bob recalls. "He asked a favor of me that I was unable to fulfill, to which he responded with a long string of profanity. Finally he spluttered, 'I'm going to get you,' and hung up." Because Bob is an easygoing guy, the call didn't really upset him that much, and he and his wife just went to bed. Fifteen minutes after they turned out the light, they heard a car screech onto their driveway. Bob got up and looked out the window. He saw a wild-eyed man with bushy hair get out of the car. It was Pete, and he was carrying a large butcher knife.

With his heart in his throat, Bob yelled to his wife, "Amy, get in the closet!" Then he ran into his son's room, told him to get under the bed, and grabbed a baseball bat out of the boy's closet. He ran past his daughter's room and told her to hide under her bed, then stopped in the foyer by the front door and waited.

"I could feel my heart racing and my ears straining to hear any noise," Bob said. "For a moment I was tempted to relax, knowing the front door was locked. Then I heard a loud thump as the man put his 200 pounds into a brutal kick. Another kick followed and the door flew open. Instantly the man sprang into the house."

Bob was waiting for him. With all his strength he sent the baseball bat crashing down on Pete's head. Blood spattered against the wall as Pete crumpled. Bob wasn't taking any chances. He hit him again and again until he was sure the guy was unconscious. Horrified at what he had done, he ran to the kitchen and called the police.

Bob finally revealed the catch to this story. "All of this took place that very night—in my mind—while I was lying in my nice, warm bed."

Pete really did call him, but the rest of the story was the fruit of his overactive imagination after Pete had said, "I'm going to get you!" Although Pete didn't follow through on his threat, Bob said his heart was pounding and his body was sweating and trembling with anger from the very thought of having to defend his family. He wrote:

> I experienced these things because of a basic fact about human beings. Our emotions can't distinguish between fact and fantasy. My emotions didn't know that there was no real danger. They simply responded to the messages sent by my brain. It was as if the events described were really happening. That's the danger with error. Whatever we put into our minds will affect our emotions. Our emotions always follow our thoughts. They are responders.[1]

I remember watching a scary movie on TV while my wife was out of town. It scared me silly, and I could hardly go to sleep for thinking about it. Have you ever had an experience like that? There was certainly no danger to me. It was just a movie, but my emotions didn't know that. They were responding perfectly to the messages being sent to them.

Our feelings are essentially a product of our thought life. We have many untrue messages engraved in our memories from past experiences.

We are not in bondage from these experiences, we are in bondage to lies we have believed as a result of the experiences. Such lies can emotionally cripple us even years later. That is why we're transformed by the renewing of our minds and why the truth can set us free.

I grew up in a home where there was no love between my mother and father. They fought violently most of the time. My worst childhood memory is of lying in bed at night, listening to them fight, yell and threaten to kill each other. I was sure I would wake up one day and find one or both of them dead. I felt very insecure, which affected every area of my life for a long time.

I still have those feelings of insecurity from time to time, but I realize now that they are just feelings left over from my past. My security is rooted in Christ, not in the past. When I find myself slipping back into my old ways of thinking, I do what Paul said: "Forgetting what lies behind and reaching forward to what lies ahead, I press on toward the goal for the prize of the upward call of God in Christ Jesus" (Phil. 3:13,14, *NASB*).

Ron Wormser, who traveled with Neil for over six years, has taken more than 700 people through the Steps to Freedom. He says that the hardest people to help are those who live by their emotions. The Christian life will be an emotional roller coaster for highly subjective people. Some have never learned the truth; others simply will not assume responsibility for what they think and will drift wherever their thoughts take them. To live victoriously in Christ, we have to learn how to take *every* thought captive in obedience to Christ (see 2 Cor. 10:5b). If it isn't true, don't think it. Instead, choose to think the truth. "Finally, brothers, whatever is true, whatever is noble, whatever is right, whatever is pure, whatever is lovely, whatever is admirable—if anything is excellent or praiseworthy—think about such things" (Phil. 4:8).

Probe

Can you trace how you feel about yourself to past experiences? Think of the most traumatic experience in your life. How did it shape what you believed about yourself, God and how you were going to live from that time on?

Journal

_____

_____

_____

_____

_____

Note

1. Bob George, *Classic Christianity* (Eugene, Ore.: Harvest House Publishers, 1989), pp. 27, 28.

DAY 89

Thought for Today: Progressive sanctification is the process of making real the truth of who you already are.

Dear friends, now we are children of God, and what we will be has not yet been made known. But we know that when he appears, we shall be like him, for we shall see him as he is. Everyone who has this hope in him purifies himself, just as he is pure.

1 J O H N   3 : 2 , 3

In the book *Voyage of the Dawn Treader* (which is part of the Chronicles of Narnia series), C. S. Lewis gives a vivid picture of our salvation experience in the character of Eustace.

Eustace was a boy who was so awful and nasty that he turned into an ugly, evil dragon. Then he met the lion, Aslan, who represents Christ. Aslan changed him from a dragon into a fine young man. At first Eustace had tried to change himself by scratching and peeling off the layers of his dragon skin. But for every layer that came off, another layer of wrinkled, scaly skin appeared underneath. Finally, Aslan stepped up to do the job. With one painful swipe of his powerful claws, the lion cut to the heart of Eustace's dragon flesh and peeled it away, and Eustace stepped out. One moment, Eustace was a dragon; the next moment, he was a boy. He wasn't part dragon and part boy; he changed from one to the other.

Once we were in the domain of darkness; now we're in the kingdom of God. Once we were in the flesh; now we're in the Spirit. Once we were darkness; now we are light. Once we were sinful by nature; now we are partakers of the divine nature.

Our spiritual identity is anchored to the truth that we are saints who sin, but we are no longer sinners. Because of God's grace and our faith in Christ, we have been born again. We are spiritually alive, and we enjoy a relationship with God like Adam and Eve did before the Fall. Being in Christ, we are forgiven, justified and acceptable to God. This truth is usually referred to as positional sanctification, which serves as the basis for progressive sanctification. In other words, we are not trying to become Christians, we are children of God who are in the process of becoming like Christ. Understanding and acting upon this truth of who we are in Christ is the basis for our growth and victory.

Every new creation in Christ is far from perfect in his or her character or behavior. Our position in Christ is settled at salvation. "Dear friends, *now* we are children of God" (1 John 3:2, emphasis added). There will be a lot of growing pains in the process of conforming to His image, just as there were growing pains in our physical maturation.

Two fundamental issues impede spiritual growth. First, we have to know who we are in Christ and accept by faith what God has already done for us. Second, we must resolve our personal and spiritual conflicts. The tool we use is the Steps to Freedom in Christ, which is a comprehensive process of repentance. In other words, to grow in Christ, we must repent and believe the truth.

We are positionally sanctified when God "delivered us from the domain of darkness, and transferred us to the kingdom of His beloved Son" (Col. 1:13, *NASB*). We have changed kingdoms—from Satan's kingdom to God's kingdom. We cannot be members of both. God declares that we "are not in the flesh but in the Spirit" (Rom. 8:9, *NASB*). We are either one or the other, not half and half. Ephesians 5:8 (*NASB*) states that "you were formerly darkness, but now you are light in the Lord."

We lack the assurance of salvation if we believe that we are part light and part darkness, part saint and part sinner. If we believe this, we will confess our sin and strive to do better but will continue to live defeated lives, thinking of ourselves as sinners saved by grace who are just hanging on until the rapture finally takes us home. Satan can do nothing about our position in Christ. But if he can get us to believe we are no different from non-Christians, then that's the way we will live.

God's work in changing sinners to saints, through Christ's death and resurrection, is His greatest accomplishment on earth. Your inner change (regeneration) happened when God gave you a new heart and a new Spirit within you. It happened the moment you trusted Christ as your Savior. That's when the dragon skin was cut away and you became a new creature. The outer change (progressive sanctification) of learning to think and act like a new creature in Christ continues throughout life. But learning to live successfully like a new creature will only happen when you accept the truth that you already are a new creature.[1] Our responsibility is to repent and believe the truth.

Probe

If we don't understand who we are in Christ, we will spend the rest of our lives trying to become somebody we already are. Why is understanding positional sanctification (who we are and what Christ has already done for us) so essential before we can conform to the image of God (progressive sanctification)?

Journal

_____

_____

_____

_____

_____

Note
1. Neil T. Anderson and Dave Park, *Stomping Out the Darkness* (Ventura, Calif.: Regal Books, 1993), pp. 65, 66.

DAY 90

Thought for Today: You must be real in order to be right with God.

Cast all your anxiety on him because he cares for you. Be
self-controlled and alert. Your enemy the devil prowls around
like a roaring lion looking for someone to devour.
1 PETER 5:7,8

Cindy was a 26-year-old university graduate with a teaching credential, but she looked more like a flower child from the '60s. She wore tattered jeans and no shoes, and she carried a well-used Bible. Cindy had been institutionalized three times in the past five years after being diagnosed as paranoid schizophrenic.

We began to meet on a weekly basis. I (Neil) assumed that her problems were either the result of moral failure or some participation in the occult. I quizzed her about the moral area but found no problems. I asked her if she had ever been involved in the occult. She had never even read a book on the subject. By this time I was scratching my head because I couldn't figure out the source of her severe and obvious conflict.

One day, she began talking about her family. She described how her father, a noted pediatrician, had divorced her mother and run off with a nurse. Cindy's mother and other family members had openly vented their hatred and frustration. But Cindy, the only Christian in the family, felt she had to be a good witness. She was determined to be the loving, conciliatory daughter. So she kept silent while her emotions tore her insides to shreds.

"Let's talk about your dad," I suggested.

"I'm not going to talk about my dad," Cindy snapped. "If you talk about my dad, I'm out of here."

"Wait a minute, Cindy. If you can't talk about your dad here, where can you talk about him? If you don't deal with these emotional issues here and now, when and where will you deal with them?"

I discovered two passages of Scripture that added significant insight to Cindy's problem-plagued life. The first one is Ephesians 4:26,27 (*NASB*): "Be angry, and yet do not sin; do not let the sun go down on your anger, and do not give the devil an opportunity." Cindy's unresolved anger toward her father was never confessed, nor had she forgiven him. Since she repressed her anger instead of dealing with it, she had given the devil an opportunity, a "foothold" (*NIV*), which literally means a place.

The second passage is 1 Peter 5:7,8: "Cast all your anxiety on him [God] because he cares for you. Be self-controlled and alert. Your enemy the devil prowls around like a roaring lion looking for someone to devour." Instead of casting her anxieties upon the Lord, Cindy tried to be spiritual by covering them up. By not giving her inner struggles to God, she became easy prey for the devil.

She began to face her unresolved feelings toward her father and to work through the issue of forgiveness, which was the crux of the problem. Within a few months, this dear lady, whom psychiatrists had given up on, made significant progress and became involved in the children's ministry at her church.

Your emotions play a major role in the process of renewing your mind. In a general sense, your emotions are a product of your thought life. If you are not thinking right, if your mind is not being renewed, if you are not perceiving God and His Word properly, your emotional life will show it. If you fail to acknowledge your emotions, you may make yourself a slow-moving target for Satan, just like Cindy did.[1]

I counseled two young men who seemed to have everything going for them. Both came from affluent Christian families and had graduated from top colleges. One was living at a downtown rescue mission, and the other was living in a halfway house. Their stories were similar. They had strong, domineering fathers whom they hated. Neither of them would admit they were angry, and they were not willing to talk to their fathers about the problems in their relationships. One of them quit coming to me for counseling because I asked him to write out a list of the people he felt anger toward and needed to forgive. The other one committed suicide by jumping off an overpass.

You are not shaped so much by your environment as you are by your perception of your environment. Life's events do not determine who you are. God determines who you are, and your interpretation of life's events determines how well you will handle the pressures of life. If what you believe does not reflect truth, then what you feel does not reflect reality.

The order of Scripture is to live by faith according to what God says is true. Your emotions will follow. If you believe what you feel, instead of believing the truth, your walk will be as inconsistent as your feelings. We don't feel our way into good behavior; we behave our way into good feeling. Jesus said: "If you know these things, you are blessed if you do them" (John 13:17, *NASB*). If you wait until you feel like doing what is right, you may never do it. Do what is right and you will feel good about it.

Which of the following best describes how you handle your emotional life?

- Readily express my emotions
- Express some of my emotion, but not all
- Readily acknowledge the presence of my emotions but am reserved in expressing them
- Tendency to suppress my emotions
- Find it safest not to express how I feel
- Tendency to disregard how I feel, since I cannot trust my feelings
- Consciously or subconsciously deny feelings because it's too painful to deal with them

Cindy had done the least healthy of all the above: She had denied her feelings because they were painful. Learning to acknowledge our emotions is a critical part of our freedom and maturity. Remember, you can't be right with God and not be real. If necessary, God may have to make you real in order to be right with Him.

Probe

Do you know someone with whom you could be emotionally honest (that is, you could tell this person exactly how you feel about yourself, life and other people)? Your God-given assignment is to be honest with Him.

Tell your loving heavenly Father exactly how you feel and be willing to share your feelings with someone you trust.

Journal

_____

_____

_____

_____

_____

Note

1. Neil T. Anderson and Dave Park, *Stomping Out the Darkness* (Ventura, Calif.: Regal Books, 1993), pp. 175-178.

DAY 91

**Thought for Today: Our emotions are to our souls what our
ability to feel is to our bodies.**

*When I kept silent, my bones wasted away through my groaning all day
long. . . . Therefore let everyone who is godly pray to you while you may
be found; surely when the mighty waters rise, they will not reach him.*

PSALM 32:3,6

Doug was attending a fine university with the hope of becoming an
architect. During his third year in school, he had some kind of breakdown. His parents brought him home, but Doug wasn't doing well. They
didn't know what to do, so they committed him to a mental hospital—
against his will—for three weeks of observation. Doug never forgave his
parents for putting him in the hospital.

By the time I (Neil) met him four years later, he was an angry, bitter
young man. He worked part-time as a draftsman but was basically being
supported by his parents. He struggled with the voices inside his head
and spent most of his time outside, talking to the air. Nobody seemed to
be able to help him. His parents asked if I would talk to him, and I agreed.

I spent three months with Doug, trying to help him accept himself
and own up to his feelings. "How do you feel about your parents?" I asked
him.

"I love my parents," he said. But the truth was that Doug loathed his
parents, and they could sense it.

"Why do you say, 'I love my parents?'"

"Because the Bible says we should love our parents."

Whenever I suggested the possibility that he hated his parents, Doug
would deny it. Finally I asked him, "Would you agree with me that it's
possible for a Christian to feel the emotion of hatred?"

"Well, maybe. But not me."

Apparently my probing crowded Doug too closely, because he never
talked to me again.[1]

Your emotions are to your soul what your physical feelings are to your body. Nobody enjoys pain. But if you couldn't feel pain, you would be in danger of serious injury and infection. In a similar way, if you didn't feel anger, sorrow, joy and so on, your soul would be in trouble. Emotions are God's indicators to let you know what's going on inside.

Someone has likened emotions to the red light on the dashboard of a car that indicates an engine problem. There are three ways you can respond to the red light's warning. First, you can cover it with a piece of duct tape. "I can't see the light now," you say, "so I don't have to think about that problem." Second, you can smash out the light with a hammer. "That'll teach you not to glare in my face!" Or third, you can respond to the light as the manufacturers intended for you to respond— by looking under the hood and fixing the problem.

You have the same three options in regard to your emotions. You can respond by ignoring or stifling them. That's called suppression. Or you can respond by expressing emotions indiscriminately. For instance, if you get angry, you can thoughtlessly lash out and give someone a piece of your mind. Or third, you can calmly acknowledge how you feel.

Suppression is a conscious denial of feelings, while repression is an unconscious denial. Those who suppress their emotions ignore their feelings and choose not to deal with them. As illustrated by Doug's experience, suppression is an unhealthy response to your emotions.

King David had something to say in Psalm 32:3,6 (see above) about the unhealthy impact of suppressing his feelings. When suppressed emotions build up within you like "mighty waters," you won't turn to God. You have emotionally lost control. It's important to open up to God while you can, because bottling up your feelings too long will disrupt the harmony of your relationship with Him.

The second unhealthy way to respond to emotions is to let it all hang out, to tell anybody and everybody exactly how you feel. The apostle Peter is a great example in this area. It was Peter who impulsively hacked off the ear of Caiaphas's servant when Jesus was arrested in Gethsemane. It was Peter who promised to follow Jesus anywhere, even to the death. Only hours later, Peter swore that he never knew Him. Indiscriminate expression may appear to be healthy for you, but it is usually unhealthy for those around you.

Psalm 109 shows that David dealt with his emotions the healthy way, by acknowledging them. He acknowledges his pain and the anger he feels against his foes by asking God to "let his children be fatherless, and his wife a widow. Let his children wander about and beg; and let them seek sustenance far from their ruined homes. Let the creditor seize all he has; and let strangers plunder the product of his labor" (Ps. 109:9-11, *NASB*). God already knew what David was thinking and feeling. David was simply expressing his pain and anger honestly to his God, who understood how he felt and accepted him where he was.[2]

God can certainly handle any emotional catharsis we may have. If we can go honestly to Him with our pain, chances are we won't have to stuff or dump our emotions in an unhealthy way. This is just honest confession that leads to cleansing and restoration.

Probe

Can you be emotionally honest with God? Doesn't He already know how you feel? Then why not be totally honest with Him?

Journal

_____

_____

_____

_____

_____

Notes
1. Neil T. Anderson, *Victory over the Darkness* (Ventura, Calif.: Regal Books, 1990), pp. 182, 183.
2. Ibid., pp. 181-187.

DAY 92

Thought for Today: Faith is the victory that overcomes the world.

For everyone born of God overcomes the world. This is the victory that has overcome the world, even our faith.

1 JOHN 5:4

In a small community outside Nashville, Tennessee, a little girl was born with major health problems that left her handicapped. She had a large, wonderful Christian family, but while her brothers and sisters enjoyed running and playing outside, she was confined to braces. Her parents took her into Nashville periodically for physical therapy. There was little hope for complete recovery. "Will I ever be able to run and play like the other children?" she asked her parents.

"Honey, you only have to believe," they said. "If you believe, God will make it happen."

She took her parents' counsel to heart and began to believe that God could make her walk without braces. Unknown to her parents and doctors, she practiced walking without her braces with the aid of her brothers and sisters. On her 12th birthday, she surprised everyone by removing her braces and walking around the doctor's office unassisted. Her doctors couldn't believe her progress. She never wore the braces again.

Her next goal was to play basketball. She continued to exercise her faith and courage as well as her underdeveloped legs. Following the example of her older sister, she tried out for the basketball team. The coach selected her sister for the team while telling this courageous girl she wasn't good enough to play. Her father, a wise and loving man, told the coach, "My daughters come in pairs. If you want one, you have to take the other one, too." Reluctantly, the coach added the girl to the team.

Her team went to the state basketball championships where one of the referees at the tournament—who happened to be the coach of the internationally famous Tiger Belles track club—noticed her exceptional ability and encouraged her to try running. So, after the basketball season, she went out for track. She began to win races and earned a berth in the state track championships.

At the age of 16, she was one of the best young runners in the country. She went to the Olympics in Australia and won a bronze medal for anchoring the 400-meter relay. Not satisfied with her accomplishment, she worked diligently for four more years and returned to the Olympics in Rome in 1960. There Wilma Rudolph won the 100- and the 200-meter-dash and anchored the winning 400-meter relay team—all in world-record times. She capped the year by receiving the prestigious Sullivan Award as the most outstanding amateur athlete in America. Wilma Rudolph's faith and hard work paid off.

When you hear inspiring stories of faith like Wilma Rudolph's, do you sometimes wonder, *Is faith really the critical element that allows some people to rise above seemingly incredible odds and achieve things others cannot? Can faith also do great things for me?* By now you should have a good idea that the answer to those questions is yes.[1]

Have you ever wondered why some Christians live in joy and victory, while others live in misery and defeat? We all have the same opportunity to believe we can do all things through Christ who strengthens us (see Phil. 4:13). The ones who gain victory in life are the ones who believe they can. "For in Christ Jesus neither circumcision nor uncircumcision has any value. The only thing that counts is faith expressing itself through love" (Gal. 5:6).

It doesn't make much difference what you do or don't do if it's not done in faith according to what God says is true. "Whatever is not from faith is sin" (Rom. 14:23, *NASB*). Paul is telling the Galatians, who had fallen back into a works-oriented approach, that it doesn't make any difference whether they are circumcised or not circumcised—faith is the only thing that counts. Paul says in Romans 2:29 that true circumcision is of the heart, not the body.

The point is not that you won't do anything, but that if you don't have faith, what you do is worth nothing. If you do have faith you will do a lot of good things. Read through Hebrews 11 and see the incredible exploits accomplished by the people of God through faith. Scripture is very clear that they did what they did because they had faith (they believed in God). They had great faith because they had a great God.

We will not have any victory if we attempt to overcome addictions or life-controlling problems by simply trying harder. Programs, methods, support groups, treatments and counseling techniques will not be very successful if they are not of faith. They may help a person cope, but they will not produce freedom. God has done everything necessary for you to walk in freedom, and you can only appropriate it by faith.

Freedom from addiction and victory over a problem come when we choose to believe the truth that sets us free. "For everyone born of God overcomes the world. This is the victory that has overcome the world, even our faith" (1 John 5:4).

Probe

Do you find it encouraging or discouraging to read that God has done everything necessary for you to be spiritually alive and free, and your only response is to believe? Why?

Journal

_____

_____

_____

_____

_____

Note
1. Neil T. Anderson, *Victory over the Darkness* (Ventura, Calif.: Regal Books, 1990), pp. 107-109.

DAY 93

Thought for Today: Nobody and nothing can keep you from being the person God created you to be if you will just let Him be your life.

The one who calls you is faithful and he will do it.
1 THESSALONIANS 5:24

It would be difficult to pick out the worst day of my life, since there were a lot of them during my struggle with alcoholism. But one does stand out—the day I woke up from a five-hour blackout to find myself handcuffed to a hospital bed and waiting for the police to pick me up.

When the police arrived, one policeman looked to be about 50 years old. As I sheepishly crawled into the rear of the police car, he said to me in a condescending tone, "Mr. Quarles, you're old enough to know better than to be out at night doing things like that."

"I know." I mumbled the words as my chin dug into my chest. I didn't want anyone to recognize me.

"Why do you do it?" he asked.

"I really don't know."

I had no logical explanation. Such behavior defied reason.

As we drove to the station, the officer filled me in on the missing five hours. "You were arrested while sitting on the floor of the parking deck at the Hilton. Your speech was completely incoherent and you didn't even know your name or what you were doing. If you had driven, the results could have been disastrous."

For some reason God protected me and I had hurt no one else while I was drunk. It was one of the many times in my life that I've experienced God's protective hand in spite of my foolishness.

Julia was waiting at the jail when we pulled into the station. She paid my fine, and the officers released me. I left the jail overcome with guilt and shame. My company expected me at the office, but I could barely hold up my head. I couldn't face anyone. When we reached home, I phoned my office. "I'm sick and I probably won't be in today or tomorrow," I told them.

After throwing some clothes into a suitcase, I drove to Atlanta to stay with some friends who knew about my struggle. I had to get away for a few days. I hated myself and what I was doing to Julia, but I had no idea how to stop my insane behavior.

What next? My only recourse was to try harder. Maybe my problem was focus. All I needed to do was give the problem more attention, then I could quit drinking. As a Christian, I knew that God didn't want me to be an alcoholic. I believed the Lord had an answer for me. As I drove to Atlanta, I honestly faced the question of how to change, but I had no idea where to find the answer.

I didn't understand that a person always acts in accordance with personal beliefs. If I was ever going to change, I needed to examine my misbeliefs (or lies) that gave me permission to continue drinking. Instead, I redoubled my efforts to focus on my behavior and change it.

During those few days in Atlanta, I followed an intense schedule of prayer and Bible reading. I vowed to God never to drink again and pleaded for Him to help me. Then I made a list of benchmarks to ensure my commitment. I continued to try to change by using my own resources, but I was setting myself up for another fall.[1]

It would be another five years of struggle, misery and bondage before I found my freedom. What was I doing wrong? I was living under the law. Telling somebody that what they're doing is wrong does not give them the power to stop doing it. The law is powerless to give life (see Gal. 3:21-25). Even worse, the law has the capacity to stimulate me to do what it was intended to prohibit. Paul said, "For while we were in the flesh, the *sinful passions, which were aroused by the Law,* were at work in the members of our body to bear fruit for death" (Rom. 7:5, *NASB,* emphasis added). If you don't believe it, go home and tell your child, "You can go here, but you can't go there." The moment you say that, where does he or she want to go? You guessed it—and they probably didn't even want to go "there" until you said they couldn't.

Bill Gillham has said that Christ didn't come alongside you or with you, above you or below you, beside you or behind you or in front of you. Instead, He came into you so that He could be in you and live His life through you.[2] That is grace, not law.

Probe

Why is the forbidden fruit always the most desirable? Does it trouble you or bless you to think that you are the only one who can keep you from being the person God has created you to be?

Journal

_____

_____

_____

_____

_____

Notes
1. Neil T. Anderson and Mike and Julia Quarles, *Freedom from Addiction* (Ventura, Calif.: Regal Books, 1996), pp. 24-26.
2. Bill and Anabel Gillham, *Victorious Christian Life* tape series (Fort Worth, Tex.: Lifetime Guarantee, n.y.), audiocassette.

DAY 94

Thought for Today: People may not live what they profess, but they will always live what they believe.[1]

You believe that God is one. You do well; the demons also believe, and shudder. But are you willing to recognize, you foolish fellow, that faith without works is useless?

JAMES 2:19, 20, NASB

When I speak at Christian treatment centers around the country, I always tell the people, "If you work this program perfectly and do everything they tell you to do, and that's all you do, you'll be drunk or on drugs shortly after you leave here." Most of them look at me incredulously. Why would I say such a thing? Because most of the people there are sincere, and "working the program" is exactly what they are planning to do. But they know that what I'm saying is true because they see it happen over and over.

When I went to my second treatment center, which was a Christian program, I was determined to do everything they asked of me and more. I desperately wanted to get out of the devastating bondage of alcoholism. It was a well-thought-out program. The director and staff were caring, competent people. Looking back, I don't think I could have gone to a better place. But many people go there and don't get free. I've talked to people who have been to 5, 10, even 20 or more treatment centers (some Christian), but have made little progress in getting out of their bondage.

This treatment center became a place of refuge, retreat and renewed hope for me. I plunged headlong into the program. I worked the discipleship workbooks and did everything they told me to do. The Bible studies were meaningful, along with my times of counseling with the director and the assistant director. Mainly I received hope that God had an answer for me. For the first time in many months, I began to experience peace and joy.

When I returned home from the treatment program, I felt encouraged that God had worked in my life. Now I could continue a normal life with my wife—and not drink. Because I had worked through several issues, I felt better about myself. I was beginning to understand repentance. I saw myself as the problem and took responsibility for myself and my failures. I made a commitment to my wife and my marriage, which felt good. I believed my answer was through God. He would enable me to live a life of freedom—without alcohol.

That was in March. The following fall I joined a ministry and began a biblical, Christ-centered ministry to alcoholics, addicts and their families. Something was still missing. Often in my thought life I would be overcome with strong feelings of guilt or insecurity. Many days I felt convinced of my failure and doubted that I could help anyone. I sat at my desk or drove around aimlessly. Finally, the inevitable happened. On one of those days I had the urge to drink. I thought, *It would take the edge off my nerves.* I gave in to the overpowering urge and was immediately overwhelmed with guilt. How could I minister freedom to people struggling with addictions if I wasn't free?

I hid the experience from Julia. I resolved that it would not happen again; but I had opened the door. Every month or so I repeated the secret pattern. I didn't go to bars because someone might recognize me. Instead, I drove around in my car or parked somewhere and drank. Each time I promised myself and God, "This will never happen again." But it always did.[2]

What was the problem? Why did working the program perfectly not work for me? Why does it not work for countless others? Because if you don't change the way you believe, what you do doesn't make much difference. If a person doesn't change what he believes about God and himself, when he walks out of the treatment center he is unchanged. Sooner or later he will go back to his old ways. As Dr. Tim Warner says: "People may not live what they profess, but they will always live what they believe." It is easy to change your behavior while you're in a treatment center. But when you get back into the world with its problems, stresses and pressures, it is impossible to live counter to what you really believe.

I taught at a treatment center for several months. There were two guys in the program who worked it perfectly and went even further. They started a prayer meeting that met every night. Both men were placed in leadership positions in the program and put on staff. But when they decided to leave, it was only a short while before both of them went down the tubes, got in trouble with the law and ended up worse off than before.

Perhaps you're thinking, *Is there hope for anybody?* Yes, but only for those who choose to believe the truth that sets us free. Unless you change your old beliefs that brought you into bondage and choose to believe the truth, you will act out what you believe.

Probe

Have you ever heard the statement, "Work the program, the program works"? Why can't a program (any program) set you free?

Journal

_____

_____

_____

_____

_____

Notes
  1. Timothy M. Warner, *Spiritual Warfare* (Wheaton, Ill.: Crossway Books, 1991), p. 25.
  2. Neil T. Anderson and Mike and Julia Quarles, *Freedom from Addiction* (Ventura, Calif.: Regal Books, 1996), pp. 83, 97, 99.

DAY 95

Thought for Today: We are saved and sanctified by faith, not by the works of the law.

Does God give you his Spirit and work miracles among you because you observe the law, or because you believe what you heard?

GALATIANS 3:5

It was official. I resigned the pastorate in Pensacola on July 2, 1979. My emotions were in turmoil as I drove home after being in Atlanta for some job interviews. My dream of serving God in ministry was over. This vision for service was the only thing in my life that I desperately wanted. It seemed unreal that it was gone.

A few of the members were genuinely sorry I was leaving, but the majority accepted it in stride, as though they weren't surprised. The long-term members knew that pastors come and go, but the church goes on. I hated giving up, but I believed I had no other choice. A friend suggested I needed to "come to grips with reality." Well, my reality was a mess. My marriage was shaky and my children didn't respect me. I had little ministry left.

How could I have failed so miserably? Before entering the ministry I had given up my business and thought I had turned my back on the world and everything it offered. Why wouldn't God bless me, my ministry and family? Seven years of my life were wasted, and now I was forced to start over again.

As I turned off the interstate for the last leg of the trip into Pensacola, a wave of depression came over me. I didn't want to return to the stock brokerage business, but it was the only option left. Julia was in Birmingham visiting her family and would be gone for several days. I thought, *I'll stop for a drink because it's Friday afternoon. Thank God it's Friday!* I stopped at a small bar to have a beer.

After a few beers, I decided to indulge myself. I asked the bartender about some local action. Who would ever know? He directed me to a place located a few miles north of town. The "action" turned out to be a roadhouse featuring a country and western band. The atmosphere and music matched my mood perfectly. I sat listening to the sad hillbilly songs and drank myself into oblivion. Finally, when the place closed, I stumbled to my car.

I was extremely drunk, but I started driving toward home. About an hour later I was in the middle of nowhere and had no idea where I was or which way to go to get home. I drove for another hour and came to Atmore, Alabama. I had left the roadhouse in Flomaton, Alabama, which was less than an hour from Pensacola. Now I was two hours from home, and I was having difficulty focusing on my driving. I began to weave all over the road.

A siren sounded from out of nowhere, and I saw blue lights in my rearview mirror. All I could think was that now I was about to be arrested for drunk driving. What a great way to end my ministry. I sent up a quick SOS prayer: "Oh God, please, please, don't let them arrest me."

I'll never know why, but God answered my prayer. Perhaps the officer felt sorry for me. He took me to an all-night restaurant. "Give this man enough coffee to sober him up," he told the waitress. After a couple of cups of coffee, I still wasn't sober, but I managed to drive home. The sun peeked over the horizon as I turned into my driveway. When I drifted off to sleep, I hoped to wake up and find my nightmare had ended. It hadn't.[1]

How could someone like me, whose consuming desire was to serve the Lord and make his life count for Christ, end up like that? I had been taught, and believed and practiced, the great deception that learning the principles of the Bible and doing your best to observe them is the Christian life. I had reaped the results of what I'd sown.

"What's wrong with that?" you might ask. Any time we focus on what we can do for ourselves instead of what God has already done for us, we will end up in failure no matter how noble or spiritual our efforts might seem. The Christian life is not about doing the best we can; it's about realizing that apart from Christ we can do nothing (see John 15:5b), and trusting Christ to be our life (see Gal. 2:20).

What's wrong with trying to do right? Nothing, except that we can't do right in our own strength and resources. Paul rebuked the Galatian Christians who were relying on their efforts to observe the law. By doing this, they were no longer relying on God. He reminded them that God gave them His Spirit and worked miracles among them only because they believed and put their faith in Him.

Galatians 3:1-5 in the *Phillips* translation puts it like this:

> O you dear idiots of Galatia, who saw Jesus Christ the crucified so plainly, who has been casting a spell over you? I shall ask you one simple question: did you receive the Spirit by trying to keep the Law or by believing the message of the gospel? Surely you can't be so stupid as to think that you begin your spiritual life in the Spirit and then complete it by reverting to physical obser-vances? Has all your painful experience brought you nowhere? I simply cannot believe it! Does God, who gives you his Spirit and works miracles among you, do these things because you have obeyed the Law or because you have believed the gospel?

Probe

Have you believed the great deception that the Christian life is about learning the principles of the Bible and doing your best to observe them? If we are not saved by the law, why are we inclined to believe that we can be sanctified by it?

Journal

_____

_____

_____

_____

_____

Note
1. Neil T. Anderson and Mike and Julia Quarles, *Freedom from Addiction* (Ventura, Calif.: Regal Books, 1996), pp. 61-63.

DAY 96

Thought for Today: The road to hell is paved with good intentions.

I do not understand what I do. For what I want to do
I do not do, but what I hate I do.
ROMANS 7:15

The most elaborate and comprehensive plan I worked out to free myself
from my addiction took me quite a few hours to put in place. I believed
my problem was that I wasn't doing what I should. I wasn't following
through and putting into practice what I knew to do. So I sat down and
made a list of all the things I should do.

This list covered the waterfront: spiritual issues, family, marriage,
business, physical, mental, financial and emotional issues. The spiritual
part of my plan included things like Bible reading, study and memorization, prayer, church attendance and discipleship groups. The business
part consisted of things such as what time I would get to work and what
I needed to do each day to be successful. Physical things included diet,
exercise and so on. As you can imagine, the list was quite long.

Then I made up a chart, divided it into the various categories and
listed each activity under each category. I assigned each activity a point
total. Performing everything on the list each week would add up to 100
points. Surely this would keep me on track.

I didn't really think I would be perfect each week, but if I could get
up in the 80s, pointwise, I knew I would be a good husband and a productive Christian. Even if I just made it to the 70s, surely I wouldn't be
drinking and messing up. Of course, if I made it up into the 90s (which
was my goal), I would have given the apostle Paul a run for his money.

The first week was very sobering (pardon the pun). I didn't even come
close to 50 points. I was failing badly. I rededicated myself and resolved that
I would do it if it killed me. The second week was a total disaster. I was
drunk several times and didn't even look at the list. I threw the chart away
before that week was over. This was probably the worst plan of any I tried.

When it came to self-help strategies, I was an expert. Almost every week or two I came up with another scheme. Countless times I ran to Julia or my minister or the assistant minister and told them about a wonderful, new spiritual plan to solve my problem. Within a week (and sometimes sooner) my plan was shattered and my life a mess again. The greater my hope, the harder I fell. Every fall validated my helplessness and inability. The road to hell is indeed paved with good intentions.

I'm actually thankful that I tried so many things that didn't work. Why? Because it convinced me that (1) there was nothing I could do to help myself, and (2) only God has a complete answer. God had to allow me to come to the end of my resources. Self-help programs are like handing someone a chain saw without gas and then encouraging him to cut down a giant sequoia tree. He may kill himself trying. Why not let the power in the gas do the work?

What's the greatest stronghold that keeps Christians from experiencing their freedom in Christ? It may vary from person to person, but one of the most formidable is the stronghold of self-help. Tom McGee, national director for Freedom in Christ Ministries, has said that he believes the stronghold of legalism (another word for self-help) is more difficult to overcome than severe abuses. That's probably true, since the people struggling with abuse know they have a problem and are usually desperate for help. The legalist is convinced that what he's doing is right, biblical and spiritual; and therefore, he doesn't need any help. He can do it himself.

We are actually being deceived if we think we will not reap what we sow. "Do not be deceived, God is not mocked; for whatever a man sows, this he will also reap. For the one who sows to his own flesh shall from the flesh reap corruption, but the one who sows to the Spirit shall from the Spirit reap eternal life (Gal. 6:7,8, *NASB*). I was just reaping what I was sowing. I had sown my good works and reaped a barren life.

The deeds of the flesh are dead. The fruit of the Spirit is the result of a living reality. The fruit comes from the life of Christ, which He came to *give* us. Nothing dead can produce fruit. Fruit is the unselfish by-product of a living organism.

Probe

Why do so many want to be self-sufficient? Why are the best of intentions not good enough by themselves?

Journal

_____

_____

_____

_____

_____

THE FREEDOM OF FORGIVENESS

DAY 97

**Thought for Today: Forgiveness is the primary ticket
that sets you free from your past.**

*Bear with each other and forgive whatever grievances you may have
against one another. Forgive as the Lord forgave you.*
COLOSSIANS 3:13

One time I counseled a woman in her late 60s who was so clinically depressed she could no longer function in life. Her mother had died while giving birth to her. Her father had blamed her for the death and had emotionally and physically abused her. When he remarried, the stepmother joined in the abuse. Her childhood was a living hell.

What really hurt her was the childhood abandonment. The father would leave her with relatives and be gone for months at a time. The worst part, though, was when her father would tell her, "I'll be back on such and such days," and then often would not show up. Her most painful childhood memories were of waiting in the yard for hours and hours for a father who never arrived.

She learned from her dad and stepmother's actions and words that she was unacceptable, unloved and unworthy. She couldn't talk about it without weeping. The depression hadn't started until her husband had died in the last year. He had been a loving and caring husband and continually affirmed her. His love enabled her to stuff the feelings she brought from her childhood. But after his death she had gone into a deep depression.

She learned that she had a lot of anger and hatred toward her dad and stepmother and needed to forgive them. On the second day of counseling she was able to do that and went from clinical depression to joy. When her son brought her back the next day, he couldn't believe it. "What did you do to her?" he asked.

"I didn't do anything," I replied. "She chose to deal with her bitterness by forgiving."

Forgiveness is the primary ticket that sets you free from your past. Forgiveness is to set a captive free and then realize that you were the captive. Choosing to forgive from the heart has proven to be the most cru-cial step in the Steps to Freedom in Christ. It is always the hardest step and takes the most time, but it's also the most liberating.

All of us have been hurt sometime in life. Such abuses can leave us angry and bitter. God's only solution? "Get rid of all bitterness, rage and anger, brawling and slander, along with every form of malice. Be kind and compassionate to one another, forgiving each other, just as in Christ God forgave you" (Eph. 4:31,32). If we are going to walk in freedom, we must choose to forgive.

Even the secular recovery people understand the devastating conse-quences of unresolved anger. Alcoholics Anonymous has an acronym, HALT: Don't get Hungry, Angry, Lonely or Tired. They know that if people get angry, it won't be long before they return to their drug of choice and get back into bondage. We can't just decide not to get angry. That's another form of emotional denial. But we can choose to forgive as Christ has forgiven us.

If for no other reason, we need to forgive because God requires it of us. When Jesus instructed us how to petition our heavenly Father in the Lord's Prayer (see Matt. 6:9-15), He says we ought to pray, "Forgive us our debts, as we also have forgiven our debtors" (v. 12). In other words, "Don't expect much results in petitioning Me if you are not willing to forgive oth-ers." We cannot have a relationship with God in exclusion of others.

After the Lord's Prayer, Jesus said, "For if you forgive men when they sin against you, your heavenly Father will also forgive you. But if you do not forgive men their sins, your Father will not forgive your sins" (Matt. 6:14,15). This model prayer was given before Christ died for all our sins, so our destiny is not at stake, but our daily victory is very much at stake. To choose to forgive is to choose freedom. To choose not to forgive is to stay in bondage to the past, even though your sins are forgiven.

Probe

Read Matthew 18:21-35 and consider the following questions:

1. Why do you think the servant who was forgiven the large debt he owed was unwilling to forgive the small debt owed him?

2. What will our heavenly Father do if we won't forgive from the heart?
3. Why is it so hard to forgive?

Journal

_____

_____

_____

_____

_____

DAY 98

Thought for Today: Unforgiveness brings misery and bondage.

"In your anger do not sin": Do not let the sun go down while you are still angry, and do not give the devil a foothold.
EPHESIANS 4:26,27

After I graduated from seminary, Julia and I moved to another state. A couple in a Sunday School class befriended us. He was the head of the Sunday School class and soon asked me to teach. He was a dedicated Christian, and there was no doubt that Christ was first in his life. His wife was one of the loveliest and most talented ladies we had ever met. They were an attractive couple, but most appealing was their love for the Lord. We were drawn to them and became close friends.

He had been a heavy-drinking businessman who owned his own company and was driven to amass wealth. She sought social status. Ultimately, their marriage couldn't stand the pressure, so they divorced.

He began dating another divorcée. They were making plans to get married when the Lord got his attention. He repented for his failure as a husband, went back to his wife and they remarried. When we met them, they had been remarried for a couple of years. They were different from most people we knew because their lives clearly revolved around Christ.

We got together on a regular basis and even took vacations together. But a few years later, I was shocked to learn that she had had a psychotic break and was in a mental hospital. This happened several times over the next few years. We kept up our friendship with them and tried to minister to them as best we could.

We also found out that her psychotic episodes were preceded by alcoholic binges. At first I was dumbfounded. How could such a lovely, talented, committed Christian end up like that? It became apparent that she was still angry at her husband for his relationship with the young divorcée. As the old saying goes, "Hell hath no fury like a woman scorned."

She would end up losing contact with reality and have to be taken to a mental hospital. One time they found her walking around in the rain in her robe. She told me she realized when she was "losing it" but was unwilling to do what she needed to do to stop it—forgive her husband.

"See to it that no one misses the grace of God and that no bitter root grows up to cause trouble and defile many" (Heb. 12:15). The one who is most defiled is the one who won't forgive, but his bitterness will spread to others and they too will suffer from the person's unforgiveness. An unforgiving spirit affords Satan his greatest access to the Church. That is why Paul said, "If you forgive anyone, I also forgive him. And what I have forgiven—if there was anything to forgive—I have forgiven in the sight of Christ for your sake, in order that Satan might not outwit us. For we are not unaware of his schemes" (2 Cor. 2:10,11).

In relating to others, Paul admonishes each of us to "Put off falsehood and speak truthfully to his neighbor, for we are all members of one body. 'In your anger do not sin': Do not let the sun go down while you are still angry, and do not give the devil a foothold" (Eph. 4:25-27). What happens if we hang on to our anger? We give the devil a foothold (literally, a place) in our lives. Once Satan has a foothold, we are in bondage.

People all over the world are taking others through the Steps to Freedom in Christ. If you asked any one of them, "What gives Satan the greatest opportunity to destroy our freedom in Christ?" they would all give the same answer—unforgiveness. Even God will turn us over to the tormentors if we will not forgive from our hearts (see Matt. 18:34,35). Why? Not because God is vindictive but because He loves us. He knows that holding on to our bitterness is a destructive poison that will only defile us and others. The only way to get rid of the mental anguish is to forgive as we have been forgiven.

Probe

Have you ever fallen into Satan's snare, like the lady who was doing a lot of good spiritual activities but neglected to forgive those who had hurt her? Have you ever tried to just forget about those who hurt you? What happened? Did you have any mental peace? Could you forget about it, or did you struggle with your thoughts?

Journal

_____

_____

_____

_____

_____

DAY 99

Thought for Today: You don't heal in order to forgive;
you forgive in order to heal.

If he sins against you seven times in a day, and seven times comes
back to you and says, "I repent," forgive him.

LUKE 17:4

Dan and Cindy were a fine young Christian couple who were preparing for ministry on the mission field. Then tragedy struck. Cindy was raped. The event devastated the couple; the trauma was so severe that they moved away from the community where it happened. As hard as she tried to get back to normal life, Cindy couldn't shake the horrible memories and feelings from her experience.

Six months after the rape, Dan and Cindy attended a church conference where Neil was speaking. During the conference, Cindy called him in tears and said, "Neil, I just can't get over this thing. I know God can turn everything into good, but how is He going to do that? Every time I think about what happened, I start to cry."

"Wait a minute, Cindy," Neil said. "You've misunderstood something. God will work everything out for good, but He doesn't make a bad thing good. What happened to you was very tragic. God's good thing is to show you how you can come out of it a better person."

"But I just can't separate myself from my experience," she said. "I've been raped, Neil, and I'll be a victim of that for the rest of my life."

"No, Cindy. The rape happened to you, but it hasn't changed who you are, nor does it have to control you. You were the victim of a terrible, ugly tragedy. But if you only see yourself as a rape victim for the rest of your life, you will never get over your tragedy. You're a child of God. No event or person, good or bad, can rob you of that."

After encouraging Cindy to deal with the emotional trauma of her rape, Neil said, "You also need to forgive the man who raped you."

Forgiveness wouldn't be easy, but Cindy—and others who have been wronged—need to hear that forgiveness is necessary. We don't forgive others for their sake, but in order to free ourselves from the past.

Forgiveness does not mean forgetting. Forgetting may be a long-term by-product of forgiveness, but it is never a means to it. You may be thinking, *But didn't God say He would remember our sins no more?* (see Heb. 10:17). God is omniscient; He couldn't forget even if He wanted to. "I will remember your sins no more" means that He will not take the past and use it against us in the future. He will remove our sins as far from us as the east is from the west (see Ps. 103:12).

Forgiveness does not mean that you tolerate sin. Isabel, a young wife and mother attending one of my conferences, said, "I know who I'm supposed to forgive—my mother. I could do that, but what am I supposed to do when I see her next week? She will just put me down again and will try to crowd between me and my family as she always does. Am I supposed to let her keep ruining my life?"

Forgiving someone does not mean that you must be a doormat to that person's continual sin. I encouraged Isabel to confront her mother lovingly but firmly and tell her she would no longer tolerate destructive manipulation. It's OK to forgive another's past sins while you take a stand against future sins and set up scriptural boundaries against future abuse.

Forgiveness doesn't seek revenge or repayment for offenses suffered. You mean we're just supposed to let them off the hook? That is precisely why you should forgive. If you don't, you are still hooked to them. If you let them off your hook, are they off God's hook? No! "Do not take revenge, my friends, but leave room for God's wrath, for it is written: 'It is mine to avenge; I will repay,' says the Lord" (Rom. 12:19).

We are supposed to forgive as Christ has forgiven us. How did He forgive us? He took our sin upon Himself. In a practical sense, forgiveness is resolving to live with the consequences of another person's sin. But that's not fair! Of course it's not fair, but you will have to do it anyway. We are all living with the consequences of Adam's sin. The only real choice is whether we live in bondage or freedom.

Suppose someone in your church said to you, "I have gossiped about you all over town. Will you forgive me?" What are your options? You can seek repayment, but how could that be repaid? Suing for damages will not take away the consequences. You can ask them to retract everything they said. But you can't retract gossip any easier than you can put toothpaste back into the tube. The point is, you will have to live with the gossip this person spread about you no matter how you respond to the gossiper. You can either choose not to forgive and live in bitterness or you can choose the freedom of forgiveness.[1]

Forgiveness is not a feeling, it is a decision, a choice, a crisis of the will. Nobody heals in order to forgive; they forgive in order to heal. The healing may take time, but the choice to forgive doesn't. You must be willing to definitively say that you forgive the person for all he or she did to you. That means specifically naming every offense and how that offense made you feel. You have to forgive from the heart, and that means letting God examine the very core of your being. If you forgive generically, you get generic freedom.

Where is the justice? It is in the Cross. Christ died for your sins, her sins, his sins and everyone else's sins. Without the Cross, forgiveness isn't possible. Someone said, "The Cross is the sternest rebuke to mankind's selfishness this world will ever see." We forgive because we have been forgiven.

Probe

If you have been hurt in the past, is the memory still painful today? For your sake, are you willing to forgive the person who hurt you? Do you think that by hanging on to your bitterness, you are getting even? Who are you really hurting? Why don't you let it go for your sake and let God deal justly with that person in His time?

Journal

_____

_____

_____

_____

_____

Note
1. Neil T. Anderson, *Victory over the Darkness* (Ventura, Calif.: Regal Books, 1990), pp. 193, 194, 200-203.

DAY 100

Thought for Today: What is gained by forgiving others is your own freedom.

Get rid of all bitterness, rage and anger, brawling and slander, along with every form of malice. Be kind and compassionate to one another, forgiving each other, just as in Christ God forgave you.

EPHESIANS 4:31,32

When Mary was nine years old, she was raped by her father while her mother held her down. Why? To train her to be a teenybopper prostitute. The reason? Money.

For almost four years, Mary was put out on the streets of Las Vegas while her father gathered up clients, selling his own daughter. At 13, she could stand it no longer and turned herself in to the juvenile authorities, who brought her to St. Jude's Ranch for Children.

After she arrived, Mary began to see Father Ward for counseling. She complained that she couldn't sleep at night. "All I can see," she said, "are the faces of those men, one after another, and the face of my father who would come home after I did at night and still he wouldn't leave me alone and would molest me. I hate them. I hate myself. I'm so dirty inside. How can I ever get over this?"

"Sweetheart," Father Ward said, "there is only one way. You'll have to pray for your father and ask Jesus to love your father and forgive him through you."

"You're crazy!" she said. "You are absolutely out of your (bleep) mind. You've flipped. I hate that dirty (bleep)! I will never love him. I will never forgive him. God couldn't exist if He allows this to happen in the world."

Mary kept returning to see if Father Ward would change his mind and give her an easier way out. Day after day he would speak to her of forgiving her father. He knew that it would be the only way she would find forgiveness, healing and restoration.

This continued for six months until one day a new and different child suddenly walked into Father Ward's office. Tears were streaming down Mary's face, but she had an inner joy.

"You'll never guess what happened, Father," she began. "This morning I got up and I was so miserable that I decided to go to Hoover Dam (just eight miles away) and jump off the top and kill myself. I decided I just couldn't live this way any longer.

"Well, I got to the front door, and as I was about to go out, I thought *What the (bleep). As long as I'm going to kill myself, why don't I give what Father Ward keeps telling me a chance?* I went back to my room, closed the door and knelt down beside my bed and said, 'Jesus, I don't believe You exist, but Father Ward says You do. I don't believe You can help me. Father Ward says You can. If You exist, I am ready to let You take charge of my life, and I am even ready to let You love and forgive my father through me.'"

After a pause, Mary said. "Father, you'll never understand. I suddenly felt these great waves pouring over me full of warmth and forgiveness and cleanliness and purity." Overcome with the peace and joy that can only come from knowing Jesus, she added, "For the first time in six years, I like myself."

That horribly abused little girl learned something that many Christians have yet to learn. She couldn't love or forgive her father because she had no power to do so. By allowing Christ to love through her, she found healing and restoration.

Is that good theology? Yes, for the apostle Paul taught that Christ is our life (see Col. 3:4). He said it is not our love, but God's love poured out in our hearts through the Holy Spirit that enables us to forgive and love others (see Rom. 5:5).

Have you been hurt badly, greatly offended or horribly abused? Many would answer yes. Is it difficult to forgive? Yes! But making the decision to forgive from our hearts is a whole lot easier than living in bondage to the past for the rest of our lives. Why is it so hard to forgive? First, our flesh wants revenge. Our old nature wants that person to pay for his or her sins. But Jesus paid for our sins. Since we have become partakers of His divine nature, shouldn't we want the same for others?

Second, Satan knows that forgiveness will be the most liberating thing we will ever do. His plan is to keep us from forgiving so we will live in misery and bondage.

You can win victory over Satan by choosing Christ and His forgiveness and then by choosing to forgive others as Christ has forgiven you. Neil has said many times that if he were reduced to being able to teach one message, it would be the message of forgiveness.

When we encourage people to forgive, we often hear, "But you don't understand how badly this person hurt me!" To which we reply, "But don't you see? They are still hurting you!" You stop the pain and gain freedom when you forgive others. When you forgive, you are no longer attached to that person. The healing of your damaged emotions will quickly follow.

There is one thing that hurts more than the pain originally inflicted on you. It will negatively affect almost every aspect of your life. It will rob you of your joy and keep you from experiencing the peace and freedom God has provided for you. It will affect other relationships in your life and keep you from experiencing love and intimacy. It will turn you into a bitter, resentful person and accomplish Satan's plan for your life. That one thing is unforgiveness.

Probe

Choosing to forgive from the heart is a battle between the Holy Spirit and your flesh. You can choose which one will be victorious. You can either live according to the Spirit or you can live according to the flesh (see Galatians 5:16-26 to discover what the results of your choice would be).

Journal

_____

_____

_____

_____

_____

DAY 101

Thought for Today: Forgiving others is an issue between you and God.

And when you stand praying, if you hold anything against anyone, forgive him, so that your Father in heaven may forgive you your sins.
MARK 11:25

In September 1984, when the discipline committee at my church recommended that I enter a secular treatment center, they knew I couldn't afford to do this. My insurance wouldn't cover the expense. Committee members assured me they understood my financial difficulty and would help me.

For some reason their help never came, and soon I was close to bankruptcy and the loss of my home. In the meantime, their recommendation obviously hadn't worked. The committee lost interest in my situation. I believe they didn't know what else to recommend. This awkward problem was very painful for Julia and me. The church had been our lifeblood and a major part of our lives. I had been a member for 14 years, and Julia had been a member for more than 20 years. Both of us grew bitter and resentful.

God graciously gave us insight about how to deal with our bitterness. If we planned to continue to walk in freedom, we needed to forgive those committee members who didn't follow through on their promises. They didn't fully understand our financial situation, nor could they predict how we would feel if their plan didn't work. They recommended what they thought was best for me, and I believed they acted in love. Regardless of their action, and regardless of their motives, Julia and I were hurt and angered by what they had done and not done. But we knew we needed to forgive from our hearts—in obedience to God—for our sake and for our own freedom. We knew that one of the most common ways Satan robs us of our freedom is through unforgiveness.[1]

When we made up our minds to forgive, God enabled us to do so and He freed us from our anger and bad feelings. No members of the pastoral staff or committee have admitted they failed to keep their promise. But I'm not waiting for them to do that. And if one should ever ask me to forgive him, I would tell him that he's already forgiven.

During the same time, I was failing even worse to keep my promises. That's the great paradox that bitter people struggle with. They are consumed by what other people have done to them and can't find the simple solution that would set them free.

There are some who believe they don't have to forgive until the guilty party admits he or she is wrong and asks for forgiveness. If that were the case, then all the sick people in the world could keep their victims in the bondage of bitterness. Had Julia and I not forgiven them, we would have missed out on the best years of our lives. We have been blessed exceedingly abundantly beyond what we could imagine (see Eph. 3:20) because we have been forgiven and have learned how to forgive others.

It is important to understand the difference between the need to forgive others who have offended you and the need to ask others to forgive you for what you have done to them. According to Matthew 5:23,24, if you have offended someone else, then don't go to God, go to that person and be reconciled. But when someone has offended you, don't go to that person, go to God and receive the grace to forgive.

The reason we're making this distinction is because many people wrongly think they have to go to the offender in order to forgive them. Your freedom in Christ cannot be dependent upon other people. It is purely an issue between you and God. After you have forgiven a person from your heart, you may or may not be reconciled to him; it is very much dependent upon the other person.

Our need to forgive others will greatly affect how well we are relating to God. If we choose not to forgive, we have chosen to disobey God and reject His Word. You cannot live in harmony with God and be an unforgiving person. Forgiveness is an essential part of being Christlike. "Get rid of all bitterness, rage and anger, brawling and slander, along with every form of malice. Be kind and compassionate to one another, forgiving each other, just as in Christ God forgave you" (Eph. 4:31,32).

I received a call from a man who has been struggling with addiction for a long time. He had gone to a Christian treatment center I recommended, but only stayed a week. I'm not sure why he called me, but it wasn't for advice or counsel. He spent the whole time telling me all his problems and lamenting that these people were treating him wrong. He blamed the treatment center for messing up his life.

"Wait a minute," I said, "no one makes you do anything or messes up your life. What you do, you choose to do." A person who insists on blaming others for his problems will never get free. We all must take responsibility for our actions and forgive those who have hurt us.

Probe

Can you see why your relationship with God will suffer if you will not forgive? How can a sick person who won't forgive keep innocent victims in bondage?

Journal

Note
1. Neil T. Anderson and Mike and Julia Quarles, *Freedom from Addiction* (Ventura, Calif.: Regal Books, 1996), p. 145.

DAY 102

Thought for Today: In order to be free, forgiving others must come from the heart.

This is how my heavenly Father will treat each of you unless you forgive your brother from your heart.
MATTHEW 18:35

What does Jesus mean when He says, "Forgive your brother from your heart?" I have encountered many Christians who still feel hurt and angry even after they say they have forgiven others. Chances are their forgiveness wasn't from the heart.

While taking a counseling training course, God began teaching me (Julia) more about forgiveness. Angry people love to talk about what others have done to them, and they get specific. But when it comes to the crisis of forgiveness, they don't want to talk about it. To forgive a person from the heart, we need to clearly specify what it is we are forgiving him or her for and what that person's sin did to us. That would include how that sin made us feel and how it affected the way we believed and lived from that time on.

Listen to how one young lady forgave her father who had sexually abused her. "Lord, I forgive my father for sexually abusing me and making me feel dirty and evil, which led me to hate sex and all men. And, Lord, I forgive my Father for abusing me. Because of that horrible experience I chose to believe You didn't love me or care for me, and I didn't see how I could ever trust You after that."

In 1985, when Mike was away for two months at a Christian treatment center, my focus had been on Mike's bad behavior. Then I realized that God wasn't just looking at Mike but at my heart as well. I saw in Galatians 5:19-21 that feelings of hate, envy, pride and anger were listed right along with drunkenness. God used that to make me see how much He had forgiven in me, and to make me willing to forgive Mike for his alcoholism and its consequences. I made the decision to forgive him for being an alcoholic, for wrecking us financially and for how I negatively processed his erratic behavior (mentally, emotionally, spiritually and physically). That decision opened the way for the restoration of our marriage.

When I first tried to forgive Mike for what he did, I didn't want to face leftover feelings. I didn't want to look at anything that may have been buried in my heart all those years. Our marriage was doing great, Mike was back in ministry and our life was much better. I didn't want to stir up any unpleasantness. But I realized that if I didn't open my heart to God, I would miss out on an opportunity to trust Him. I thought my only feelings were mad, glad or sad. I didn't want to consider how "mad" felt or how "sad" felt. Those underlying feelings were what I had stuffed for years.

One weekend, Mike was going to be out of town speaking. I decided to use that time to deal with this issue. I thought, *Since forgiveness is between me and God, Mike doesn't have to be here; he doesn't even have to know I am doing it.*

I had been taught that it might be helpful to put an empty chair in front of me and picture the person I needed to forgive sitting there. As I started thinking back to the drinking years, I remembered how I felt when Mike would call and say he had to work late and wouldn't be home for dinner. I knew he was lying to me. I felt so helpless to coerce him to come home or to stop him from lying. I would hang up the phone and fling myself down on the sofa and sob. I felt abandoned, rejected and undesirable.

Now I wept bitterly as I remembered the awful feelings of those nights. I pictured Mike sitting in that chair, and I said, "Mike, you made me feel rejected, undesirable, abandoned and unloved. But I forgive you."

I continued into the next day, and many painful memories returned. I remembered how it felt to have a creditor call. I said to the chair, "Mike, when we were hounded for payments we couldn't make and I had to answer about them, I felt so deserted and dishonored by you. I was ashamed. I felt that people looked down on me. I felt so insecure think-ing we might lose our house. But I forgive you for the way I felt, and I release you from any debt to me."

I remembered that I often felt I would drown in his selfishness as he pampered himself with nice clothes and new cars and whatever his heart desired. I said, "Mike, you made me feel inferior to you and to other people. I felt unloved and uncared for; but I forgive you."

This went on for two very difficult days. I allowed God to dig up, one by one, those long-hidden feelings. By Sunday I felt empty and exhausted, but I also felt a freedom I had never experienced. I even felt a fresh love for Mike. I was no longer holding anything against him.

Now, when any of those old feelings come up—and they do—I remind myself that those issues have been forgiven. I choose not to think about them. I realize they are part of the process I went through to experience the freedom I now enjoy. I don't want to let any root of bitterness grow in my heart, so I have learned to take my thoughts captive and not dwell on issues I have already dealt with. Because I have forgiven Mike from my heart, I am now free to write about this and to speak and teach along with Mike. I couldn't do that if I were still in bondage to unforgiveness. God healed me from those painful memories when I chose to forgive from my heart.

Probe

Do you need to place an empty chair in front of you? We keep trying to push painful memories down, but God is trying to surface them one by one, so that we can choose to forgive from our hearts. Hasn't there been enough pain? You know how to stop it. Will you?

Journal

_____

_____

_____

_____

_____

DAY 103

Thought for Today: Forgiving is not denying how we feel.

If an enemy were insulting me, I could endure it; if a foe were raising himself against me, I could hide from him. But it is you, a man like myself, my companion, my close friend, with whom I once enjoyed sweet fellowship as we walked with the throng at the house of God.

PSALM 55:12-14

Author and preacher Malcolm Smith, who has taught the message of freedom and grace to thousands, shares the following story on forgiveness. It was a major turning point in his ministry.

A person who had been a close friend grew jealous of Malcolm's success. He began to spread lies in an attempt to destroy Malcolm's ministry. It all came to a head one evening when the man's vicious lies were aired before the congregation. Malcolm felt helpless against the attack. He was thrown into such despair that he felt his ministry was over and he walked away from the church.

He found himself walking down a deserted country road, his spirit as dark as the night about him. Angry, bitter thoughts raged within, and endless questions bombarded him. How could his former friend have stooped so low? Resentment and hatred welled up in Malcolm's heart. He knew that unless he dealt with his feelings that very night, he could be destroyed by an unforgiving spirit. He wrote:

> Stopping on the road, I called out the name of the man who had been my friend and was now my would-be destroyer. And then, I said, "I forgive you in the Name of the Lord Jesus Christ. Father, do not lay this sin to his charge. I recognize it was laid on Jesus and put away . . . I do not hold it against him any more." I turned and walked on down the road. By faith, I had drawn my line and the matter was settled in my heart with God.[1]

Only minutes later, Malcolm began to feel the anger, self-pity and resentment rising in his heart again. *How could he do it?* his hurt spirit whimpered. He stopped and said aloud, "Ten minutes ago he was pronounced forgiven, the case is closed and I am not discussing it with myself or anyone again."

Malcolm repeated that declaration many times during the next days and weeks. He had to stop what he was doing and state aloud that final decision in spite of his recurring feelings of resentment. He had forgiven the man, even though feelings would come back whenever his thoughts would drift back to the injustice of it all. Malcolm recognized the battle for his mind and would not give in to the resultant feelings! He knew that God had forgiven both himself and the person who sought to harm him. Old thoughts and emotions will try to recycle themselves, but when they do, take those thoughts captive in obedience to Christ, choose the truth and get on with your life in Christ.

Malcolm recalls that he felt no "warm, gushing feelings" toward the man after he forgave him. In fact, he felt nothing about the man, because he was free from the past and he was trusting Christ for the future. Gradually, the intervals of peace between those negative tempting thoughts and feelings grew longer. "I can still remember those days," Malcolm writes. "In fact, I can vividly remember the history of that night; but I remember it as history, nothing more. I have no emotional attachment to it. It has no power to hurt me or anyone else."

One night, while having dinner with a family after church, the wife asked me, "Do you find it hard or painful to share all of the struggles and problems you went through? Do you sometimes not want to do that?" A lot of people ask me (Mike) that question or one very similar to it. My answer is always an unqualified no. Actually, I enjoy telling about my struggles and my brokenness. I have no emotional baggage left over from my past.

As Malcolm Smith said, "[The past] has no power to hurt me or anyone else." Also, my past is not an unresolved conflict, because I have found my own forgiveness in Christ and I have forgiven those who hurt me. Now I view the past in the light of my identity in Christ. I have an answer for people in bondage; and I know it works because it is God's answer, and it worked for me.

Some people say, "I don't want to talk about that. It's in the past, and it's too painful." That's because they really haven't dealt with all their issues, and the problem isn't really in the past. The abuse may be in the past, but the problem is still present. It may take some time for damaged emotions to heal, but once you have dealt with the pain and forgiven those who hurt you, the healing begins.

Our emotional life is real, and we can't ignore it, but we can't let it control us either. One young lady said, "I can't forgive my mother; I hate her."

"Now that you've admitted that," I replied, "you can forgive her. I'm not asking you to change how you feel or to deny your emotions; they have correctly revealed that you haven't forgiven your mother yet, but now you can. If you couldn't be totally honest about how you felt about your mother, you probably couldn't forgive her from your heart."

I remember a time when I was angry at Julia about something (I can't recall now what it was). I decided I would wait until I felt like it before I forgave her. The longer I waited the angrier I got, until I had worked myself into a rage. I was losing control and it scared me. So in the midst of my anger I said aloud, "Lord I don't feel like it, but I choose by faith to forgive Julia and release her." Almost immediately the anger subsided. The issue had been dealt with. If you wait until you feel like forgiving, you will never get there.

Probe

When Stephen was being stoned to death, he chose to forgive those who were murdering him (see Acts 7:59,60). How was he able to do that and why did he do it? What is the difference between the lasting effects of an incomplete forgiveness and the tendency for our thoughts and emotions to recycle after we have truly forgiven someone?

Journal

_____

_____

_____

_____

_____

Note
1. Malcolm Smith, *Spiritual Burnout* (Tulsa, Okla.: Honor Books, 1988), pp. 190,
   191.

DAY 104

Thought for Today: Forgiveness is letting go of the past
and grabbing hold of God.

While they were stoning him, Stephen prayed,
"Lord Jesus, receive my spirit." Then he fell on his knees and cried out,
"Lord, do not hold this sin against them."

ACTS 7:59,60

One of the best examples of true forgiveness is the story of Corrie ten
Boom, the famous Dutch author of *The Hiding Place*.

It was 1947. I had come from Holland to defeated Germany with
the message that God forgives.

And that's when I saw him, working his way forward against
the others. . . . It came back with a rush; the huge room with its
harsh overhead lights; the pathetic pile of dresses and shoes in
the center of the floor; the shame of walking naked past this
man. I could see my sister's frail form ahead of me, ribs sharp
beneath the parchment skin.

Betsie and I had been arrested for concealing Jews in our home during the Nazi occupation of Holland; this man had been a guard at Ravensbruck concentration camp.

Now he was in front of me, hand thrust out: "A fine message, Fraulein! How good it is to know that, as you say, all our sins are at the bottom of the sea!"

And I who had spoken so glibly of forgiveness, fumbled in my pocketbook rather than take that hand. . . .

"You mentioned Ravensbruck in your talk," he was saying. "I was a guard in there." No, he did not remember me. "But since that time," he went on, "I have become a Christian. I know that God has forgiven me for the cruel things I did there, but I would like to hear it from your lips as well, Fraulein,"—again the hand came out—"will you forgive me?"

And I stood there—I whose sins had every day to be forgiven—and could not. Betsie had died in that place—could he erase her slow, terrible death simply for the asking?

It could not have been many seconds that he stood there, hand held out, but to me it seemed hours as I wrestled with the most difficult thing I had ever had to do. For I had to do it—I knew that. . . .

And still I stood there with the coldness clutching my heart. But forgiveness is not an emotion—I knew that too. Forgiveness is an act of the will, and the will can function regardless of the temperature of the heart.

Even as the angry, vengeful thoughts boiled through me, I saw the sin of them. Jesus Christ Himself had died for this man; was I going to ask for more? *Lord Jesus,* I prayed, *forgive me and help me to forgive him.* I tried to smile. I struggled to raise my hand. I could not. I felt nothing, not the slightest spark of warmth or charity. And so again I breathed a silent prayer.

Jesus. I cannot forgive him. Give me your forgiveness.

As I took his hand, mechanically, woodenly, a most incredible thing happened. From my shoulder along my arm and through my hand a current seemed to pass from me to him, while into my heart sprang a love for this stranger that almost overwhelmed me.

And so I discovered that it is not on our forgiveness any more than on our goodness that the world's healing hinges, but on His. When He tells us to love our enemies, He gives, along with the command, the love itself.[1]

Corrie ten Boom's story reminds me of a lady who came to my conference. She was deep in the bondage of bitterness. Ten years ago her best friend had run off with her husband. I had a picture of her stretched between heaven and her past, one arm extended upward. She wasn't trying to grasp hold of God, but He had her firmly by the hand. Her other arm was holding on to her past with all her might and she was unwilling to let it go. I told her the picture I saw and said, "Why don't you let go? You're only hurting yourself."

I spoke the following morning in her church and saw her singing in the choir. I asked the pastor if he knew who she was. He said, "I can't keep my eyes off her. She is a completely different person. What happened to her?"

"She let it go," I said.

Probe
Why don't people "let it go"? What are the consequences of not letting go? What will happen if we do?

Journal

_____

_____

_____

_____

_____

Note
1. Corrie ten Boom, *Tramp for the Lord* (Old Tappan, N. J.: Revell, 1974), pp. 53-55.

DAY 105

Thought for Today: Forgiveness is the spiritual glue that holds relationships together.

Do not judge, and you will not be judged. Do not condemn, and you will not be condemned. Forgive, and you will be forgiven.

LUKE 6:37

He was a top-ranking officer who had a brilliant career in the military for nearly 20 years. He was a committed Christian with a loving wife and children who loved and respected him. He looked forward to the day when he would be able to retire.

One indiscretion in a weak moment turned it all upside down. He knew he shouldn't have done it, but he had given in to the temptation. Another person who knew about it could have overlooked it. After all, such indiscretions are committed every day in the military. But the other person didn't overlook it. He reported it to his commanding officer. The CO could have dismissed it, but he didn't. A court-martial was called for.

Surely the other officers who had worked so closely with him and seen his dedication and commitment would come to his aid and testify for him. They didn't. In fact, it looked as though everyone had turned against him. The whole trial was an unbearable nightmare. He felt vilified and castigated. His wife was there and heard everything.

He was court-martialed, dishonorably discharged and deprived of his pension. But the worst part was that everyone—his wife, children, relatives, friends and associates—knew about it. His life was ruined—all because of one stupid indiscretion.

His worst fears were confirmed. His wife was so hurt she could no longer relate to him. It seemed as though he had lost all his friends overnight. Even the people at church were distant. Some of his relatives and friends made it clear they no longer wanted to have anything to do with him.

He spent thousands of dollars and many hours on secular counseling and treatment. He went to the church seeking for help. The pastor and elders started working with and counseling both him and his wife, but they were heavy-handed and judgmental. It seemed to him they were part of the process to destroy him. And to make it worse, they came down hard on his wife. She was devastated. The marriage deteriorated further.

His children were also hurting. One of them reached out to the youth pastor, but he just didn't have time for the hurting youth and never followed through. This son felt rejected, uncared for and alone.

The man tried to go to the pastor and share his pain and grief with him, but it seemed the pastor didn't want to discuss it and wished he would go away. That was one of the most hurtful experiences in this nightmare. If he couldn't find any help in the church, where would he ever find any?

I took the man through the Steps to Freedom in Christ. We were doing well until we got to the third step—forgiveness. As I was going over the step and explaining it, he stopped me and started asking a lot of questions about forgiveness. Most of his questions seemed off base, and I sensed strong resistance. We hit a major roadblock.

I suggested we break for lunch. When we came back together, he said, "You're right, my problem is that I don't think I can forgive my pastor. He hurt me and my wife so deeply and was never there for us."

I pointed out to him that even though he didn't want to and didn't feel like it, he could choose to forgive because he was a child of God, and God would enable him. He said he would think about it and let me know if he wanted to proceed with the Steps. In a few minutes he came back and said he was ready to go on.

It wasn't easy, but he did choose to forgive. He found his freedom that day. His wife's biggest struggle was also to forgive, but she was able to fight through many tears and she too found her freedom. God has restored their marriage and they are heavily involved in the ministry of sharing the truth that sets people free.

It seems that we all face a crossroads in life where we can choose to forgive and release the bitterness, or continue to live in it. We tend to think God's commands are too hard, too burdensome. But they aren't: "This is love for God: to obey his commands. And his commands are not burdensome" (1 John 5:3).

When you say you can't forgive, you are believing a lie. You have the ability to forgive because Christ is your life and He lives in you. Martin Luther put it this way: "The promises of God give what the commandments of God demand."[1] The commandments of God are not restrictive, they are protective.

Probe

Since we live in a fallen world and have to relate to imperfect people, can we have any meaningful relationships without forgiveness? Why or why not?

Journal

_____

_____

_____

_____

_____

Note
1. Harold J. Grimm, ed., *Christian Liberty* (Philadelphia: Fortress Press, 1957), p. 12.

DAY 106

Thought for Today: Self-condemnation is the lack of assurance that our sins are forgiven.

This is my blood of the covenant, which is poured out for many for the forgiveness of sins.
MATTHEW 26:28

The following letter was written to Neil after a Living Free in Christ conference:

I am writing in regard to your recent conference. The day your conference was supposed to start, I was to be admitted to the hospital for the fourth or fifth time for manic depression. I had been dealing with this for one and a half years. My wife was by my side every step of the way.

We had gone to several doctors and tried just about every drug they could think of. I also had shock treatments. I attempted suicide twice. Unable to work any longer, I spent most of my days downstairs, wishing I were dead or planning the next attempt. Also, it was a good place to protect myself from people and the world around me. At that point I had a history of self-abuse. I spent 30-odd years in jails and prisons. I was a drug addict and alcoholic. I had been in drug and alcohol treatment 28 times. I lived under bridges and tracks for several years. I ended up becoming a Christian several years ago, but always lived a defeated life. No matter how hard I tried I would always fall way short of what God wanted.

Now I was going back into the hospital to try new medication or talk about more shock treatments. My wife and some very good friends convinced me your conference would be of more value. The hospital was concerned because they thought I should be there because of the shape I was in. As the four days [of the conference] progressed, my head started to clear up. The Word of God was ministering to me, even though I was confused and in pain. My wife and friends kept encouraging me to come back and go to the day sessions. I did, and your staff was great. I attended Hal Parks' workshop. The second day I went up to him and said, "I am in the 11th hour of my life, what will God do for me?" He left and came back and said I could have a Steps to Freedom in Christ appointment at 2:00 p.m. on Sunday, and to just keep coming to the conference. I did, and through you, God brought me joy.

When it came time for my Freedom appointment on Sunday, I was in a place to deal with it. The session lasted seven hours. The people I was with didn't leave a stone unturned. Things were going great until I came to forgiveness and bitterness. You see, the three things that motivated my life were low self-worth, anger and bitterness, which were caused from being molested by a priest several times and being beaten regularly and verbally abused for six or so years. It took a long time in that session to honestly say I forgave them. But when I did in truth, God moved right in. The depression lifted and my eyes were opened to the truth in God's Word. I felt lighter than before. I did go to the hospital and after two days they said I didn't need to be there. My doctors said I was a different person. They had never seen a person change so fast. They said, "Whatever you're doing, don't stop."

This man didn't get justice from his offenders who molested him, beat him and verbally abused him. But he did find freedom and joy because he was able to forgive them.

If God gave us what we justly deserved, we would all get hell. To satisfy the justice of God, Jesus took the consequences of our sins upon Himself. God the Father "made Him who knew no sin to be sin for us, that we might become the righteousness of God in Him" (2 Cor. 5:21, NKJV). It's the Cross that makes forgiveness legally and morally right: "The death he died, he died to sin once for all" (Rom. 6:10).

Some people are unable to forgive because they haven't experienced forgiveness themselves. God is able to accept us just the way we are because He has dealt with our sins on the Cross. All of our sins have been nailed to the Cross. "When you were dead in your sins and in the uncircumcision of your sinful nature, God made you alive with Christ. He forgave us all our sins, having canceled the written code, with its regulations, that was against us and that stood opposed to us; he took it away, nailing it to the cross" (Col. 2:13,14).

People who are judgmental and unforgiving toward others are often struggling with their own lack of forgiveness. The unforgiven become the unforgiving. We consistently come across people who need to forgive themselves. They stand self-condemned and often say when they come to their name, "This will be the hardest one to forgive." They are forgiven but they haven't appropriated it. There is no condemnation for those who are in Christ Jesus (see Rom. 8:1). Let yourself off your own hook. The devil may accuse you day and night, but God will remember your sins no more.

Probe

Are you your own worst critic? Why don't you let yourself off your own hook? Pray, "Lord, I forgive myself for (specifically identify every issue of self-condemnation). I thank You for Your forgiveness and I now receive it as your child. I submit myself to You and I resist the devil and all his accusations. In Jesus' name I pray. Amen."

Journal

_____

_____

_____

_____

_____

DAY 107

Thought for Today: Forgiveness is the fragrance the violet leaves on the heel that crushed it.

Jesus said, "Father, forgive them, for they do not know what they are doing." And they divided up his clothes by casting lots.
LUKE 23:34

One of the greatest personal crises I (Neil) have faced in the ministry revolved around the issue of forgiveness and a board member I'll call

Calvin. I was struggling to relate to this man, so I asked if he would meet weekly with me. I had only one goal: to try to establish a meaningful relationship with him.

About four months after Calvin and I started meeting, I asked the board if I could lead a tour group from the church to Israel. Calvin's hand shot up. "I'm against it because, as the tour leader, the pastor will go free, and that's like giving him a bonus." I didn't want any kind of a board crisis, so I withdrew the request and used my vacation time to go with another tour.

Despite the burden I carried in my heart over my conflict with Calvin, the trip to Israel was a tremendous spiritual experience for me. On one of my free days in Jerusalem, I spent one afternoon alone in the Church of All Nations that enshrines the rock where Jesus struggled with His greatest crisis. I sat there staring at the rock where Christ reportedly sweat great drops of blood as He anticipated taking upon Himself all the sins of the world. All Jesus was asking of me was to take the sin of one man upon myself. I decided I could do that. If Jesus could take all the world's sins upon Himself, I could surely endure the sins of one difficult person.

I left there with a sense of resolution and went home feeling pretty good. Not having me to pick on anymore, Calvin shifted his attack to our youth pastor. That did it! I could handle Calvin's resistance to me. But when he attacked my youth pastor I had reached the end of my patience. The board of the church wouldn't do anything about it, so I decided to resign.

One morning I wrote out my resignation. By that evening I was flat on my back with a temperature of 103.5 degrees, and I had totally lost my voice. It doesn't take a genius to recognize that God was not pleased with my decision. When you are flat on your back, there is no way to look but up. So I began reading the Gospels. I came to Mark 8:22-26, where Jesus healed the blind man. After Jesus touched the man the first time, he asked, "What do you see?" "I see men like trees," he responded (v. 24). The Lord touched him a second time, and now he could see men clearly. I suddenly realized that I saw Calvin like that: an obstacle in my path.

I thought Calvin was blocking my goals as a pastor, but he wasn't. God actually used that man, more than any other, to make me the pastor God wanted me to be. I prayed, "Lord, I don't love that man, but I know You do, and I want to. There is no way I can love him in my present state. I'm asking You to touch me like You did that blind man." And God did! I also chose to forgive Calvin from the heart.

The next Sunday I went to church not to resign but to preach. My text was Mark 8:22-26. I talked about three types of people. Some are blind and need us to take them by the hand and lead them to Jesus. Then there are those who see people like trees, but we aren't trees. We are children of God, and only those who have been touched by Him can see people clearly. I confessed to the congregation my own independence and my desire for the Lord to touch me, to see people as people, not as obstacles in my path.

At the end of the sermon I invited everyone who desired a second touch from the Lord to join me at the altar. We sang a hymn and people streamed forward. Soon the altar area and the aisles in the front were packed with people. We opened the side doors and people spilled out onto the lawns. Only about 15 people remained in their seats. It was a revival!

Guess who was one of the few holdouts? To my knowledge, Calvin never changed; but I did. I continued to take a stand against what I believed was wrong, because I was not about to tolerate sin. But I no longer responded in bitterness. I thank God to this day that He struck me down. If I had had my way, I would probably be out of ministry, struggling with bitterness.[1]

We all come to crossroads in our lives where we could choose to forgive or continue to live in bitterness. The number one reason that people fail in ministry is because they can't get along with others. Their bitterness will torpedo every relationship. How much easier life would be if they would just be willing to forgive.

God will allow or place a few trees in our path and say, "There; what are you going to do about that?" The flesh will reach for a chain saw, but the Spirit will reveal the true condition of our hearts. At that moment, the difficult other person isn't the issue, because nobody and nothing on planet Earth can keep us from being the people God created us to be. The issue is our relationship with God and our growth in character. Such trials are not intended to destroy us, but they do reveal who we are. We can choose to grow through the crisis by the grace of God.

Probe

What is your natural tendency when somebody seems to block your goals? Do you try to remove the obstacles by trying to change or control others, or do you try to change yourself? What is God trying to accomplish in your life?

Journal

_____

_____

_____

_____

_____

Note
1. Neil T. Anderson, *Victory over the Darkness* (Ventura, Calif.: Regal Books, 1990), pp. 206, 207.

DAY 108

Thought for Today: You are most like Christ when you forgive.

You, with the help of wicked men, put him to death by nailing him to the cross. But God raised him from the dead, freeing him from the agony of death, because it was impossible for death to keep its hold on him.

ACTS 2:23,24

Ruby had experienced more rejection in 40 years than anyone I (Neil) have ever heard about. She was rejected by her unmarried mother before she was born, miraculously surviving an abortion six months into her mother's pregnancy. Ruby's mother then abandoned her to her father, who in turn gave her to his mother. Ruby's grandmother was involved in a bizarre mixture of religious and occult practices, so Ruby was raised in an atmosphere of seances and other weird demonic experiences.

Ruby married at 14 to escape her grandmother's home. By the time she was 21 she had five children, all of whom were convinced by their father that Ruby was no good. Eventually her husband and five children all deserted her. Feeling totally rejected, Ruby unsuccessfully attempted suicide several times. She received Christ during this time, but those who knew her were still afraid she would take her own life. "Don't commit suicide," they urged her. "Hang on; life will get better." Yet voices inside her head taunted Ruby, and an eerie, dark spiritual presence infested her home.

It was in this condition that Ruby came to a week-long conference I was conducting at her church. On Wednesday night I spoke on forgiveness, encouraging people to list the names of people they needed to forgive. In the middle of the session, Ruby left the room with what appeared to be an asthma attack. In reality, Satan was frantically trying to keep her from experiencing the freedom in Christ I was speaking about.

The next afternoon, one of the pastors and I met privately with Ruby to counsel her and pray with her. When we began to talk about forgiveness, Ruby brought out the list of names she had compiled—four pages of people who had hurt her and rejected her over the years! No wonder Satan was having such great success in her life. Virtually everyone else had turned her away.

We led Ruby through the steps to forgiveness, and she walked out of the office free. She realized for the first time that God loves her and will never reject her. She went home thrilled and excited. The evil voices inside her and the evil presence in her home vanished.

Most of us haven't suffered the pervasive rejection Ruby experienced. But everyone knows what it feels like to be criticized and rejected, even by those who are supposed to love and care for us. We were born and raised in a worldly environment that chooses favorites and rejects seconds. Since nobody can be the best at everything, we all were ignored, overlooked or rejected at some time by parents, teachers and friends.[1]

The greatest evil ever perpetrated against an innocent man would have to be the crucifixion of Christ. Wicked men nailed the sinless Son of God to a cross, where He died a horrible, cruel death. But it was also the greatest act of love and kindness the world has ever seen. "The God of our fathers raised Jesus from the dead . . . God exalted him to his own right hand as Prince and Savior that he might give repentance and forgiveness of sins to Israel" (Acts 5:30,31).

God is the Redeemer. To "redeem" means to rescue, recover, deliver and liberate. "In him we have redemption through his blood, the forgiveness of sins, in accordance with the riches of God's grace" (Eph. 1:7). The death of Christ on the cross redeemed us from sin, bondage, evil, death and hell.

The grace of God overcomes sin. "But where sin increased, grace increased all the more" (Rom. 5:20). When we are sinned against, we want justice. We want the guilty one punished. We think that to forgive him or her would be to overlook sin. But unforgiveness is the opposite of grace. If we choose not to forgive, we are ignoring and rejecting what Christ's death accomplished.

If we choose not to forgive, we buy into Satan's schemes and fall for his number one method of keeping us in bondage. Paul urged the Corinthians to forgive a man who had sinned greatly by committing adultery with his "father's wife" (see 1 Cor. 5:1; 2 Cor. 2:5-11). The apostle then warned them about the satanic trap of unforgiveness, "in order that Satan might not outwit us. For we are not unaware of his schemes" (2 Cor. 2:11).

The story was told of a little girl who was deathly afraid of bees. One day when the girl was riding in a car with her dad, a bee flew in the window and she went berserk. Her dad quickly grabbed the bee and held it in his hand. Then he released the bee. The little girl was terrified again. The father gently said, "There's nothing to be afraid of. Look—the stinger is in my hand. He can't hurt you anymore."

The devil is roaring around like a hungry lion seeking someone to devour, but his "stinger" has been removed. We have victory in Christ, but we can't be ignorant of Satan's schemes. To hold on to our bitterness is to give the devil an opportunity. You are most like Christ when you forgive.

Probe

Do you know someone who is locked in the bondage of bitterness? How can you help this person get over the bitterness? Would you be willing to try? There is no greater privilege than to help someone else find freedom in Christ.

Journal

_____

_____

_____

_____

_____

Note
1. Neil T. Anderson, *Victory over the Darkness* (Ventura, Calif.: Regal Books, 1990), pp. 209, 210.

WINNING THE BATTLE FOR THE MIND

DAY 109

**Thought for Today: Freedom comes when we take every thought
captive in obedience to Christ.**

*The evening meal was being served, and the devil had already prompted
Judas Iscariot, son of Simon, to betray Jesus.*

JOHN 13:2

Before he met Christ, Rick's life was an endless quest for intimacy. As a
child, he was sexually abused by his grandmother. After his father committed suicide, his mother became increasingly involved in religious
activities, devoting her life to ministry. So as a young man, Rick
embarked on a desperate search to fill the hole that the sins of others had
left in him. Even after his marriage to Emily, his college sweetheart, he
kept trying to cover his bitterness and hurt with sexual encounters, work
and the approval of others, but without success. Emily lost patience and
left him.

One day, while listening to a tape by Dr. Charles Stanley, Rick fell to
his knees and asked Jesus to save him from himself and the sinful lifestyle
that had never delivered what it promised. He and Emily were reconciled
and eventually had four children. They seemed to be the model Christian
family.

But deep inside, Rick was still taunted by the lie that sex, food, work
and other people could meet his needs more fully than Christ could. He
began listening to that lie and fell back into his old patterns of immorality. He became sexually involved with numerous partners. For years he
rode a spiritual and emotional roller coaster. Rick recalls:

The pimp in my mind repeatedly promised me fulfillment if I
would only prostitute myself one more time. But he never fulfilled his promise. . . . My sexual addiction ruled everything in
my life. I hated it. I knew it was destroying me from the inside
out—but I kept heeding the pimp in my mind again and again.

Rick's mother invited him to attend Neil's conference on resolving personal and spiritual conflicts. He consented to go, but during the first evening of the conference he was harassed by sexual fantasies prompted by Satan, the "pimp" in his mind.

Rick's mother set up an appointment for Rick to meet with Neil privately during the conference. He continues his story:

> As Neil led me through the Steps to Freedom in Christ, I could hear the pimp's insistent lies in my mind. The inner battle was intense, but I was ready for the shackles to be broken. So I repented of my sin, renounced all the lies I had believed, renounced every sexual use of my body as an instrument of unrighteousness and forgave all those who had offended me. As I did, peace began to roll in and drown out 37 years' worth of lies. I heard holy silence. The pimp was gone and, praise God, I was free.

Rick's freedom was tested right away. The next day, during the conference, he was bombarded by immoral thoughts. But he stood firm in the power of the blood of Christ to resist them. That night he was strongly tempted to pursue another destructive relationship. But the moment he called on Christ's all-powerful cleansing blood, the holy silence returned. "It's a miracle!" Rick says. "I have been set free from that lying pimp in my mind."[1]

How does Satan deceive you into believing his lies? Does he show up in a little red suit, carrying a pitchfork, and say, "Hey, I've got a great idea for you?" No, he is far more deceptive than that. Scripture reveals that he is capable of putting thoughts in our minds in such a way that we think they are our own.

In the Old Testament, Satan rose up against Israel and incited David to take a census of the people, and David did it even though his military commander told him it was sinful to do it (1 Chron. 21). Thousands died as a result of David's belief in a lie. In the Gospels, the devil "prompted Judas Iscariot, son of Simon, to betray Jesus" (John 13:2). In the Early

Church, God struck down Ananias and Sapphira because Satan had filled their hearts to lie to the Holy Spirit (Acts 5:3). God had to send a powerful message to the Early Church, because He knew that if Satan deceived any of His children into believing a lie, he could control their lives.

We don't know how Satan put thoughts into David's, Ananias's and Judas's minds, but Scripture clearly reveals that he can and he did. It can also happen to us, especially in light of the age in which we are living. "The Spirit clearly says that in later times some will abandon the faith and follow deceiving spirits and things taught by demons" (1 Tim. 4:1). To guard against this we are admonished to "take captive every thought to make it obedient to Christ" (2 Cor. 10:5).

"You have to get rid of that 'stinking thinking,'" is the advice you'll hear in many AA meetings. They also say, "Don't pay attention to the committee in your head." They have correctly analyzed the problem, but unless they understand the spiritual battle for their minds, they will lack an adequate answer. Many alcoholics hit the bottle to drown out negative thoughts. They have no mental peace.

Rick really didn't have a sexual problem, he had a thinking and believing problem. So does everyone in bondage. That's why it is essential that we renew and discipline our minds to the truth of God's Word.

Satan's power is in the lie. It's the only weapon he has against the believer, because Satan is a defeated foe. We have the authority over him because we are seated with Christ in the heavenlies (see Eph. 2:6) and He is "far above all rule and authority, power and dominion" (Eph. 1:21). If we can expose the lie and choose the truth, we can win the battle for our minds.

Probe

Do you struggle in your thought life? Why do you need to take *every* thought captive and make it obedient to Christ? Rather than trying to analyze every thought to see where it comes from, why not just choose the truth and not pay attention to tempting and accusing thoughts? Try it.

Journal

_____

_____

_____

_____

_____

Note

1. Neil T. Anderson, *A Way of Escape* (Eugene, Oregon: Harvest House Publishers, 1994), pp. 51-55.

DAY 110

Thought for Today: Freedom comes when we choose the truth and live accordingly.

How long, O men, will you turn my glory into shame? How long will you love delusions and seek false gods?

PSALM 4:2

During World War II, Lieutenant General Jonathan Mayhew Wainwright was commander of the Allied Forces in the Philippines. Following a heroic resistance of enemy forces, on May 6, 1942, he was forced to surrender to the Japanese the island of Corregidor.

For three years General Wainwright suffered as a prisoner of war in a Manchurian camp. During his internment, he endured the incessant cruelties of malnutrition, physical and verbal abuse, and psychological mind games. Through it all, he maintained his dignity as a human being and a soldier. After the Japanese surrendered, his captors kept Wainwright and the other prisoners incarcerated—the war ended, but the bondage continued.

One day, an Allied plane landed in a field near the prison. Through the fence that surrounded the compound, an airman informed the general of the Japanese surrender and the American victory. Wainwright immediately pulled his emaciated body to attention and marched toward the command house. He burst through the door, marched up to the camp's commanding officer and said, "My commander in chief has conquered your commander in chief. I am now in charge of this camp." In response to Wainwright's declaration, the officer took off his sword, laid it on the table and surrendered his command.

The Christian's commander in chief has conquered Satan. I am certain that General Wainwright did not feel victorious and in charge as he marched up to the commander of the prison camp. But he chose to believe the truth and act on it. Satan has deceived many Christians who still believe they are under the authority of the god of this world. As long as they believe it, their bondage will continue. Perhaps you are one of them. It is time for you to stand up and claim your rightful victory. The war has been won; Satan is defeated. You are now alive and free in Christ, and in Him you are more than a conqueror (see Rom. 8:37)!

Bondage is nothing but lies that comprise strongholds in your mind. Freedom is believing the truth that sets you free.[1] When General Wainwright believed the truth and decided to act on it, he took a great risk. Even though what he said was true, his actions could have cost him his life. It would have been relatively easy for the Japanese commander to have had him killed on the spot. To believe and act on the truth is never easy. It always involves a risk. It usually means going against your feelings and circumstances and is the only means to set you free.

I was preaching at a church several years ago and was struck by the fact that every family in the church was sitting by themselves. The sanctuary seated more than 500, but since only about 100 were in attendance, they were able to do this. When they sang the hymns, only a few were actually singing. It was the deadest church I have ever seen.

I felt like shouting, "What's wrong with you people? Don't you know that Christ is risen from the dead? Satan has been defeated and we have been given the victory!" They didn't act like they knew that.

For 2,000 years, orthodox Christianity has used a refrain where the pastor says, "Christ is risen!" and the people respond in unison, "He is risen indeed!" Do you believe it? Do you believe that you are alive in Christ and seated with Him in the heavenly places (see Eph. 2:6)? Do you believe that the kingdom of darkness has been placed under His feet and that He is head over everything (see Eph. 1:22; 2:6)? Do you believe that you have been given the victory (see 1 Cor. 15:57) and that you are always led in triumph (see 2 Cor. 2:14)?

A man called me about a friend of his who went through a Christian treatment center I had recommended. After returning home, his friend returned again to alcohol and cocaine. I wasn't surprised to get the call, because I had talked to his friend several times and urged him to do two things: (1) learn the truth that sets you free and (2) deal with his root issues by going through the Steps to Freedom in Christ.

Unfortunately, the man was unresponsive; he was trying to "work the program" rather than be transformed by the renewing of his mind (see Rom. 12:2). He went down in flames. There was nothing really wrong with the program he was following, but his efforts ended in failure because he never truly changed what he believed. Programs don't (can't) set you free. Truth sets you free. The exciting revelation of God's Word says that "You will know the truth, and the truth will set you free. . . . So if the Son sets you free, you will be free indeed" (John 8:32,36).

Probe

What do you think would have happened if General Wainwright had asked a guard if the Japanese had surrendered? The devil has no positional authority over you, but as long as you don't know it, he will continue to rule. What lies have you believed about yourself, God and Satan that have negatively affected your life?

Journal

_____

_____

_____

_____

_____

Note
1. Neil T. Anderson and Mike and Julia Quarles, *Freedom from Addiction* (Ventura, Calif.: Regal Books, 1996), pp. 186, 187.

DAY 111

Thought for Today: The key to victory is to practice "threshold thinking."

No temptation has seized you except what is common to man.
And God is faithful; he will not let you be tempted beyond what you can bear.
But when you are tempted, he will also provide a way out
so that you can stand up under it.

1 CORINTHIANS 10:13

Anabel Gillham tells a story of the time when she was cooking dinner and heard what she thought were her two young sons at the front door. She called out, "Come on in, dinner's almost ready." However, it wasn't her two sons. It was a vacuum cleaner salesman. Once he entered the house it took them almost two hours to get him out.

We have all unwittingly invited intruders into our minds. Once we allow a tempting or deceiving thought to enter, it is very difficult to get it out. One casual look at pornography can stay in our memory banks for years. Martin Luther's adage is true: You can't stop birds from flying over your head, but you can stop them from building a nest on your head.

The spiritual battle is in the mind, and if we don't renew and discipline our minds by choosing the truth, we will likely lose the battle. The stakes are huge. To lose could mean personal destruction, alienation and bondage. It is a battle, not a game, and Satan is determined to inflict as much damage as he can.

The good news? God has promised to provide a way of escape for every temptation (see 1 Cor. 10:13). We are promised that no temptation will come our way that is not common to everyone else, and God will enable us to withstand every one. The key to victory is to practice threshold thinking.

Every temptation comes by way of an initial thought to your mind. It matters not whether the thought is from your own carnal nature, the world or the devil. If you ruminate on that thought and consider it an option, you will eventually act on it, and that's sin. Instead, Paul instructs us to take every thought captive to the obedience of Christ (see 2 Cor. 10:5b). The first step for escaping temptation is to apprehend every thought as soon as it steps through the doorway of your mind.[1]

If it isn't true, don't think it.

The way of escape is not a physical door you run out of if you're tempted to lust, drink or do drugs. The way of escape is to choose the truth when any tempting, accusing or deceiving thought first enters your mind. If you do that you will never enter the doors of a porno shop or tavern. The way of escape came long before you got to such places. To think that we can frequent such places and not sin is to be deceived. "Do not be misled: 'Bad company corrupts good character'" (1 Cor. 15:33).

You have heard that the Bible will keep you from sin, and sin will keep you from the Bible. But it's not that simple. Nothing you can do is more encouraging, profitable and uplifting than to spend time with God in His Word. It's a great start for every day, but when you leave your quiet time is when you will be tested. Having the Word of God tucked in your heart and on the top of your mind will help you choose the way of escape.

When I was in bondage to alcohol, I would sometimes study the Bible for an hour or two in the morning, then be drunk that very same night. Why? I didn't know how to take every thought captive and I don't think I was even aware of the need to. Daily Bible reading is not some magical manna that once digested will sustain us for the rest of the day (like the manna did for the Israelites in the wilderness). We have to practice the presence of God and assume 24-hour responsibility for our thoughts. Hannah Whitall Smith said that our thoughts are what we feed on and what determines our spiritual vitality. Hannah wrote:

> Very few persons realize the effect of thought upon the condition of the soul, that is in fact its food, the substance from which it evolves its strength and health and beauty, or upon which it may become weak and unhealthy and deformed. The things we think about are the things we feed upon. If we think low and corrupt thoughts, we bring diseases upon our soul, just as we bring diseases upon our body by eating corrupt and improper food. If

we will take the words of God, that is, His revealed truth, into our lips and eat it; that is, if we will dwell upon His words . . . we will find that our soul-life is fed and nourished by them, and is made strong and vigorous in consequence.[2]

Probe

Have you understood how important your thought life is for living a responsible and victorious life? What negative patterns of thinking get you into trouble or weigh you down? Can you identify these thoughts and stop them at the threshold of your mind?

Journal

_____

_____

_____

_____

_____

Notes
1. Neil T. Anderson, *The Bondage Breaker* (Eugene, Ore.: Harvest House Publishers, 1990), p. 138.
2. Hannah Whitall Smith, *The Common-Sense Teaching of the Bible* (Old Tappan, N.J.: Fleming H. Revell Company, 1984), pp. 25-28.

DAY 112

Thought for Today: What you do is what you think.

Therefore, prepare your minds for action; be self-controlled; set your hope fully on the grace to be given you when Jesus Christ is revealed.

1 PETER 1:13

There it was again—the thought to pull off the freeway and rent a sexually explicit video. Even though Scott was married, with two children still living at home, he continually battled the urge to fantasize sexually. He had prayed repeatedly against the impulse, but as he sped closer to the off-ramp, a conflict raged within him. He knew his actions wouldn't be pleasing to God. He knew he would be embarrassed if his wife or children came home unexpectedly and found him acting out his fantasy. But he was propelled to the video store like a heroin addict to a fix.

Scott had found many ways to satisfy his secret craving for sexual excitement and release: pornographic paperback novels and magazines, textbooks on the subject of sexuality, sexual fantasies while in the shower, and steamy videos featuring nudity and sex. (He avoided more obvious X-rated films, reasoning that the R-rated ones were easier to explain if he got caught.)

Once he took the off-ramp, Scott had stepped over the line. He passed by the "way of escape." He made his selection in the video shop and headed home for an afternoon of self-gratification. After watching the movie, he was again flooded with shame and guilt. *How did I get sucked into this pattern again?* he cried. *Lord, what am I going to do?* He had told no one about his ongoing struggle and repeated failure—not his wife, not his pastor and not the two Christian counselors he had seen in the past for other problems. He felt weak and alone. Even God seemed distant and unavailable.

So Scott did what he always did: He stuffed his feelings and guilt deep inside and went on with the charade of being a successful Christian man. Eventually his despair would dissipate and he could relax until the old urges returned and pulled him under again.[1]

Most people who struggle with chemical addictions also struggle with sexual problems. Sexual temptation is the plight of nearly every Christian man. At a retreat for Christian leaders, all of the men who were struggling with sexual problems were asked to stand up if they wanted prayer; 75 percent of the men stood up. The other 25 percent were probably too embarrassed to stand up. Of the thousands of people who have gone through the Steps to Freedom in Christ, it is rare to find one not struggling with a sexual problem.

A few years ago there was a story in the newspaper about the president of a Bible college who had embezzled several hundred thousand dollars from the school. He had used it on gambling and prostitutes. The story concluded by saying that he "must have snapped." The truth is that people don't live a holy life and then one day just snap. Years of fantasies led him to the point of public exposure.

No one wakes up one morning and has a thought out of the blue: *I think I'll have an affair with my secretary today.* Nobody becomes an addict by suddenly deciding on impulse to do drugs or get drunk. The mental strongholds of addiction are developed over much longer periods of time.

When Christians ask me, "Aren't you tempted to drink, and don't you struggle with it on a daily basis?" then I know they don't understand freedom and the importance of taking thoughts captive. The answer to that question is "No, not anymore." Before I found my freedom in Christ, I did struggle on a daily basis, but now I make it a priority every day to walk by faith in the truth and to take every thought captive. If I didn't do that, and I started paying attention to tempting and accusing thoughts, it wouldn't be long before avoiding alcohol was a struggle again.

Some people think, *There's no harm in thinking about it if I don't do anything about it.* That's the lie Satan wants you to believe. Everything we do is a product of our thought life. If you spend too much time and energy thinking about something, it won't be long before you act it out. For instance, three viewings of hard-core pornography have the same lasting effect on a person as the actual experience does. "For as he thinks within himself, so he is" (Prov. 23:7, *NASB*).

The mind is unable to distinguish between what is real and what is vividly imagined over time. If you tell a lie long enough, you will begin to believe it is true. Eventually we will live out our thought life. Our thoughts fuel our emotions and they drive our will. You prepare your mind for the right action by choosing the right thoughts. Paul's prescription for choosing the right thoughts is found in Philippians 4:8,9:

> Finally, brothers, whatever is true, whatever is noble, whatever is right, whatever is pure, whatever is lovely, whatever is admirable—if anything is excellent or praiseworthy—think about such things. Whatever you have learned or received or heard from me, or seen in me—put it into practice. And the God of peace will be with you.

Probe

Mentally speaking, what is the one essential discipline you must have if you are going to live a responsible life? How can you cultivate a pure mind in order to live a pure life? What practical steps can you take to ensure it will happen?

Journal

_____

_____

_____

_____

_____

Note
1. Neil T. Anderson, *A Way of Escape* (Eugene, Ore.: Harvest House Publishers, 1994), pp. 76, 77.

DAY 113

Thought for Today: Garbage in, garbage out!

We demolish arguments and every pretension that sets itself up against the knowledge of God, and we take captive every thought to make it obedient to Christ.

2 CORINTHIANS 10:5

The following testimony, from a man who was formerly trapped in nearly every form of sexual bondage mentioned in Neil's book *A Way of Escape,* illustrates the process of securing freedom in Christ.

I believed that I was different from most boys. I started playing sexually with some of my male friends during grade school. Voices in my head told me it was okay because I was born that way. I had a terrible male void in my life and my heart burned with desire. The memory of seeing my grandfather with an erection prompted a fascination with seeing boys and men naked. Voyeurism became a way of life for me. . . .

As an adolescent and young adult, I threw myself into the gay world. I was addicted to watching men in public restrooms and I visited gay bars almost every night. . . .

I finally started reading the Bible and attending church. I accepted the Lord at a baptism service and left the gay lifestyle completely. I studied the Word seriously, but with my background it was easy to fall into legalism. I didn't understand grace and forgiveness. I asked myself, *If I am a Christian, why do I still feel the same homosexual tendencies?* The more I tried to do what the Bible said and what others expected of me, the more guilty I felt. I didn't dare tell anyone what I was feeling. The voyeurism became intense and triggered an uncontrollable bondage to masturbation.

A friend who was aware of my struggle gave me a copy of *Victory over the Darkness* by Neil Anderson. As I began reading it, the book seemed to be written about me. For the first time I understood how I got into my horrible condition and how I could get out of it. No one had ever told me that I was a child of God, that God had chosen me as His friend and that He loved me specifically. I had learned about God intellectually, but through reading this book I finally met my gentle and loving heavenly Father personally. . . .

I attended one of [Neil's] conferences and my entire life was changed. One of his staff met with me in a four-hour session. No one has ever wanted to spend that much time with me. I felt free for the first time in my life. Still my desperate need for affirmation prevented me from being totally honest in the counseling session. . . .

After a couple of months, the glow of my freedom subsided. I started to backslide and return to voyeurism. I read Neil's books, *Released from Bondage* and *Walking in the Light*. I fought back against the attack and worked through the issues . . . I felt renewed again, but also worn out from the battle. I wasn't reading the Word or praying much. I didn't feel like doing it.

So I started Neil and Joanne's devotional *Daily in Christ*. I was filled with guilt because of my mental lapses into voyeurism and masturbation. How could I teach Sunday School and be such a hypocrite? I told the Lord that I really loved Him and wanted to serve Him. Then I decided to prove it. I was always fearful of vows, but I made one. I told the Lord that I was His child and that I was going to be baptized again. I knew I didn't have to and that baptism didn't save me, but I wanted to erect a milestone for the Lord like the Israelites did when they crossed the Jordan.

I made the vow and the Lord honored it beyond my wildest anticipation. He confirmed in me that I was a child of God and that He loved me. Once I submitted myself completely to Him and stopped trying to fix myself, He could do it for me.

The masturbation stopped instantaneously and has never come back. The voyeurism has also stopped. I have learned what it means to take every thought captive in obedience to Christ. Now I measure everything that comes into my mind against what the Lord says in His Word, and the truth has set me free.[1]

There is a computer term—GIGO—that means "garbage in, garbage out." In other words, what you put in the computer is what you're going to get out of it. It's the same with us. Our lives will eventually reveal what we have put into our minds and what we have chosen to think about.

I was discussing this principle with a man over lunch. He leaned across the table and asked, "You mean I have to take every thought captive?"

"Only if you want to be free," I replied.

Julia summed it up when she said, "You know, it's an overwhelming task when you think about taking every thought captive, until you consider the alternative." In the long run, it is far easier to live a righteous life than a sinful one. Most Americans spend at least 12 years in school learning how to live a responsible life for the next 40 or 50 years. Those who do it well never regret the years they spent educating their minds. Those who never took learning seriously will find life much more difficult.

Think how little time the average Christian takes to learn how to live for eternity. What we learn now and choose to believe doesn't just affect us for the next 40 years, but for all eternity. As Neil so often states during his Living Free in Christ conferences:

Whoever sows a thought, reaps an action.
Whoever sows an action, reaps a habit.
Whoever sows a habit, reaps a lifestyle.
Whoever sows a lifestyle, reaps a destiny.

Probe

Have you ever considered that what you think today may have implications for all eternity? If you have developed poor habits of thinking, can you start to change that? Will you?

Journal

_____

_____

_____

_____

_____

Note
1. Neil T. Anderson, *A Way of Escape* (Eugene, Ore.: Harvest House Publishers, 1994), pp. 184-189.

DAY 114

Thought for Today: Mental illness or a battle for your mind?

Do not conform any longer to the pattern of this world, but be transformed by the renewing of your mind. Then you will be able to test and approve what God's will is—his good, pleasing and perfect will.
ROMANS 12:2

It was 1993, and I was on staff with Grace Ministries International, a counseling and counselor-training ministry. A young woman came in for counseling who was obviously in bondage. She had spent six months in a psychiatric ward. She was a professing Christian, but she could no longer function as a wife and mother. The psychiatrist at the mental hospital told her husband that she would have to be institutionalized for the rest of her life. She had been diagnosed with multiple personality disorder. (As it turned out, the diagnosis was wrong, but she did have severe spiritual conflicts.)

This woman had been victimized by incest and satanic ritual abuse. She was suicidal and extremely depressed. I knew that if anything was to happen, God would have to do it. When I tried to counsel her, she couldn't finish a sentence without crying. I had taken only one or two people through the Steps to Freedom in Christ and I knew I had to try it with her. I was not experienced, but she agreed to do it. I had a photocopy of the Steps that one of the counselors had brought back from a conference he attended with Neil. After making a copy for her, I just read aloud through the Steps and she followed along.

She was so dramatically freed and changed that it's still hard for me to believe it even as I think about it today. She was so excited that she brought her sister to me and sat in as a prayer partner while I took the sister through the Steps. She shared the following letter with me:

> My sister Sandra visited for three days. She is so changed from six months ago—you wouldn't believe your eyes! Not only did she shed 34 pounds, but she shed depression, anxiety and fear which completely changed her countenance. No panic attacks or suicidal thinking—just peace. Her husband reported such a difference in her since December (after going through the Steps) that he thought something was wrong. He was accustomed to crying fits and hysteria. Her calmness caused him to ask many questions. He is now considering Jesus Christ as the answer. Praise God! My heart was overjoyed to hear him testify to her transformation and to sense his openness to the Lord. Being set free seems to have a ripple effect on those around us, doesn't it?
>
> God has given me a vision that is about to burst in my heart, because He has called me to write about the freeing of my mind. Satan, however, is doing all he can to inflict discouragement. But I'm learning to put on my armor daily, and stand in the truth of God's Word. What a difference it has made in my daily living! To think a psychiatrist diagnosed me as mentally ill, with no hope of functioning in the real world, seems like a very bad dream. Praise God, I no longer depend on antipsychotics, antidepressants, or tranquilizers, but am clear-minded, victorious and healed from the repercussions of incest and child abuse. I'm free from suicidal depression, self-mutilation, dissociation and

worm theology. I'm free from condemning voices and confusion. I am fulfilling God's purpose for my life, which is not doing time on a psych ward plotting my own death.

There is much to rejoice about. Today I feel like my life is one big kick in Satan's teeth! He has no power over me. Christ has totally set me free. Even during times I don't feel particularly free, I know I am. Thank you for your devotion to sharing the Truth with others. I am one life that was remarkably changed because of it.

All I did was share the truth with this woman and help her resolve her personal and spiritual conflicts. God set her free, not me. How's she doing today? Great. She headed up the prayer team for our ministry for a while and we still stay in contact.

Secular psychologists would diagnose such a person as mentally ill because they believe such a person is out of touch with reality. In many cases, secular counselors are the ones who are out touch with reality. The spiritual world is as real as the one we see, and the voices these people struggle with are also real. People such as David, Judas and Ananias were not mentally ill, but they were deceived, as any believer can be. Much of what is diagnosed as mental illness is nothing more than a spiritual battle going on for the patients' minds.

Good mental health begins with a true knowledge of God, a true knowledge of who we are in Christ and a recognition that "our struggle is not against flesh and blood, but against the rulers, against the authorities, against the powers of this dark world and against the spiritual forces of evil in the heavenly realms" (Eph. 6:12). The battle for our minds is winnable if we know the truth. The truth according to 1 John 5:18-21:

> We know that anyone born of God does not continue to sin; the one who was born of God keeps him safe, and the evil one cannot harm him. We know that we are children of God, and that the whole world is under the control of the evil one. We know also that the Son of God has come and has given us under-

standing, so that we may know him who is true. And we are in
him who is true—even in his Son Jesus Christ. He is the true God
and eternal life. Dear children, keep yourselves from idols.

Probe

Have you ever thought you were losing your mind? Looking back, do you
think it was mental illness or a battle for your mind? How can you win
the battle for your mind?

Journal

_____

_____

_____

_____

_____

DAY 115

Thought for Today: Greater is the One who is in you
than the one who is in the world.

Since, then, you have been raised with Christ,
set your hearts on things above, where Christ is seated at the right hand
of God. Set your minds on things above, not on earthly things.
For you died, and your life is now hidden with Christ in God.

COLOSSIANS 3:1-3

When I (Neil) was a boy on the farm, my dad, my brother and I would
visit our neighbor's farm to share produce and labor. The neighbor had
a yappy little dog that scared the socks off me. When it came barking
around the corner, my dad and brother stood their ground, but I ran.

Guess who the dog chased! I would escape to the top of our pickup truck while the little dog yapped at me from the ground.

Everyone except me could see that the little dog had no power over me except what I gave it. Furthermore, it had no inherent power to throw me up on the pickup; it was my belief that put me up there. That dog controlled me by using my mind, my emotions, my will and my muscles, all of which were motivated by fear. One day I finally gathered up my courage, jumped off the pickup and kicked a small rock at the mutt. Lo and behold, the mutt ran!

Satan is like that yappy little dog, deceiving people into fearing him more than God. His power is in the lie. He is the father of lies (see John 8:44) who deceives the whole world (see Rev. 12:9), and consequently the whole world is under the influence of the evil one (see 1 John 5:19). He can do nothing about your position in Christ, but if he can deceive you into believing his lies about you and God, you will spend a lot of time on top of the proverbial pickup truck!

You don't have to outshout or outmuscle Satan to be free of his influence. You just have to out-truth him. Believe, declare and act upon the truth of God's Word, and you will thwart Satan's strategy. Truth is the liberating agent. The power of Satan is in the lie, and the power of the believer is in knowing truth.[1]

Many Christians are not living a victorious life because they focus on negative thoughts and circumstances (yappy little dogs) instead of fixing their eyes on Jesus, the author and finisher of our faith (see Heb. 12:2). When people focus on the dogs, their emotions follow suit and they feel powerless and defeated. If they feel like that long enough, they begin to believe that's the way it is, so they continue to live that way.

Scripture has a different order. We have to know the truth; then believe the truth; then live accordingly, by faith, and our feelings will follow. When our Christian experience doesn't match the truth, we wrongly ask, "What experience must I have in order for that to be true?" Experience will never get you there. You walk by faith according to what God says is true, and your experience will work out.

The same order applies to our relationship with God and our works of service. I don't labor in the vineyard, hoping that someday God will accept me. I am already accepted by God; that is why I labor in the vineyard. I don't do the things I do, hoping that God will someday love me. God loves me; that is why I do the things I do. Remember, it is not what you do that determines who you are. Who you are determines what you do.

Paul admonishes us in Colossians 3:5-14 to put to death whatever belongs to our earthly nature; to rid ourselves of anger, rage, malice, slander and filthy language; to refrain from lying and to practice compassion, kindness, humility, gentleness and patience; and, most difficult of all, to bear with each other and forgive whatever grievances we may have. How are we going to do that?

The first three verses of Colossians 3 tell us that we should set our minds on the things above and our new life within. If we set our minds on the truth that our old self has died, that a new self has been raised up with Christ and that Christ is now our life, then we can walk by faith. The remnants of our old self will fall away and we will become more and more like Christ.

Of course Satan will oppose this, because he's a deceiver and he prowls around like a roaring lion seeking someone to devour (see 1 Pet. 5:8). The devil can't do anything about your position in Christ, but if he can get you to believe that it isn't true, you will live as though it isn't. Like a yappy little dog, he chases all those who will run. He devours the person who will not stand firm in the truth of God's Word.

In 2 Kings 6:8-23, the King of Aram sent an army to do away with Elisha the prophet. Elisha's servant went out early in the morning, saw that an army had surrounded them and said, "'Oh, my lord, what shall we do?' . . . And Elisha prayed, 'O Lord, open his eyes so he may see.' Then the Lord opened the servant's eyes, and he looked and saw the hills full of horses and chariots of fire all around Elisha" (2 Kings 6:15,17).

The negative circumstances of this world do not give us a clear picture of the truth. The truth is, Satan is a defeated foe. God is omnipresent, omniscient and omnipotent, and we are seated with Him in the heavenlies. We need to have our eyes opened to the truth as God sees it. "You, dear children, are from God and have overcome them, because the one who is in you is greater than the one who is in the world" (1 John 4:4).

Probe

Have you given the devil too much credit or too little? Do you fear the demonic or do you fear God? How is the fear of Satan mutually exclusive from having faith in God?

Journal

_____

_____

_____

_____

_____

Note
1. Neil T. Anderson, *The Bondage Breaker* (Eugene, Ore.: Harvest House Publishers, 1990), pp. 23, 24.

DAY 116

Thought for Today: The Spirit of Truth will lead us into all truth.

Because you are sons, God sent the Spirit of his Son into our hearts, the Spirit who calls out, "Abba, Father." So you are no longer a slave, but a son; and since you are a son, God has made you also an heir.
GALATIANS 4:6,7

Earlier, I (Neil) told about how it was customary when I was in the Navy to refer to the captain of our ship as the Old Man. The first captain I had was a lousy Old Man. He belittled his officers and drank excessively with the senior enlisted men. I had to learn to cope and defend myself on board that ship.

One day the Old Man was transferred. He was gone forever, and I no longer had any relationship with him. I was no longer under his authority. We got a new Old Man, and he was a good one. But how do you think I continued to live on board that ship? I lived the way I was trained under the former Old Man until I got to know the new captain. Then I slowly began to realize that my old means of coping was no longer necessary. I had to learn a new way to live under the authority of my new captain.

As Christians, we are no longer under the authority of the god of this world, because our relationship with him has been severed. We are children of God. Our greatest priority is to get to know the new captain of our souls. That is why Paul wrote, "I consider everything a loss compared to the surpassing greatness of knowing Christ Jesus my Lord" (Phil. 3:8).

The fall of Adam caused us all to be born physically alive but spiritually dead in our trespasses and sins (see Eph. 2:1). At birth we have neither the presence of God in our lives nor the knowledge of God's ways.

During our early formative years, we learn how to live our lives independently from God. We have no choice. Then one day we hear the gospel and decide to invite Jesus into our lives. We are born again; we are brand-new creations in Christ. But everything previously programmed into our memory banks is still there. Nobody pushed the "clear button"!

Unfortunately, these tremendous computers we call our minds are not equipped with an erase feature. That is why Paul said, "Do not conform any longer to the pattern of this world, but be transformed by the renewing of your mind. Then you will be able to test and approve what God's will is—his good, pleasing and perfect will" (Rom. 12:2).

Like a computer, our brains have recorded every experience we have ever had. These impressions have a lasting impact on our physical bodies. I have seen adults recoil in physical pain as they get in touch with childhood memories of abuse, because strongholds were raised up in their minds against the knowledge of God. These strongholds have affected their temperament. It takes time to renew their minds and to replace the lies they have believed with the truth of God's Word.

The good news (the gospel) is that we have every resource we need to break strongholds. The Lord has sent us the Holy Spirit, who is the

"Spirit of truth" (John 14:17), and "He will guide [us] into all the truth" (16:13). Because we are one with God, "We have the mind of Christ" (1 Cor. 2:16). We have superior weapons to win the battle for our minds. Paul said:

> For though we live in the world, we do not wage war as the world does. The weapons we fight with are not the weapons of the world. On the contrary, they have divine power to demolish strongholds. We demolish arguments and every pretension that sets itself up against the knowledge of God, and we take captive every thought to make it obedient to Christ (2 Cor. 10:3-5).[1]

A very poignant scene appeared in the TV miniseries "Queen," the sequel to "Roots," when it was aired several years ago. A former slave and his wife were talking about sending their son to high school. The man said, "No, we can't do it. It's just not done. It's never been done. A black has never gone to high school." His wife replied, "You were born a slave; you have lived as a slave most of your life, and you still think like a slave."

Paul echoes this when he says we were all born as slaves and have lived like slaves. "As for you, you were dead in your transgressions and sins, in which you used to live when you followed the ways of this world" (Eph. 2:1,2). Then he says that although we learned to think like slaves, we "must no longer live as the Gentiles do, in the futility of their thinking. They are darkened in their understanding and separated from the life of God" (4:17,18). The reason many Christians are not free is because they are still thinking like slaves.

Perhaps you're saying, "I can't help what I think, that's just the way I am." That's not true. Being able to choose what we think is part of what being created in the image of God means. Even the secular world teaches the freedom to choose what we think. Secular bookstores in America are loaded with self-help books. Secular programs such as "Think and Grow Rich" and "Psychocybernetics" admonish their followers to make positive mental choices. All these programs can do, however, is transform a person from one earthly creature to another earthly creature.

We have something far better to guide us than external gurus. We have the Spirit of Truth within us. He will guide us into all truth. As we renew our minds to the truth of God's Word, we are transformed from earthly creatures to mature children of God.

Probe
How have you been transformed by the renewing of your mind? Think back to when you were young. How have your beliefs changed, and in what ways are you different today?

Journal
_____

_____

_____

_____

_____

Note
1. Neil T. Anderson and Mike and Julia Quarles, *Freedom from Addiction* (Ventura, Calif.: Regal Books, 1996), pp. 275-277.

DAY 117

Thought for Today: You are transformed by the renewing of your mind.

Brothers, stop thinking like children. In regard to evil be infants,
but in your thinking be adults.
1 CORINTHIANS 14:20

I had just finished speaking at a Sunday evening service in a church in San Diego, when a friend of mine who attended there passed me a note: "I brought a family with me to church tonight. Will you please see them before you leave?" I was dead tired from a weekend of speaking, and I still had at least an hour of ministry ahead of me with people who wanted to talk after the service. But I agreed to see the family if they could wait until I was finished.

Unknown to me, my friend had practically dragged 26-year-old Alyce and her parents to the service. They were Christians. But as I sat down with them it was obvious they had a problem. Alyce was one of the most pathetic-looking young women I have ever met. She was so skinny that she literally had no more body fat to lose. She had lost her job three days earlier and her vacant eyes conveyed that she had lost all hope for her life.

Alyce's father told me she had suffered terribly from PMS during adolescence and had become addicted to prescription painkillers. She was a very talented girl and a committed Christian in many ways, but she was also a Darvon junkie. She had even been arrested once for illegal possession of prescription drugs. As her father told me her sad story, Alyce sat nodding to herself as if to say, "Yes, that's me, and life is the pits."

Finally I turned to Alyce, took her by the hands and said, "I want you to tell me who you think you are."

"I'm just a no-good failure," she whimpered.

"You're not a failure," I said. "You're a child of God." She continued to pour out the negative self-talk and evidences of demonic deception she had been living under, and I continued to counter her negativism with the good news of her identity in Christ. The hour was late and I was tired, but the more we talked the more aware I became of Christ's presence ministering to Alyce. We tested the spirit that was harassing her in this area, and she saw firsthand that she had been subject to demonic influence.

Finally she said, "Do you mean to tell me that all these negative thoughts about myself are nothing but satanic deception?"

"That's right, Alyce, And as you begin to learn the truth about your identity in Christ, you will be free from the bondage of Satan's lies."

Two weeks later, Alyce enrolled in an intensive 12-week, live-in, spiritual-growth course at the Julian Center near San Diego. At the end of the course, Alyce began to take the initiative in her life instead of remaining a victim of Satan's deception. She got a job. She gained about 25 pounds. And today she's free.

The prevailing theme of the New Testament is the position we enjoy in Christ through our faith in Him. That's the good news: Christ in you and you in Christ. If there is a prevailing negative theme in the New Testament that capsules the opposition we face in Satan, I believe it is deception.[1]

If the primary truth we need to know is who we are in Christ, then it stands to reason that this is the main truth Satan wants to hide from us. One of the most effective lies of Satan is to convince believers they are the same old people they once were. If he can do this, he has succeeded in his plan, because the same old person will act the same old way.

"But I just don't feel dead to sin and alive to God." That's right. You probably don't always feel that way, and you can't control your feelings. But you can control your thinking. Scripture tells us: "Brothers, stop thinking like children. In regard to evil be infants, but in your thinking be adults" (1 Cor. 14:20).

Our feelings are primarily a product of our thought life. What we believe, how we think, and how we perceive ourselves and the world around us determines how we feel. Our feelings can be distorted by what we choose to think or believe. If what we choose to believe and think does not reflect truth, then what we feel will not reflect reality. If what we see or mentally visualize is morally wrong, then our emotions are going to be violated. If you want to feel right, you must think right and act right.

Satan doesn't want you to think or believe the truth about God, yourself and how to live the Christian life. Paul writes, "The Spirit clearly says that in later times some will abandon the faith and follow deceiving spirits and things taught by demons" (1 Tim. 4:1). We have counseled hundreds of people who struggle with such deceiving thoughts or literally hear voices. In every case the root problem has been a spiritual battle for their minds. To walk free, you must discipline your mind, take thoughts captive and choose to live by the truth. The alternative is bondage.

Probe

How can you personally be transformed by the renewing of your mind (that is, what is your personal strategy for growth)? How much time are you giving each day in order to do that? What kinds of books should you be reading or not reading? What kinds of local church involvement would help you renew your mind?

Journal

_____

_____

_____

_____

_____

Note
1. Neil T. Anderson, *The Bondage Breaker* (Eugene, Ore.: Harvest House Publishers, 1990), pp. 153, 154.

DAY 118

Thought for Today: What we have learned wrongly can be relearned rightly.

But I am afraid that just as Eve was deceived by the serpent's cunning, your minds may somehow be led astray from your sincere and pure devotion to Christ.

2 CORINTHIANS 11:3

Charles, a 52-year-old pastor, admitted to me (Neil) that he had struggled with homosexual tendencies for as long as he could remember. More than once he had given in to those urges. He begged God to forgive him and take the feelings away. He had attended healing services and self-help groups for those in sexual bondage. Nothing worked. To his credit, Charles never once got mad at God. He was married, and somehow had kept his struggle a secret from his family. Most people in sexual bondage struggle privately. It is an extremely lonely battle.

I asked Charles what his earliest childhood memory was. He went right back to the age of two. His birth father left before he was born, and his Christian mother raised him. She had a boyfriend who occasionally came over and spent the night. On those nights, two-year-old Charles had to share a bed with this man. Charles's earliest childhood memory was of this man, whom he admired so much, turning his back to him and going to sleep. The little boy was desperately looking for affirmation from a male figure, wanting so much to be loved, accepted and appreciated. As an adult he found that affection in homosexual men.

As I walked Charles through the Steps to Freedom in Christ, he broke down and cried. He forgave his birth father for abandoning him and forgave his stepfather for never really accepting him. Then he renounced every sexual use of his body as an instrument of unrighteousness and gave himself and his body to the Lord. I also encouraged him to renounce the lie that he was a homosexual and declare the truth that God had created him to be a man. As he finished the Steps, the bondage to homosexuality was broken.[1] The path to wholeness and maturity would take much longer.

Ed Silvoso defines a stronghold as "a mind-set impregnated with hopelessness that causes us to accept as unchangeable what is known to be contrary to the will of God."[2] How are these destructive strongholds established in our minds? Usually, they are the result of subtle steps that lead us away from God's plan for our lives. Nobody is born an alcoholic. The alcoholic develops that addiction over time. Sometime in their development, they discovered alcohol could be a means to get rid of inhibitions or to cope with physical and emotional pain.

How did I become an alcoholic? As a teenager I was a very insecure person who felt guilty because of my failures. I felt inferior to my friends who had money, were good at sports and had good-looking girlfriends. I felt unaccepted and worthless, and desperately needed something to help me feel better about myself.

When I was 17 years old, my two best friends and I decided we would celebrate our upcoming graduation from high school by going out and getting drunk (something we had never done before). It was a life-changing experience for me. Not for the good, but it was life changing. I was able to get out of my self-conscious shell and cut up and be one of the guys. I was able to relate to the girls and talk to them. I felt better about myself. Drinking did something for me that nothing else had been able to do. I wouldn't give it up easily. It became a major part of my life for many years.

Charles was introduced into homosexuality because he was looking for male affirmation. I embraced alcohol because it did something for me that nothing else had been able to do. The essence of all temptation is to live independently of God. The basis for temptation is legitimate needs. The question is, who is going to meet those needs—the world, the flesh and the devil, or Christ? Satan knows which buttons to push to tempt you away from depending on Christ. He has observed your behavior over the years and he knows where you are vulnerable. That's where he will attack. Your temptations will be unique to your area of vulnerability.

For many people, homosexuality and addiction would not even be a consideration. I don't think you could hold a gun to Julia's head and make her get drunk. But she has her own areas of vulnerability. The strongholds she had to tear down were codependency, the desire to control and perfectionism. Satan knows each of us well and knows where to attack us, but God knows us infinitely better.

Satan is the father of lies, and he will work on our minds to destroy our concept of God and our understanding of who we are as His children. People in bondage don't know who they are in Christ. That is the one common denominator in every person we have been privileged to help find freedom in Christ. Remember, Satan can't do anything about our position in Christ, but if he can get us to believe it isn't true, we will live as though it isn't true, even though it is.

Can strongholds of bondage in the mind be broken? Yes! If our minds have been programmed wrongly, they can be reprogrammed. If we learned something the wrong way, we can learn it the right way. Will this take time? Yes, it will take the rest of our lives to renew our minds and to develop our character. But nothing you do will prove more rewarding.

Probe

What mental strongholds in your mind are keeping you from being free in Christ? What tempting or accusing thoughts does Satan give you to trigger your life-controlling problem or addiction? Does he accuse you about how bad you are and beat you down? Does he remind you of past failures? Does he tell you that God has given up on you? Does he tell you that it's hopeless, that you will never be free? What does your addiction or life-controlling problem do for you that nothing else has been able to do?

Journal

_____

_____

_____

_____

_____

Notes
1. Neil T. Anderson, *A Way of Escape* (Eugene, Ore.: Harvest House Publishers, 1994), pp. 112, 113.
2. Ed Silvoso, "Setting Your Church Free" conference, March 1994, Minneapolis, Minn.

DAY 119

Thought for Today: The Spirit of truth will lead you into all truth.

But solid food is for the mature, who by constant use have trained them-selves to distinguish good from evil.

HEBREWS 5:14

One of my students exemplified how deceptive Satan's thoughts can be. Jay came into my office one day and said, "Dr. Anderson, I'm in trouble. When I sit down to study I get prickly sensations all over my body, my arms involuntarily rise, my vision gets blurry and I can't concentrate."

"Tell me about your walk with God," I said.

"I have a very close walk with God," Jay boasted.

"What do you mean?"

"I look to Him for guidance every day. For instance, when I leave school at noon each day, I ask God where He wants me to go for lunch. If the thought comes to my mind, *Burger King*, I go there; and when I come to the counter to order, I ask Him what He wants me to eat. If the thought comes to order a Whopper, I order a Whopper."

I was beginning to question this undiscerning method of divine guidance. He had asked God where to go to church the last three Sundays and ended up in a Mormon church. This wasn't divine guidance, this was pure deception.

Jay sincerely wanted to do what God wanted him to do. But he was listening to his subjective thoughts as though they were God's voice instead of "taking every thought captive to the obedience of Christ" (2 Cor. 10:5, *NASB*). In so doing he had opened the door to the father of lies, and he was being defeated in his studies.

We have to assume responsibility for our own thoughts. It takes only about six weeks of thinking wrong thoughts to develop a habit, and if you exercise a sinful habit long enough, a stronghold will be established in your mind. Tearing down strongholds is far harder than not giving in to the original tempting thought.[1]

How do you tell if the thought is from God or from your flesh or the enemy? The first step is to "let the word of Christ dwell in you richly as you teach and admonish one another with all wisdom, and as you sing psalms, hymns and spiritual songs with gratitude in your hearts to God" (Col. 3:16). You are more likely to recognize Satan's thoughts if you allow God's thoughts, through His Word, to dwell in you. If you know God's Word, you will be able to distinguish between the truth and lies.

Second, are your thoughts constructive or destructive? Are they biblical and positive or worldly and negative? God doesn't give you negative thoughts about yourself and others, Himself or your circumstances. Secular psychiatrists conclude that 90 percent of what people think is negative. Maybe unbelievers who have no hope should be thinking negatively, because apart from Christ there is no hope. But Christians are filled with the God of all hope. If you want to think truthfully, then be filled with the Spirit of truth. It's hard to be negative while you're singing with gratitude in your heart to God.

Third, is your thought a source of encouragement to you and others? Martin Luther and Hannah Whitall Smith say that all discouragement is of the devil. Does God give you discouraging thoughts? Does He tell you how bad you are? Does He tell you how hopeless your situation is? No. Scripture says that we are to encourage one another (see 1 Thess. 4:18).

Fourth, we are not called to dispel the darkness; rather, we are called to turn on the light. It would do little good to encourage others not to believe lies. That is a negative orientation that doesn't work. We are admonished to choose and believe the truth. In Philippians 4:8, God tells us to think about things that are true, noble, right, pure, lovely, admirable, excellent and praiseworthy. How do we do that? We let the Word of God dwell in us richly (see Col. 3:16a).

The prophet Habakkuk knew how to choose the truth and be an encouragement when external circumstances were stacked against him. As he waited for a nation to invade and take them captive, he wrote: "Though the fig tree does not bud and there are no grapes on the vines, though the olive crop fails and the fields produce no food, though there are no sheep in the pen and no cattle in the stalls, yet I will rejoice in the Lord, I will be joyful in God my Savior" (Hab. 3:17,18).

Fifth, we need to learn the difference between the conviction of the Holy Spirit and the accusations of Satan. The difference is revealed in 2 Corinthians 7:9,10:

> Yet now I am happy, not because you were made sorry, but because your sorrow led you to repentance. For you became sorrowful as God intended and so were not harmed in any way by us. Godly sorrow brings repentance that leads to salvation and leaves no regret, but worldly sorrow brings death.

The conviction of sin makes us feel sorrowful like the accusations of Satan, but the end result is totally different. One leads to repentance without regret. The other leads to death. The devil deceived Judas into betraying Christ, and Judas went out and hung himself. Satan demanded the right to sift Peter like wheat because of his pride. Peter denied Christ three times; then He repented and became the spokesperson of the Early Church.

Probe

Have you ever thought you were hearing from God only to find out later it wasn't God you were listening to, but the devil? How can you discern between the deceiver and the guidance of the Holy Spirit?

Journal

_____
_____
_____
_____
_____

Note
1. Neil T. Anderson, _The Bondage Breaker_ (Eugene, Ore.: Harvest House Publishers, 1990), pp. 53, 54.

DAY 120

**Thought for Today: Disciplining your mind requires
a lifelong commitment.**

*For those who are according to the flesh set their minds on the things of
the flesh, but those who are according to the Spirit, the things of the Spirit.
For the mind set on the flesh is death, but the mind set on the Spirit is life
and peace, because the mind set on the flesh is hostile toward God; for it
does not subject itself to the law of God, for it is not even able to do so.*
ROMANS 8:5-7, NASB

As a young Christian, I (Neil) decided to clean up my mind. Do you think
the battle became easier or more difficult after I made that decision? Of
course it became more difficult. Temptation is not much of a battle if we
easily surrender to it. It is fierce when we decide to stand against it.

Although I had gone to church all my life, I did not become a
Christian until I was in my 20s. Fortunately, I had a very clean upbring-
ing; but after four years in the Navy, my mind had been exposed to a lot
of junk. I didn't drink for the first two years, but eventually I began to
join my friends. I didn't drink long enough or often enough to establish
any kind of a drinking habit, but I had seen enough pornography to
develop a problem. Images would dance in my mind for months and
years after one look. I hated it. I struggled every time I went anywhere
pornography was available. Let me share how I found victory.

Think of your mind as a coffeepot. You desire the water inside to be
pure, but unfortunately you have put in some coffee grounds. There is no
way to filter out the grounds. So the water inside is dark and polluted.
Sitting beside the coffeepot is a huge bowl of crystal-clear ice, represent-
ing the Word of God. Let's say you are able to place one or two cubes of
ice a day in the polluted water. It may seem a little futile at first. If you
keep up that process long enough, eventually you won't be able to see,
taste or smell the coffee, even though it is still in there. That process
works, provided you stop putting in more coffee grounds. If you are read-

ing your Bible 10 minutes a day and looking at *Playboy* magazine 10 minutes a day, you are going to lose more than you will gain.

For most people, winning the battle for their minds will initially be two steps forward and one step back. Slowly it becomes three steps forward, as we learn to take every thought captive in obedience to Christ. We may despair from all the backward steps, but God is not going to give up on us. Remember, our sins are already forgiven. We need only fight for our own personal victories over sin. We can win the war because we are alive in Christ and dead to sin.

Freedom to be all God has called us to be is the greatest blessing we can have in this present life. This freedom is worth fighting for. As we learn more about who we are as children of God, and the nature of the battle going on for our minds, the process gets easier. Eventually it will become 20 steps forward and one step back, until finally the steps are all forward with only an occasional slip in the battle for the mind.

We have to fill our minds with the crystal-clear Word of God. He has no alternative plan. Merely trying to stop bad thoughts won't work. Should we rebuke all those tempting, accusing and deceiving thoughts? No. If we attempted to win the war for our minds that way, we would be doing nothing but rebuking thoughts every waking moment for the rest of our lives.

It would be like telling a man in the middle of a lake to keep 12 corks submerged by hitting them with a small hammer. He would spend his entire life treading water and bopping down corks. What should he do? He should ignore the stupid corks and swim to shore. We are not called to dispel the darkness. We are called to turn on the light. We overcome the father of lies by choosing the truth![1]

There is no quick fix for maintaining our freedom in Christ. A lifelong commitment to renewing our minds is required. Americans are programmed for the quick fix. At this writing, the Power Ball Lottery is worth $250 million. People are driving across several states to buy a $1 ticket, and they are selling 1,000 tickets a minute. The odds are 80 million to one. The odds are not even that good if we try to walk in freedom without disciplining our minds!

Christ has already paid the price for us to be free. What kind of a price are you willing to pay to experience His peace, freedom and joy? Life is not a lottery; the odds are all in our favor. All we have to do is believe the truth and be transformed by the renewing of our minds. "It is for freedom that Christ has set us free. Stand firm, then, and do not let yourselves be burdened again by a yoke of slavery" (Gal. 5:1).

You can learn from the context that the "yoke of slavery" is the yoke of legalism. Don't go back to trying to live the Christian life in your own strength and resources. "For the mind set on the flesh is death, but the mind set on the Spirit is life and peace" (Rom. 8:6, *NASB*). The Christian life can only be lived by faith in God and in the power of the Holy Spirit. Walking by faith is believing the truth and setting your mind on it. When you do that, you will experience the freedom God has already made possible for you.

Probe

Now that you have developed a habit of doing a daily devotional, I would like to suggest two other devotionals by Neil: *Daily in Christ,* which is a one-year daily devotional, and *Living Free in Christ,* which has 36 short chapters on who you are in Christ and how He meets your most critical needs of acceptance, security and significance. These books will help you to stay free in Christ. May the good Lord bless you and keep you in His perfect peace.

Journal

_____

_____

_____

_____

_____

Note

1. Neil T. Anderson and Mike and Julia Quarles, *Freedom from Addiction* (Ventura, Calif.: Regal Books, 1996), pp. 295, 296.

WHO I AM IN CHRIST

I Am Accepted

John 1:12	I am God's child.
John 15:15	I am Christ's friend.
Romans 5:1	I have been justified.
1 Corinthians 6:17	I am united with the Lord, and I am one spirit with Him.
1 Corinthians 6:20	I have been bought with a price. I belong to God.
1 Corinthians 12:27	I am a member of Christ's Body.
Ephesians 1:1	I am a saint.
Ephesians 1:5	I have been adopted as God's child.
Ephesians 2:18	I have direct access to God through the Holy Spirit.
Colossians 1:14	I have been redeemed and forgiven of all my sins.
Colossians 2:10	I am complete in Christ.

I Am Secure

Romans 8:1,2	I am free from condemnation.
Romans 8:28	I am assured that all things work together for good.
Romans 8:31-34	I am free from any condemning charges against me.
Romans 8:35-39	I cannot be separated from the love of God.
2 Corinthians 1:21,22	I have been established, anointed and sealed by God.
Colossians 3:3	I am hidden with Christ in God.
Philippians 1:6	I am confident that the good work God has begun in me will be perfected.
Philippians 3:20	I am a citizen of heaven.
2 Timothy 1:7	I have not been given a spirit of fear, but of power, love and a sound mind.
Hebrews 4:16	I can find grace and mercy to help in time of need.
1 John 5:18	I am born of God and the evil one cannot touch me.

I Am Significant

Matthew 5:13,14	I am the salt and light of the earth.
John 15:1,5	I am a branch of the true vine, a channel of His life.
John 15:16	I have been chosen and appointed to bear fruit.
Acts 1:8	I am a personal witness of Christ.
1 Corinthians 3:16	I am God's temple.
2 Corinthians 5:17-21	I am a minister of reconciliation for God.
2 Corinthians 6:1	I am God's coworker (see 1 Corinthians 3:9).
Ephesians 2:6	I am seated with Christ in the heavenly realm.
Ephesians 2:10	I am God's workmanship.
Ephesians 3:12	I may approach God with freedom and confidence.
Philippians 4:13	I can do all things through Christ who strengthens me.

THE OVERCOMER'S COVENANT IN CHRIST

1. I place all my trust and confidence in the Lord, I put no confidence in the flesh and I declare myself to be dependent upon God.

2. I consciously and deliberately choose to submit to God and resist the devil by denying myself, picking up my cross daily and following Jesus.

3. I choose to humble myself before the mighty hand of God in order that He may exalt me at the proper time.

4. I declare the truth that I am dead to sin, freed from it and alive to God in Christ Jesus, since I have died with Christ and was raised with Him.

5. I gladly embrace the truth that I am now a child of God who is unconditionally loved and accepted. I reject the lie that I have to perform to be accepted, and I reject my fallen and natural identity which was derived from the world.

6. I declare that sin shall no longer be master over me because I am not under the law, but under grace, and there is no more guilt or condemnation because I am spiritually alive in Christ Jesus.

7. I renounce every unrighteous use of my body and I commit myself to no longer be conformed to this world, but rather to be transformed by the renewing of my mind. I choose to believe the truth and walk in it, regardless of my feelings or circumstances.

8. I commit myself to take every thought captive to the obedience of Christ, and choose to think upon that which is true, honorable, right, pure and lovely.

9. I commit myself to God's great goal for my life to conform to His image. I know that I will face many trials, but God has given me the victory and I am not a victim, but an overcomer in Christ.

10. I choose to adopt the attitude of Christ, which was to do nothing from selfishness or empty conceit, but with humility of mind. I will regard others as more important than myself; and not merely look out for my own personal interests but also the interests of others. I know that it is more blessed to give than to receive.